FEARING GOD

The Key to the Treasure House of Heaven

DR. ROBERT MOREY

DAVIDSON PRESS™

Yorba Linda, CA

Edition 1
Version Number: 1.00
Build Number: 1
Build Date: 15 May 1999

Reference Number: 1
Release Date: 15 July 1999
CAM Format: Logos, PDF, STEP, XML
Document Format: MS Word 97 SR-1

Library of Congress Catalog Card Number: 99-63297
ISBN 1-891833-52-9 Hardback US$21.00

Cover Design: Larry Vilott (copyright © 1999
Davidson Press, Inc.). Layout: Charles Welty &
Larry Vilott. Document Processing: Charles
Welty.

23621 La Palma Avenue, #H460
Yorba Linda, CA 92887-5536
email: info@davidsonpress.com

Table of Contents

PUBLISHER'S PREFACE

Robert Morey has an amazing ability to communicate truth, but unfortunately, what he has to say often irritates people. A number of Muslims, for example, weren't too happy about Dr. Morey's excellent work *The Islamic Invasion* (Harvest House of Eugene, OR, ISBN 0890819831). And some Unitarians didn't take too well to what Dr. Morey had to say in his definitive work on the subject of the trinity entitled—what else?—*The Trinity* (World Publishing of Grand Rapids, MI, ISBN 0529106922).

As the publisher for Dr. Morey's new work *Fearing God*, I think this book may irritate Christians this time. But I don't think the irritation will come from any confrontational writing style. I think people just don't want to hear about Dr. Morey's subject. Too bad. What Dr. Morey has to say in *Fearing God* needs to be said. In fact, I think it should have been said a long time ago. And with over 40 books to his credit (some of which are used as theological text books), Dr. Morey has the credibility to speak about his subject. It's just that most of the publishers of Christian books today don't want to "rock the boat." They want to publish books that make you feel good.

You might not "feel good" after you read this book. In fact, you're going to feel more than a bit challenged. I suspect that you will either embrace *Fearing God* out of a sense of humility or you will throw it against the wall out of a burning sense of irritation. Here's an example of what you're going to find in these pages (page 62, to be exact):

> Could it be that modern Christians are shallow in their lives and sloppy in their beliefs because they do not fear God? If we take the Bible seriously, the

reason that most Christians today are weak, carnal, spineless, and mindless is rooted in the fact that they do not fear God!

As I said in my preface to N. Allan Moseley's ground-breaking work *Worldviews at War* (ISBN 1891833537), say what you will about Jesus of Nazareth, but you cannot say that He never irritated people, or that His message does not continue to irritate people today. He irritated the scribes and Pharisees so much they handed Him over to be crucified. He irritated the people in His own home town such that they mocked Him, refused to believe His message, and then threw him out of the town. Even his own brothers did not believe in Him. And so Jesus continues to irritate people to-day.

A few years ago, a couple of books became widely read by people in search of a deeper relationship with God. These two books were entitled *Knowing God* by J. I. Packer and *Loving God* by Charles Colson. They were marvelous works as far as they went, but I'm not convinced they went far enough. They left out a important piece of the puzzle— God's holiness. *Fearing God* completes the picture and completes an "unofficial trilogy" to the other books.

We need *Fearing God* preached from the pulpit of our churches. We need *Fearing God* in our home libraries. We need *Fearing God* in our hearts. We need it in our obedience.

Charles Welty, *Publisher*
Davidson Press
Yorba Linda, California

INTRODUCTION

Stop for a moment and meditate on the following questions:

- Have I ever resisted the temptation to sin because I feared the wrath of God?
- Will God really judge me if I cheat on my wife or husband?
- Does the God I worship ever get upset or angry with me because of my sins?
- Does God really punish people today?
- Does the idea of fearing God ever enter my mind?

I can hear some people protesting vigorously, "Wait a minute, you are asking me to think negatively about God! Since God is love, the idea of fearing Him never crosses my mind. Anyway, why would I fear sweet Jesus, meek and mild? He would never do anything to hurt me."

When the average "born-again" Christian does not fear the Lord, things have gotten completely out of hand. Is it any wonder that adultery and divorce are as common among church goers today as it is in the world? Immorality, drugs and sheer wickedness can be found today in our families, churches, Bible colleges and seminaries across the land. But this was not always so.

Evangelicals used to be called "a God-fearing people" and we pointed out to unbelievers with pride that fornication, babies out of wedlock, adultery and divorce were rarely seen in our circles. Church discipline was swift and sinners were rebuked for their wickedness. We even had high standards for the ministry and when a pastor fell into adultery and divorce, he left the ministry in disgrace. Today, we tolerate pastors who have gone through the cycle of adultery and divorce two or three times. Even when one pastor was caught on video tape "entertaining" hookers at a cheap motel, he is not only still pastoring his church, but back on TV as if there was nothing wrong!

Paul's condemnation, "There is no fear of God before their eyes" (Romans 3:18), was originally aimed at unbelievers. It explained why unbelievers were going to suffer the eternal wrath of God in hell. But it would have come as a complete surprise to the apostle Paul to find that his condemnation now describes the church as well as the world.

When was the last time you heard a sermon on the necessity and nature of fearing God? Why is it never discussed in Sunday School? The Bible talks about it all the time. So, why is it that we never hear about it in church?

Does this situation bother you at all? Or has your conscience been totally hardened on this issue? Has your heart burned within you confirming the truth of what we are saying? Do you want to know what the Bible means when it tells you to "fear the Lord in the beauty of holiness"?

By now it is clear that the fear of the Lord is the missing note in Evangelical theology today. There have been no major works on this subject in this century. The last full book on the fear of God was written by John Bunyan in A.D. 1688!

An examination of the theology textbooks used in Evangelical colleges and seminaries today reveals that the fear of God has been almost completely ignored. The last popular systematic theology textbook to devote an entire chapter to the fear of the Lord was John Gill's *Body of Divinity* which was written in 1770.

Since the textbooks used by most Christian colleges and seminaries do not teach the fear of the Lord, an entire generation of pastors and missionaries have never been taught the fear of God. And they, in turn, have never taught the people of God that the Lord should be feared as well as loved. Is it any wonder then that Christians are no longer referred to as "God-fearing" people? Indeed, who today views himself or herself as "God-fearing"? Do you?

We have moved so far away even from the idea of fearing God that the very words "God-fearing" seem strange to our ears. Most Christians today assume that "fearing" God is no longer necessary. This situation cannot and must not be allowed to continue. *The fear of the Lord is absolutely necessary for the spiritual health of our nation, our churches and our families as well as for our personal lives.* Any nation, church, family or individual that ceases to fear the Lord will fall into gross sins.

In order to revive the Biblical teaching on the fear of God in our own day, we have decided to present anew the words of John Bunyan, John Gill, Charles Spurgeon and others on the subject. From the earliest Church Father to the present day, the fear of the Lord is the beginning of wisdom.

The positive effects of fearing God are many. The blessings that come our way as we fear the Lord benefit the individual, the family, the church, and the nation. What it means to fear the Lord and how to put it into practice in our daily lives is the focus of this study. May God use it to revive the fear of the Lord in our day.

FEARING

GOD

The Key to the Treasure House of Heaven

DR. ROBERT MOREY

DAVIDSON™ PRESS
Yorba Linda, CA

Part One:

A Modern Analysis of the Fear of God

Chapter 1: WHAT HAS HAPPENED?

W hy is the fear of God no longer preached or practiced today? Is it because the Bible is silent on the subject? No! As a matter of fact, one thing is abundantly clear: *The entire Bible from Genesis to Revelation is filled with commands to fear the Lord.* But this is not something that most of God's people understand today. Thus a brief survey of some of the biblical material which teaches us to fear God is necessary.

The Old Testament

In the Old Testament, the fear of God was viewed as *the fundamental attitude of the believer to his God.* The fear of God was honored and practiced by prophets, priests, and kings throughout the entire Old Testament. Indeed, King Solomon declared, "The fear of the Lord is the beginning of knowledge" (Proverbs1:7).

The New Testament

When we turn to the New Testament, the fear of God is taught from Matthew to Revelation. It is not negated, lessened or down played in the New Testament in any sense whatsoever.

In the Gospels, the fear of God played a significant role in the life and teachings of Christ.

> Stop being afraid of those who kill the body but can't kill the soul. Instead, *be afraid of the one who can destroy both body and soul in hell.* (Matthew 10:28)

1

The fear of God was preached as part of the early Church's proclamation of man's duty to God.

As it continued to be built up and *to live in the fear of the Lord*, it kept increasing in numbers through the encouragement of the Holy Spirit. (Acts 9:31)

In the Church Epistles, the Apostle Paul viewed sanctification as taking place in the context of the fear of God.

Since we have these promises, dear friends, we should cleanse ourselves from everything that contaminates body and spirit by perfecting holiness *in the fear of God.* (2 Corinthians 7:1)

The Apostle Peter in the General Epistles commanded all Christians, "Fear God" (I Peter 2:17). Even in the last book of the Bible, the Book of Revelation, heaven itself is filled with the glorious hymn that all nations should fear the Lord.

"Your deeds are spectacular and amazing, Lord God Almighty.
Your ways are just and true, King of the nations.
Lord, who won't fear and praise your name?
For you alone are holy,
and all the nations will come and worship you
because your judgments have been revealed." (Revelation
15:3-4)

Historic Christianity

Since the golden thread of the fear of God runs through the entire Bible, the fear of the Lord has always been a vital part of the historic Christian understanding of God. It does not matter what period of Church history we study, people were taught to fear the Lord. From the Apostolic Fathers to the Pilgrim Fathers, the fear of God was part of fundamental Christian belief and practice.

Our Puritan and Pilgrim Fathers delighted in the fear of the Lord. They were a "God-fearing" people and the high moral and ethical lives they led was a direct result of their fear of God. The necessity and nature of the fear of the Lord filled their hymns and theological works as well as their daily lives.

Something Has Happened

Obviously, something has happened to change the way people think about God. People today no longer fear God. How has this come to pass? What has happened to the fear of the Lord?

The Sad Answer

Historically, it was during the late 18th Century and prominently in the early 19th Century that a drastic change took place in the way the average person viewed God. Before the last part of the 18th century, the average person living in America generally held to a Puritan view of God, which they inherited, from their Pilgrim Fathers.

The God of the Pilgrims was a mighty God who was "tough" in the sense that He was aggressive in rewarding saints and punishing sinners. The Almighty Jehovah was not a wimp or a pushover. He was a righteous and holy God who would not let sin go unpunished. He was Holy as well as Loving.

In short, the God of the Pilgrims was a God who was worthy to be feared. He was mighty to save and mighty to judge. This God held all men accountable for the way they lived and would one day judge all men for their sins. He was enthroned in the Heavens and laughed at the puny efforts of rebel sinners to throw off His sovereign rule (Psalm 2). His justice would be fully vindicated by His divine judgment on the Last Day. To the Pilgrims, hell was not an empty threat and heaven an empty dream. To them there was a hell to shun and a heaven to gain. *This was the soul and substance of the Gospel. Salvation made sense only upon the assumption of the fear of God.*

The Great Awakening

It was in this context that the greatest revival in America's history took place. During the Great Awakening, Jonathan Edwards preached his famous sermon, "Sinners in the Hands of An Angry God." Revival broke out in his church that day, and, before it was over, it turned America into the church-going nation it is today.

Have you ever heard preaching like Edwards? Given today's man-centered theology, we are more likely to hear a sermon entitled, "God in the Hands of Angry Sinners!" No wonder we do not see true revival today. In Edwards' day, people in general believed that God would indeed punish men for the evil they do. They firmly believed that there was going to be a Day of Judgment. This meant that sinners must prepare to meet their God.

Now, to be sure, the Pilgrims did not deny the love of God. They had a profound understanding of the love of God that far exceeded the "cheap" love preached today. They understood that the wrath of God was the black velvet pillow on which the jewel of divine love shined its brightest. Without the wrath of God, divine love becomes lifeless like a diamond on white paper. This is why in Scripture God's wrath always forms the context of His love.

In the third chapter of John's Gospel, we find the most well known verse in the Bible.

> For this is how God loved the world: He gave his only Son so that everyone who believes in him would not perish but have eternal life. (John 3:16)

The love of God in the gift of His only Son remains the core of the gospel. But what is the context of God's love? It is the wrath of God that rests upon unrepentant sinners.

> The one who believes in the Son has eternal life, but the one who disobeys the Son will not see life. Instead, the wrath of God remains on him. (John 3:36)

But what if you do not fear the wrath of God? Then you will not appreciate the love of God. This is why cheap grace and cheap love are so popular today.

The fear of God is not limited to conversion. It is the foundation of holy living. It is a sign of spiritual maturity and depth in the Christian life. The lack of it is a sign of spiritual immaturity and shallowness.

Conclusion

What has caused a major shift in the way we think of God? What happens when a nation or a church no longer fears the Lord? Iniquity will abound and lawlessness will prevail. The only real and lasting cure for all the violence and crime in modern society is a return to the biblical understanding of the fear of God.

Chapter 2: THE LIBERALIZATION OF CHRISTIANITY

The demise of the fear of God in modern society can be traced back to several great mega-shifts that took place in Western society during the 18th and 19th centuries. A "mega-shift" is a radical change that alters a culture or society to such a degree that it becomes something new and different.

The Industrial Revolution

Sociologically speaking, the industrial revolution of the 18th and 19th centuries was a mega-shift which uprooted millions of people from their ancestral homes and rural churches and plunged them into inner-city slums that were ruled by crime, poverty, filth, ignorance, alcohol, and immorality. They often worked twelve to sixteen hours a day, seven days a week. Even the children worked as virtual slaves in the factories.

The churches were few and attendance was meager. An entire generation grew up that had never been in a church or sat under the Gospel. They lost any sense of the fear of God and the Judgment Day. They sinned boldly and cursed God while they did so.

Darwinianism

Philosophically speaking, Darwin's theory of evolution gave people the excuse to live as they pleased. It led to the rise of secular humanism which openly denied there was a God to fear. Darwinianism led to both Marxism and Nazism which sought to destroy the Church and its gospel.

The Church's Condition

Ecclesiastically speaking, the Christian Church became more interested in buildings, numbers, and money than solid doctrinal preaching. As a result, they failed to preach and teach the whole counsel of God. Confessions, creeds and catechisms were laid aside in the vain pursuit of carnal goals. Churches became places of entertainment instead of repentance and conversion. There was little concern or compassion for the millions of poor people trapped in the filth and wickedness of the slums.

The Root Cause

While all these things contributed to the loss of the fear of God, the main cause of the demise of the fear of God in Western culture was the rise of religious Liberalism in the 19th century. To put it bluntly, liberal theology proclaimed that *there was nothing in God to fear!*

Liberalism's denial of the supernatural in general and the inspiration of the Bible and miracles in particular, paved the way for the triumph of secular humanism and Darwinianism. The famous 19th century preacher, Charles Spurgeon, stood virtually alone in the fight against liberalism in the famous "Downgrade Controversy."

A typical liberal clergyman from that period would preach, "Is there is a hell? No! God is too loving and man is too good for any divine judgment to take place. As a matter of fact, God is the Father of all mankind; all men are the children of God and are brothers. If there is a Heaven, we are all going there. Hell cannot exist in the same universe with a God of love. There is nothing to fear in God. He is all love."

The God of Liberalism was often pictured as being so loving that "he would never hurt a fly." Because he would never really damn anyone, hell was only an empty threat. The denial of eternal conscious punishment became the theological fad of the day. Since God was viewed as sensitive, compassionate, tender, loving, kind, non-aggressive and non-threatening, there was nothing left in God to fear.

The Hard Attributes of God

All the "hard" attributes of God such as His power, justice, holiness, righteousness, judgment, and any other attributes which were "threatening" were jettisoned from God's nature. Only the "soft" attributes such as love and mercy were preached.

The Feminization of God

The next step was only logical. God was now recast into the mold of being a divine "Mother" instead of a divine "Father." It is no surprise to find that the process of the feminization of God began in the 19th century when God was reduced to a sentimental blob of "love." It was not long before liberals, cultists, and occultists were praying to the "Mother God" instead of God the Father. For example, Mary Baker Eddy, the founder of Christian Science, preached that we should address the divine Mind as a "Mother-God." She was later followed by such radical feminists as Mary Daly who openly called for the castration of the Father and the Son!

From New Thought to New Age

The feminization of God from a "father" into a "mother" became part of the 19th century movement called "New Thought." But old heresies never die; they just change names. Thus the "New Thought" movement of the 19th century became the "New Age" Movement of the 20th century.

The teachings of both movements were embraced by the liberal theologians who control the seminaries and colleges in mainline Protestant denominations. Today the theology of the Christian Science Church, New Thought, and the New Age Movement have taken over most mainline liberal Protestant schools and churches.

As we pointed out in the book *Battle of the Gods*, modern liberal theologians assume that "God" is whatever you want "he," "she" or "it" to be. In other words, whatever "god" makes you "feel good" about yourself is acceptable. The only god that is "bad" is the God of the Bible. Any other god will do but the One revealed in Scripture.

A Word of Clarification

Before we go any further, let us clarify this point: We believe in *all* the attributes of God regardless if they are viewed as "hard" or "soft." We believe in the love and mercy of God as well as His holiness and wrath.

What we are objecting to is the assumption that all the "hard" attributes of God such as His justice and holiness should be ignored or rejected and that we must somehow re-shape God, the Bible, Jesus, the clergy, preaching and the church to reflect only "soft" attributes.

The "hard" attributes are often described by liberal and feminist theologians as "male" qualities which need to be rooted out of our understanding of God. The "soft" attributes are in turn described as "feminine" qualities which need to emphasized in order for women to feel good about God.

Male and Female

Let us state for the record that there is nothing inherently wrong or evil with the qualities of maleness or

9

femaleness. According to the Bible, God made us "male and female." Thus there is nothing "evil" about being either gender (Genesis 1:27). Thus the qualities that characterize maleness are not inherently evil, despite what "feminazis" say. Maleness is as inherently good as femaleness.

Mother or Father

Feminist theologians claim that referring to God as "Father" hurts the self-image of women. If this were true, then referring to God as "Mother" would likewise hurts the self-image of men. Men and women will have to worship different deities! But God cannot be reduced to what makes us feel warm and fuzzy! The attempt to create a goddess or god in our own image is futile as well as blasphemous.

The God who revealed Himself in the Bible by "hard" or "male" attributes does not want or need radical feminists to rewrite the Bible in order to get rid of those very attributes. We must accept God as He has chosen to reveal Himself or be guilty of gross idolatry.

The Feminization of Jesus

During the 19th century, Jesus was feminized. Several famous paintings of Christ became popular which depicted Him as a weak, effeminate, white European male with a pale complexion and long hair set in a womanly manner. None of these portraits of Christ looked like someone who could have survived in the wilderness for forty days without food!

Jesus was no longer viewed as someone who was so strong and virile that He commanded the allegiance of other men. He did not look like someone who had been a carpenter for many years or who was strong enough to knock over the tables of the money changers and drive them out of the temple. Nor was He the kind of man who was likely to throw anyone into Hell! He was too "sweet" to do something so horrible. He was now depicted as an effeminate white male whose appearance was not threatening. There was nothing left in Jesus to fear.

It has gotten only worse. We were shocked to see a new picture of Christ on the wall of a church in which he is portrayed as a white, long-haired, blond, blue-eyed California surfer! Besides being blatantly racist, this "Jesus" is not the "mighty God" of Isaiah 9:6.

The Feminization of Hymns

The historic hymns of the Christian Church were strong in doctrine and majestic in style. They emphasized God's sovereignty, power and judgment as well as His love and mercy. But, after the rise of liberalism, a whole new generation of hymns were written which were often marked by romantic terminology, erotic expressions, and gushy sentimentality. Many of these hymns were written by well-meaning single Christian women who were guilty of unconsciously fantasizing a romantic love to Jesus which was clearly sexual in nature.

Whereas the great hymns of the church were marked by strong doctrinal content and a majestic style, the hymns of the 19th century were generally shallow in content, sticky sweet in terminology, and sloppy in style. One searches in vain to find any references to the fear of God or the final Judgment in such hymns. Even the doctrine of the Trinity is replaced by a romantic "loving" Jesus theme.

It is thus no surprise to find that it was during this time that the fear of the Lord disappeared from modern hymnody. This also explains why so many men began to feel uneasy with hymns which portray a sticky romantic love to an effeminate "sweet" Jesus.

One modern example of a "romantic" hymn is the popular song, "You Light Up My Life." It has been sung to Jesus, to boyfriends, to lovers and to husbands. The fact that it can be equally applied to all romantic and erotic relationships reveals that the author was under the mistaken impression that her love to Jesus Christ could be erotic in nature.

There are three different words for "love" in the Greek language. The Greek word *philos* describes the love between brothers and is used in the New Testament to describe Christian fellowship (Titus 3:15). Our love for fellow Christians is not romantic or sexual in nature.

The second Greek word for love is *agape* which refers to our pure devotion to and worship of God (John 14:23). There is no erotic, romantic or sexual element in this kind of love.

The third Greek word is *eros* which refers to the sexual and romantic relationship between lovers. This is why the word *eros* is NEVER used in the Bible to describe our love to Jesus or to the other members of the Trinity. Thus it is simply wrong when our love to Jesus is expressed in an erotic or romantic manner. *Jesus is not our male lover*. Thus any song or hymn which expresses a romantic love to Him borders on blasphemy.

The Feminization of Christianity

As God, Jesus, and Christian hymns were feminized, the secular literature of the 19th century began to picture Christianity as a religion fit only for "women, children and sissies." Magazine stories, fiction novels, and theatrical productions pictured Jesus as effeminate. He was no longer someone to be feared. All His "fangs" had been pulled and He was as harmless as an old toothless tiger.

As a liberal view of God swept through Protestant churches, the men stopped going to church because "religion was for women and children." Even Jesus lost respect in the eyes of men as He was now perceived as weak and effeminate. For example, men in the military were told that if they wanted to be "like Jesus," they could not fight for justice or kill the enemy. Jesus was pictured as a harmless pacifist who would not fight for what He viewed as right. If you "really loved the Lord," you would not be a policeman or a soldier. Thus those careers were now abandoned to unbelievers.

This is why so many police departments came to be run by Roman Catholics even in Protestant communities. The Protestants were told from the pulpit that if Jesus would never hurt anyone, then how could those who believe in Him be a policeman or soldier?

In many novels of that period, Christianity became a religion for "sissies" and no "macho" man would ever attend church. Mark Twain's *Tom Sawyer* pictured religion as something fit only for the "Aunt Polly's" of this world. Real men could safely ignore it.

A Mega-shift

A mega-shift in the way people thought about God was the end result of the rise of liberalism. We no longer needed to fear God because His holiness and wrath had been eclipsed by His love and mercy.

The same mega-shift which took place in mainline Protestant churches during the 19th century is happening today in evangelical seminaries, colleges, and churches. The feminization of evangelical theology is taking place at a rapid rate. God's people must wake up and realize the danger of what is happening all around us today. Should we worship the God revealed in Scripture or the goddess of modern liberalism?

Conclusion

What is your view of Jesus? Is He sweet or strong? Do you fear Him? Is He a forceful and commanding figure? Or, is He just "meek and mild"? Does He sit on the throne as the Judge of all the earth? Or, is He just a sweet savior? Would your Jesus take a whip and use it to beat the money changers in the temple? Will your Jesus really throw people into an eternal hell on the last day?

If you feel uncomfortable with a strong Jesus, your view of Jesus is a product of 19th century liberalism and not the Bible.

Chapter 3: THE FEMINIZATION OF THE CLERGY

In our last chapter, we saw how the feminization of Christianity corrupted our view of God and even debased our hymns. The feminization of God is a process once started that cannot stop until the biblical God is totally eradicated and the goddess reigns supreme. Thus it is no surprise that this process also altered how people viewed the clergy. But this is only what we would expect. A change in the way people view God will change the way they view those who represent Him.

Masculine Pastors

Before the feminization of Christianity, pastors were viewed as strong men who preached strong sermons and who had strong ministries. They were soldiers, judges, mayors, hunters, and pioneers as well as preachers. They were not afraid to stand up for the truth. Throughout church history, many pastors died in battle defending their home, their church, and their nation.

The Swiss Reformer Swingli died in battle after leading his people in the defense of their lives and liberties from an invading army. The great Oliver Cromwell and his army of godly Puritans included many clergymen such as the great John Owen.

The Puritans and the Pilgrims always had "fighting pastors" who did not hesitate to take up arms when needed. In the American Revolution, the clergy were at the forefront of the battle. Several of the outstanding generals in Washington's army were clergymen.

In a famous Lutheran Church near Gettysburg, Pennsylvania, after the pastor preached his Sunday morning sermon, he opened his gown to reveal that he had on a soldier's uniform. He was answering Washington's call to become one of his generals. When he called for volunteers to follow him into battle, most of the men in his congregation rose up and went into battle with their pastor.

The average Puritan or Pilgrim clergyman shared a common life with his men. He went hunting, fought wars, and served as a soldier, a judge, a mayor, etc. In short, a pastor's masculinity was never put in question. He was not passive or retiring in the face of evil. He was a "real" man in the popular meaning of the word.

Feminized Pastors

With the rise of religious liberalism, the role of "pastor" was feminized. Clergymen were discouraged from all "manly" activities, and it became "unseemly" for a clergyman to hunt or fish, fight in war, hold a political office, or even physically defend himself. His place was now restricted to the parlor where he read poetry to the Ladies' Afternoon Literary Society. He was no longer feared or respected. He was now "sweet."

As a result of this, a new picture of clergymen appeared in the literature of the 19th Century. Pastors were held up to ridicule and described in various novels and short stories as weak and effeminate. They wore fancy clothes and spent their time going to teas for bored women. They were scorned as sissies and pansies.

During the Civil War, for the first time in American history, clergymen were forbidden by law from fighting on the front lines with their men. Instead, they were stationed at the rear of the battle with the women, reduced to giving comfort to the wounded and dying. Even today, our chaplains in the military are not allowed to fight. They are denied the right to fight for their God and their country.

The feminization of the clergy became so dominant that several States passed laws forbidding clergymen from holding public office! Do you understand how outrageous this is? Pastors were denied their civil rights by law and could not run for political office. This was in stark contrast to Colonial America where clergymen such as Cotton Mather served as mayors and judges or to the Revolutionary War where pastors were generals and officers.

Even today, when conservative pastors get involved in politics, liberals will accuse them of "mixing politics and religion." They are told that it is not "right" for them to get involved in such issues. Clergymen should be restricted to "soul winning." The "separation of church and state" usually means that conservative clergy are denied their freedom of speech.

Those who have a feminized view of the clergy were shocked and outraged when pastors were arrested during abortion demonstrations, not because they were arrested, but because they were fighting for civil rights! They do not understand that their bigoted and narrow view of what pastors can or cannot do comes from the liberal process of the feminization of God.

Sissy Sermons

As the role of the clergy grew more effeminate in character, preaching styles began to change. The bold, strong, virile, doctrinal preaching of the Puritans—who were not afraid to warn people of hell and judgment to come—was now looked upon as unkind, unloving, uncouth and, worst of all, insensitive to people's feelings.

People wanted soothing sermons and "quiet talks" on love. Doctrinal preaching was no longer acceptable. Strong theology and bold preaching became out of fashion for clergymen. Thus any pastor who was bold and assertive when dealing with sin and heresy was condemned as "unloving."

People also no longer wanted sermons that made them *think*! Instead, they wanted sermons that made them *feel* warm and happy. To raise your voice or to pound on the pulpit was no longer acceptable. The use of logic and argumentation in sermons was frowned upon.

This is why many seminaries tell their students not to be bold, authoritative or doctrinal in their preaching. They are told to keep to those topics which make people feel good about themselves and not to be so rude as to tell them that they are depraved sinners or to frighten them with the doctrine of hell.

Today, if a pastor is strong and outspoken in his preaching and pastoring, he will be accused of pride and beaten down with accusations that he is not loving, kind or sensitive to people's feelings. The glory of God and biblical truth have been eclipsed by church growth techniques that focus only on the felt needs of the people in the community. Today, giving people what they want is more important than obeying God and preaching the truth.

Lesbian Pastors

In liberal Protestant denominations and organizations such as the National Council of Churches, feminist and lesbian clergy have taken over. As these women "pastors" fill the pulpits, the last of the men are leaving the main line churches in droves. Men find their masculinity under attack from the pulpit. Why go to church to hear that being a male is the root of all evil?

In one liberal church near us, the lesbian pastor took the feminization of God to its ultimate conclusion by changing hymns and even Scripture to reflect her radical feminist views. In her church they sang, "Lead On, O Queen Eternal" and prayed to "Our Mother Which Art In Heaven!"

Bible translators have even dared to rewrite the Bible to conform to the demands of radical feminists. So-called "neuter gender" hymnals and prayer books have been produced to further feminize liberal churches.

The Return of the Goddess

Where will this all end? It will end in what took place in a Boston church in 1989. Over four hundred women met to worship Diana of Ephesus and to proclaim that the biblical view of God as "Father" was now "dead" and that the time had finally come to worship ancient pagan goddesses such as Diana!

Some "evangelical" churches have also bowed before the goddess. In their rush to be "inclusive" and politically correct, they have fallen for the lie that the Father and the Son have had a sex-change operations and have become a Mother-Daughter team!

Anyone who claims to be a Christian should take a long and hard look at what the feminization of Christianity has done to liberal churches. Do we really want to drive the men out of our churches; to put lesbians in the pulpit and gays in charge of our young people? Is this honoring to God or to His Word? NO! It is blasphemous to say the least and heretical to say the best. How can anyone who claims to be a Christian do such wicked things? God gives us the answer in His Word: "There is no fear of God before their eyes" (Romans 3:18).

Conclusion

The fear of the Lord vanished as God, Jesus, the clergy, hymns, the church and preaching were first liberalized and then feminized. The kind of god that is preached in most churches today is not worthy of awe, wonder or worship. "She" or "it" is thus not worthy of our fear.

The liberals have already emptied their churches. Should evangelicals allow them to empty our churches as well? Theologians and pastors must once again with vigor proclaim the biblical view of God as found in Holy Scripture. They must stand up to the politically correct crowd and condemn them as heretics, sodomites and wolves in sheep's clothing. We need to cleanse our colleges and seminaries of heretical professors. The fundamental principle that should guide us in all this is: *Any view of God, which does not lead us to fear God, cannot be a biblical view of God.*

Chapter 4: THE WORLD MOLDING THE CHURCH

In Romans 12:1-2, the Apostle Paul warned us not to let the world squeeze us into its own mold.

> Therefore, brothers, because of God's mercies, I urge you to offer your bodies as living sacrifices that are holy and pleasing to God, for this is a reasonable way for you to worship. Stop being conformed to this world, but continue to be transformed by the renewing of your minds so that you may be able to determine what is God's will—what is proper, pleasing, and perfect.

Down through the centuries, the surrounding pagan culture with its are, music, manner of dress, and social standards has always been a snare to the people of God. This was true of Israel in the Old Testament as well as of the Christian Church throughout its history.

While the typical Bible-believing church has not fallen into the error of liberal theology, it has, at times, fallen under the spell of the cultural norms which liberalism has spawned. At times we have failed to preach the Truth as it is in Jesus because we were afraid of being ridiculed by the world. We have been intimidated into silence.

Hell Fire Sermons

The doctrine of hell is a good example of how liberal theology can influence Christians to become silent on various doctrines. As we pointed out in the book *Death and The Afterlife*, while evangelicals still believe in the eternal conscious punishment of unbelievers, they rarely preach it today. After all, when was the last time *you* heard a sermon on hell? Why do we fail to preach it? How did we end up in this situation?

Liberal theologians frown upon the doctrine of hell as being "unkind" and "insensitive" as well as morally repulsive. The liberal controlled media has depicted anyone who preaches "hell and damnation" as a wild-eyed illiterate preacher with dirt between his toes, a bloody ax in one hand, and a KJV pulpit Bible in the other hand! Hollywood has produced thousands of radio/TV programs and movies, which ridicule anyone who, believes in hell.

Given the dominance of liberalism in our culture today, the doctrine of hell is no longer "acceptable" or "proper." Thus while evangelicals still believe in hell as a doctrine, they do not preach it much today because the surrounding liberal culture is opposed to its mention except in cursing.

The Raw Truth

The raw truth is that we have avoided preaching those doctrines such as hell, the sovereignty of God, the lost condition of the heathen, etc., because we are afraid of the mockers and scoffers of this world. We have allowed the world to squeeze us into its own mold! Peter warned us that this was going to happen.

> First of all you must understand this: In the last days mockers will come and, indulging in their own lusts, will ridicule us by saying, "What happened to his promise to return? Ever since our ancestors died, everything continues as it did from the beginning of creation." (2 Peter 3:3-4)

Did Peter stop preaching the Second Coming of Christ because some people were mocking it? No! To the apostles, the truth was the truth, and they did not care what the mockers said. The apostle Paul had the same attitude when he said,

> God is true, even if everyone else is a liar. (Romans 3:4)

He told young Timothy to preach the Word regardless of "whether or not the time is convenient" (2 Timothy 4:2). When the frown of the world is more influential than the frown of God, the fear of the Lord needs to be revived.

What Ever Happened To Sin?

The same process has made it "out of place" today to preach on sin. The "popular" thing is to talk about various psychological sicknesses, addictions, and problems.

Have you noticed that today people are no longer viewed as sinners? If you watch the TV talk shows, you will hear that adulterers, rapists, and child molesters are not *sinners* who need to *repent*. They are only *sex addicts* who need *therapy*! They are only "sick"—not sinful. They are the "victims" of society, racism, abuse, neglect, etc. What they need is a "twelve step" program. We should not condemn them as sinners but "feel their pain" and have compassion on them! Such wickedness and downright stupidity comes from a lack of fearing God.

Doctrinal Preaching Today

The same liberal cultural process has made strong doctrinal preaching "out of fashion" today. What has happened to the good old-fashioned concern for the Truth as it is in Jesus?

Instead of preaching the truth of God, too many pastors give "relational" sermons, which focus on the feelings of man. Any doctrine that might hurt someone's feelings is either denied or ignored.

If you want to get people mad today, just preach the truth of Scripture that the man is the head of the home and his wife should submit to him; that children should obey their parents; that criminals should be punished; that the death penalty should be used more frequently; that we are not part of God; that we cannot be all that we want to be; that we do not have infinite potential; that all things are not possible with us; that being positive will not do much for you; that we are not all created equal because some people are smarter or stronger than others; that adultery and divorce disqualify you for the ministry; and that the heathen are lost.

The Price of Discernment

The moment you point out all the false teachings heard on popular "Christian" radio and TV programs, you are told to shut up for the sake of peace and unity. "Don't rock the boat!" "Don't make any waves!" These maxims seem to be the ultimate virtues today.

If you stand up for the truth of God's Word, you are called a "trouble maker" who is not "sensitive" to the feelings of people. You are accused of pride and conceit if you defend the fundamental doctrines of the Bible.

The Church Growth Movement

One movement today which clearly reveals how far we have drifted from the fear of the Lord is the "church growth movement." They would have us believe that numbers, money, and buildings are the only goals that count; that the New Testament is irrelevant when it comes to the nature, structure and programs of the local church; that we should take surveys in the community and ask the heathen what kind of church service they want and what sermon topics they are willing to hear. Then we should build a church that reflects the counsel of the ungodly! Never mind what the Bible says about how a church is to be structured and run. The sociologists are better equipped to tell us what to do than the Apostles!

I Will Build My Church

In Matthew 16:18, Jesus said that He was going to build His Church His way. He did not ask the Pharisees what kind of church they wanted and then set up a church according to their desires. Did the Apostles in the Book of Acts run around taking surveys of the heathen to see what they wanted? No!

The New Testament tells us the nature and structure of a local church. We can create any organization we want and call it a "church" but that does not mean it is a true church of the Lord Jesus Christ. The Bible is the only rule of faith and practice—not pragmatism.

The Whole Counsel of God

The Bible tells us in such passages as Acts 20:27 that "the whole counsel of God" must be preached. If the "church growth movement" is of God, why is the doctrine of hell never preached? Why isn't the reality of sin and depravity proclaimed? The answer is quite simple: The heathen do not want to hear that they are sinners under the wrath of God. They hate the very idea that they need to repent and turn to Jesus. They do not want to hear it. If you build a church to suit their tastes in sermons, you will not warn them to flee the wrath to come. Since the cross is a stumbling block to the heathen, some churches will not display a cross or even sing hymns as "The Old Rugged Cross!"

The Cult of Happiness

Because the fear the Lord is no longer preached, most Christians today do not understand that their purpose in life is to glorify God. Instead, their own personal happiness has become the all consuming theme of the Christian life. Happiness has become an idol before whom all must bow. Anything such as the fear of God which would tend to make people feel unhappy at times is frowned upon.

We have heard far too many sermons, which focused on "How Jesus can make you happy." It is time to tell people the truth that God is more concerned with their holiness than their happiness. Sadness and sorrow are good things if they bring you to repentance.

Come close to God, and he will come close to you. Cleanse your hands, you sinners, and purify your hearts, you double-minded. Be miserable, mourn, and cry. Let your laughter be turned into mourning, and your joy into gloom. Humble yourselves before the Lord, and he will exalt you. (James 4:8-10)

Instead of preaching that we exist for God's glory and that we are His servants, we are told today that God exists for our happiness and He is our servant! He is supposed to "fetch and carry" wealth and health for us whenever we demand it!

Dedicated to Jesus?

This is why dedication to Christ has fallen on hard times. The "Me-First" generation is not interested in the personal sacrifice that is required to serve Christ. When was the last time you heard a sermon calling upon you to be totally surrendered to Christ?

The biblical demand of the total dedication of everything you are and have to the Lord Jesus Christ is rarely preached today. Instead, people are told that the Christian life is easy and fun. You can lie, cheat, steal and even commit adultery and still be a pastor! Morality and truth do not matter anymore.

Let Us Entertain You

Because people no longer fear God, too many churches are involved in entertainment instead of biblical preaching. The worship service has become an off-off-Broadway musical production instead of being centered on the preaching of the Word of God. Have you ever noticed that as more and more entertainment is included in a church service, the shorter and the shallower the sermons become?

Crowds of people are willing to attend church if it is long on entertainment and short on preaching. With church programs and services designed to make everyone feel good about themselves, is it any wonder that we no longer hear sermons that convict us of sin? When is the last time you heard a sermon that pricked your conscience; that caused you to weep before the Lord in repentance; or that made you rededicate your life to Christ?

The End Result

Is it any surprise then, given the liberal cultural context, that most evangelical Christians have never heard a single sermon on fearing God? The very word "fear" itself is viewed as a "bummer." It does not fit into the "positive thinking" movement. It is not politically correct.

How can we tell people to fear God when we are trying to convince them that Jesus will make them happy all the time? If we told people the truth that they should fear the just judgment of Almighty Jesus, how can we con people into joining our "warm and fuzzy" churches where everything is "nice" and "sweet?" We have sold our birthright for a bowl of mush.

Conclusion

The Church at the beginning of the twenty-first century, despite all its wealth and power, is actually desperately sick and weak. The man in the pulpit is far too often more carnal and immoral than those who sit in the pew! Why? There is no fear of God before their eyes.

The wickedness that is carried on in the name of the Lord today is a blight upon the testimony of the Church. *If the Church is to regain its spiritual strength and power, we must begin with the fear of God. Why? Those who fear the Lord will depart from evil.*

Part Two:

The Importance of Fearing God

Chapter 5: How Important Is It?

In order for us to overcome a century and a half of liberal thinking, we must be convinced that the fear of God is important and essential to true biblical religion. The first observation is this: *The frequency of its mention in Scripture, as compared to other aspects of vital piety, reveals the importance of the fear of God.*

Training Children

This observation is based upon the assumption that when someone tells you to do something over and over again, it is evidently important to him or her that you do it.

Every parent knows that this principle is true. As soon as your children start crawling, they automatically go for the electrical cords of lamps, radios, etc. They desperately want to chew those wires! You have to tell them, "No wires!" over and over again. As children grow, you have to tell them repeatedly not to go near the swimming pool without an adult; do not to talk to strangers; do not fight with your sister or brother, etc. It was even by repetition that you taught them the alphabet and how to read.

In short, we have to repeat things to our children over and over again. In order for them to learn something we must repeat it until they catch on to it. Why? Because this is human nature. Sometimes the only way that we can get something into our thick sculls is to have it pounded into it again and again. What is so surprising is that when we study the frequency of the mention of the fear of God in Scripture and then compare it to the other aspects of vital piety, we discover that God is overwhelmingly concerned that people fear Him.

Our Love of God

For example, the Bible speaks of our love to God, His name, His law, and His Word, a total of 88 times. This is the sum total of both the Old and New Testaments, counting every verse that speaks of man's love toward God. This breaks down to 45 references in the Old Testament and 43 references in the New Testament.

Since man's love toward God is mentioned 88 times in the Bible, it is rather obvious that it is very important to God that we love Him personally and also love His name and His Law. David proclaimed,

> I love the Lord, because He hears my voice and my supplications. (Psalm116:1)

> Oh, how love I your Law! It is my meditation all the day. (Psalm 119:97)

God repeatedly tells us in the Bible that we should love Him with all our heart, soul and mind. The Lord Jesus said,

> You must love the Lord your God with all your heart, with all your soul, and with all your mind. (Matthew 22:37)

The mere fact that He had to tell us to love Him 88 times reveals that He is concerned that we do so.

Trusting in God

Secondly, the Bible speaks of our trusting in God (Proverbs 3:5-6), His name (Psalm 33:21), and His Word (Psalm 119:42) ninety-one times. This breaks down to 82 times in the Old Testament and 9 times in the New Testament.

But lest someone be tempted to say that since trusting God is mainly found in the Old Testament, it is not really important today, we must emphasize that the New Testament often assumes what the Old Testament has already established. Thus the New Testament assumes such virtues as trusting God because it was clearly taught in the Old Testament.

Fearing God

When we come to the subject of the fear of God, the Bible speaks of it 278 times! We are referring to all the places in Scripture where it speaks of men fearing God, His name, His Law or His Word.

In the Old Testament there are 235 references to the fear of God. In the New Testament there are 43 references to the fear of God which, by the way, is the same number of references as man's love to God.

From Genesis to Revelation, the Bible proclaims that the fear of the Lord is a fountain of life and those who drink deeply of it shall have the blessings of God in this life and in the life to come. However, those who reject the fear of the Lord will end up in the ways of death.

A Logical Conclusion

What is the only logical conclusion we can draw from the frequency of the mention of the fear of God in Scripture? *The fear of God is the predominant response to and fundamental attitude toward God, His Word, His Law and His name, that God desires.* This is why it is mentioned more times than any other aspect of vital piety.

Ever Hear about It?

Given the scriptural importance of the fear of the Lord, most of us must confess that although we have been going to church for many years, we have never heard a single sermon on the fear of God! When was the last time you had a Sunday School lesson on the fear of God? Have you ever seen a book on the fear of God? The typical Christian today has heard many sermons on the love of God but absolutely nothing about the fear of God. This is sad as well as unbiblical.

What We Are Not Saying

We must emphasize that we are NOT saying that the fear of God is the ONLY way to relate to God. Please do not misunderstand what we are saying and run off thinking that we are denying the importance of loving God.

Of course you should love God. That is not the issue. What we are saying is that we must relate to God in more than one way. Loving God is not enough according to the Bible. We must also FEAR Him.

Just as a diamond has many facets, so our relationship to God has many different aspects. It is multi-dimensional. While we believe in loving God, we also believe that there is more to walking with God than loving Him. We must also trust Him, believe in Him and fear Him! The modern church's failure to teach the average Christian this truth is what has led to the sloppy and disobedient lifestyle of most Christians today.

The Fundamental Aspect

If we take the Bible seriously, the fundamental aspect of our relationship to God should be the fear of the Lord! We should fear the Lord, trust Him, love Him, obey Him, honor Him, etc. Anything less than this is not true saving religion.

The Psalms

The Book of Psalms is the record of man's intimate and personal relationship with God. These hymns and prayers express the subjective experience of what it means to walk with God. Thus it is not surprising to find that the Psalmist declares 62 times that the fear of the Lord is the pinnacle of that personal relationship.

Entire Psalms are dedicated to the subject of the blessedness which results when someone fears the Lord.

Psalm 112

In Psalm 112:1, the Psalmist states,

Praise the Lord! How blessed is the man who fears the Lord, who greatly delights in His commandments.

In Hebrew poetry, the second phrase often deepens our understanding of the first phrase. In this verse, the fear of God is not a negative or a slavish fear. It is a "delight!" The Psalmist says, "who *greatly delights* in His commandments."

This is the kind of awe or reverence which actually draws you into God's presence where you experience delight in the Law of God because you fear the Lord. The Psalmist goes on to say,

His descendants will be mighty on earth. The generation of the upright will be blessed. Wealth and riches are in his house and his righteousness endures forever. Light arises in the darkness for the upright; he is gracious and compassionate and righteous. (Psalm 112: 2-4)

Carnal Blessings

Under the Old Covenant, the word "blessing" sometimes had a carnal meaning. A "blessing" was not so much "heavenly" as it was "earthly." It was usually more "carnal" than it was "spiritual" (2 Corinthians 3:1-11).

Under the Old Covenant, material prosperity was the reward for fearing the Lord. They were promised many children; their barns would be full; their cattle would gave birth in due season; they would inherit the land; they would live a long time, etc. The word "blessing" mainly referred to the carnal gifts of God.

No, we are not saying the same thing that the "blab it - grab it" prosperity preachers on TV are saying! What we are saying is that the Old Covenant was a carnal covenant which focused on such material things as land, children, money, health, etc.

Spiritual Blessings

In distinction, the New Covenant is as spiritual as the Old Covenant was carnal. In the New Testament, we are told to focus on "things above" instead of carnal "things below" (Colossians 3:1-2). We are not looking for a land here on earth but a heavenly home where Christ dwells (John 14:1-2).

Psalm 128

Again, in Psalm 128, we find another entire Psalm dedicated to the blessedness of fearing the Lord.

> Blessed are all who fear the Lord, who walk in His ways. You will eat the fruit of your labor. Blessings and prosperity will be yours. Your wife will be like a fruitful vine within your house. Your sons will be like olive shoots around your table. (Psalm 128:1-3)

The olive tree was so important to the Jews that they would often bring the young shoots into the house where they could watch over them until they were strong enough to be planted outside. This is why David says that our children are so precious that they are like olive plants sitting around our table because we fear the Lord.

Psalm 111

In Psalm 111:10, we read,

> The fear of the Lord is the beginning of wisdom. All who follow His precepts have good understanding. To Him belongs eternal praise.

Do you want to be a wise person? Do you seek after understanding? Do you search for wisdom as you would for a hidden treasure? Then you must begin with the fear of the Lord.

Psalm 130

In Psalm 130:3-4, we find,

> If you, oh Lord, kept a record of our sins, who could stand? But there is forgiveness with you that you may be feared.

God is keeping a record of every evil thought that passes through your mind. He has taken note of every evil deed you have ever done and of every idle word that you have ever spoken. There is a coming Day of Judgment on which He will hold you personally accountable for all the evil you have ever thought, felt, spoken, or done.

Do you think that you will be able to stand on that Day and successfully defend your sins before God? No, all would be lost! There would be no hope for you because your sins are like the sands on a seashore. You cannot even count them.

If the Psalmist were simply to leave it there, we would be able to out-existentialize the existentialists! Christians would have to tell Kafka and Sartre to move over because we are going to preach a real theology of despair. But look at verse 4, "but with You there is forgiveness."

What? Forgiveness? Despite the fact that we sinned against God's grace and provoked Him to His face? Even when we have trampled His Law under our feet? Despite all the rebellion, the hatred, and the spite? "Yes!" the Psalmist says, "There is forgiveness with God. There is an infinite amount of forgiveness in God, and you may receive this forgiveness without cost and price to yourself."

But what is the GOAL of God's forgiveness? WHY does He forgive us? WHAT is He seeking to accomplish by forgiving us? David states that the purpose of God's forgiveness is to usher us into a new relationship to Him, and that new relationship is the fear of God: "that You may be feared."

God does not just forgive you and then, willy nilly, let you run off and live like the devil. He is not interested in people who want to play games trying to keep one foot in the world and one foot with God. He does not play that kind of game with people. He is either Lord of all or not Lord at all.

Psalm 34

We are also told that the fear of God brings special protection and provision. In Psalm 34:7-16, we read,

> The angel of the Lord encamps around those who fear Him and He delivers them. Fear the Lord, you His saints, for those who fear Him, lack nothing. Come my children, listen to me, I will teach you the fear of the Lord, whoever of you loves life and desires to see many good days, keep your tongue from evil, and your lips from speaking lies, turn from evil and do good, seek peace and pursue it. The eyes of the Lord are on the righteous and His ears are attentive to their cry. The face of the Lord is against those who do evil, to cut off the memory of them, from the earth.

Psalm 33

The same thing is said in Psalm 33:18-19,

> The eyes of the Lord are on those who fear Him, on those whose hope is in His unfailing love, to deliver them from death and keep them alive in famine.

Psalm 111

Or again, in Psalm 111:5, we are told, "He has given food to those who fear Him." This is why we are told in Deuteronomy 6:24,

> The Lord commanded us to obey all of these decrees and to fear the Lord our God so that we might always prosper and be kept alive as is the case today.

The book of Ecclesiastes reflects the same idea:

> Although a wicked man commits a hundred crimes, and still lives a long time, I know that it will go better with God-fearing men who fear God. — Ecclesiastes 8:12

Psalm 103

The fear of the Lord also secures the compassion and love of God, as David explains in Psalm 103:11,17,

> For as high as the Heavens are above the earth, so great is His love toward those who fear Him. As far as the east is from the west, so far has He removed our transgressions from us. As a father has compassion on his children, so the Lord has compassion on those who fear Him. From everlasting to everlasting, the Lord's love is with those who fear Him.

Do you want to secure the love and the compassion of the forgiveness of God? You must fear God in order to have it.

Proverbs

In the book of Proverbs, the fear of the Lord is referred to 15 times as being the source of wisdom, knowledge, discretion, truthfulness and morality. Thus the fear of the Lord should not be limited to "inner" piety. It is truly practical and enables us to live a godly life in a sinful world.

What is wisdom? The ability to see something from God's viewpoint. And what is understanding? The ability to respond to what you have seen according to God's Word. We are told in Proverbs 14:27,

The fear of the Lord is a fountain of life, turning a man from the snares of death.

The fear of God is a fountain of life! Would it not be a blessing to have such a fountain and to be able to put in your cup and lift it up and drink of the waters of life? Would you like to have "a fountain of life" in your home; an artesian well that is bubbling up with the water of eternal life for you and your family? Would you rejoice in such a fountain? This is what the fear of the Lord is all about!

More than simply promising a long life if you fear the Lord, Solomon says that the fear of the Lord will enable you to escape from "the snares of death" when you and your family are tempted to do evil in the sight of the Lord.

Practical Stuff, Too

But someone may say, "This is all theological stuff. Do I get anything practical out of fearing God?" Well, what about a good night's sleep? Proverbs 19:23 says,

The fear of the Lord leads to life. The one who fears God can sleep satisfied, untouched by any evil.

Would you like to have a nice sleep untouched by the evils of night? Solomon said that the fear of the Lord is the very essence of life. You can lie down safely, rest contented, and sleep satisfied, unmolested by evil, because the Lord encamps around those who fear Him.

In Isaiah 33:6, we read,

And He will be the sure foundation for your times, a rich store of salvation, wisdom and knowledge. The fear of the Lord is the key to this treasure.

God is pictured as a great and glorious King whose treasure house is filled with all of the glories and benefits of salvation. The prophet Isaiah says that there is a key that unlocks the door to the treasure room.

All of God's treasures can be ours if we have the key that unlocks the door. What is this key? Where can we find it? This key is the fear of the Lord. *It is the key that unlocks the door to the treasure house of God.* Is it not amazing that what Isaiah proclaimed as the "key" to the blessings of God is totally ignored today? Have you used the key of the fear of the Lord to unlock the storeroom of blessing for you and your family?

A Defective Covenant

The book of Hebrews tells us that there was a fundamental defect in the Old Covenant (Hebrews 7:18-8:13). What was this defect? The Old Covenant could not provide a redeemed heart to fear God. It was a carnal, legal covenant that dealt with such external things as land, wealth, health and one's children. The constant lament throughout the Old Testament was,

> Oh, that they had such a heart in them, that they should fear Me, and keep all my commandments always, that it may be well with them and with their sons forever! (Deuteronomy 5:29)

A Superior Covenant

The superior nature of the New Covenant is that it provides man with a new heart to fear God.

> "Behold, the days are coming," declares the LORD, "when I will make a new covenant with the house of Israel and with the house of Judah, not like the

covenant which I made with their fathers... I will put my law within them, and on their heart I will write it... They shall all know Me. And they shall be My people, and I will be their God; and I will give them one heart and one way, that they may fear Me always... I will put the fear of Me in their hearts so that they will not turn away from Me. (Jeremiah 31:31-33; 32:38-40)

All the gracious provisions of the New Covenant, from knowing God to forgiveness of sins, are given to usher us into the fear of the Lord. This last insight provides us with the link between the fear of God and the New Testament.

The New Testament

The authors of the New Testament apply the prophecy of the New Covenant to the Church in such places as Hebrews 8:8-13 and Hebrews 10:11-18. Indeed, the New Testament is itself the record of the establishment of the New Covenant through the person and work of Christ. This New Covenant is a covenant of grace wherein God graciously provides man with a new heart to fear Him always. Thus the fear of God is the stated goal of the New Covenant.

But why is this a "new" concept to so many Christians today? The liberals have always claimed that the Old Testament deity was a primitive savage god you had to fear. The New Testament, they claimed, did away with the fear of God and substituted the love of God in its place.

Since the goal of the New Covenant is to bring sinners into a permanent relationship with God in which they fear Him and keep His commandments forever, there is no way that the Liberals can legitimately pit the Old Testament against the New Testament.

The Frequency of Mention

Even more to the point, there are 43 references in the New Testament to the fear of God. This means that *there are as many references to the fear of God as there are references to the love of God!* For example, in Acts 9:31, we are told that the church enjoyed a time of peace:

> So the church throughout Judea, Galilee, and Samaria enjoyed peace. As it continued to be built up and to live in the fear of the Lord, it kept increasing in numbers through the encouragement of the Holy Spirit.

In the Greek text, we are told by way of participles, how and why they obtained this peace. The text states that the Church "continued to be built up." It was increasing in numbers. Why?

Luke tells us that this was happening because the Christians were going on in the fear of the Lord. Thus the fear of the Lord was the divinely appointed means by which the church experienced peace and growth. Luke also tells us that as they went on in the fear of the Lord, they experienced the comfort of the Holy Spirit. Thus the fruit of the Spirit is rooted in the fear of God.

Do you want to see your church prosper in the things of God? Then learn to fear the Lord. All of these things happen as people live in the fear of the Lord.

No Fear of God

One last principle can be drawn from Romans 3:18. In speaking of those who are not Christians, the Apostle Paul tells us, "There is no fear of God before their eyes."

If you are truly converted, you already fear God to some degree. You know that He is mighty to save and mighty to

Chapter 5: How Important Is It?

judge. You realize that the Lord is a great King. He is not sitting in a wheelchair waiting for you to wheel Him around. He is a great King, sitting high and lifted up on a throne, ruling the universe.

But to those who do not know the Lord personally, they have no fear of God. If they were honest, they would say, "No, I do not fear God. To fear God never enters my mind. Since God is all loving, what is there to fear? If I want to steal something, I steal it. If I want to say something, I say it because I do not fear God." When men no longer fear God, there is no restraint upon their lusts.

Conclusion

The fear of the Lord is the recognition that God is holy as well as loving, and thus He is to be feared as well as trusted. God is the Righteous Judge of all the earth who sits upon His throne judging the nations with equity. If we make the mistake of neglecting or denying this biblical view of God, we will suffer in our spiritual life. *Since God has revealed Himself in Scripture, to worship any other God than the One revealed in Scripture is the essence of idolatry.*

Chapter 6: THE IMPORTANCE OF WISDOM

The Beginning of Wisdom

One of the Biblical phrases that most Christians memorize is found in the Psalms as well as in Proverbs. Both David and Solomon proclaimed, "The fear of the Lord is the beginning of wisdom." (Psalm 111:10; Proverbs 9:10). What most people do not understand is that in Psalm 111:10 and Proverbs 9:10, two different Hebrew words are translated by the word "beginning." Why this is never brought out in English translations is a mystery to us.

Psalm 111

Psalm 111 is entirely dedicated to the subject of the fear of the Lord. In verse 10, David tells us that the fear of the Lord is the *"beginning"* of wisdom. In the Hebrew text, David uses the word רֵאשִׁית (*re-sheet*) when he says that the fear of the Lord is the "beginning" of wisdom.

The Chief Aspect of Wisdom

The Hebrew word רֵאשִׁית is translated elsewhere in the Bible in other ways than by the word "beginning." For example, in 1 Samuel 15:21, it has been translated as the "best," i.e. the highest quality, the chief, the choicest.

The people took some of the spoil—sheep, cattle, and the best (רֵאשִׁית) of what was to be completely

46

destroyed—to sacrifice to the LORD your God at Gilgal. (1 Samuel 15:21)

The story is well known. God had ordered Saul to kill all the Amalakites because their "Judgment Day" had come early. When Samuel met Saul, he said, "Did you obey the Lord and all that He commanded?" Saul replied, "Sure, we did it all. We did it just like God said." But he was lying through his teeth. He had let King Agag and the best of the animals live.

Samuel had told them to destroy all the possessions of the Amalakites including their sheep and oxen. When Samuel heard the bleating of the sheep and the lowing of the oxen, he said, "Now, if you have obeyed God, why am I hearing sheep and oxen over across that hill?" We can imagine some of the soldiers saying "Oh no, Samuel's coming. Get those oxen and sheep quiet!" But Samuel heard them, and he knew that they had not obeyed the Lord.

Saul tried to defend himself in verse 20, "I did obey the Lord, and went on the mission on which the Lord sent me. (1 Samuel 15:20)" He then tried to blamed the "people" for keeping the "choicest" of the sheep, oxen and plunder for themselves. The same Hebrew word רֵאשִׁית, which was translated as "beginning" in Psalm 111:10, is now translated in 1 Samuel 15:21 as "best" or "choicest," depending on which translation you use.

What did the people steal from Jehovah? They did not choose some old scrawny sheep with one blind eye and one ear flopping down! They took the best and killed the rest! But Samuel said in verse 22, "Does the Lord delight in burnt offerings and sacrifices as much as in obeying the voice of the Lord? To obey is better than sacrifice."

It is thus no surprise to find that the word רֵאשִׁית is used to describe the "best" fruit and animals (Exodus 23:19; Ezekiel 20:40), the "foremost" nation (Amos 6:1), and the "best"

part of a land (Ezekiel 48:14). In Proverbs 4:7, the word רֵאשִׁית
is translated as the "beginning" of wisdom. In this passage,
Solomon says that the fear of the Lord is the "best" or
"chief" aspect of wisdom. Therefore, above all else in life,
make sure you fear God, for it is the chief, the best, the
choicest and the supreme part of wisdom.

The First Step

In Proverbs 9:10, Solomon used the Hebrew word תְּחִלָּה.
(*te-chil-lah*) when he wrote the statement, "The fear of the
Lord is the *beginning* of wisdom." This word refers chrono-
logical to the "first" item in a succession of things (ex. Hosea
1:2). Thus in Proverbs 9:10, Solomon is saying that the fear
of the Lord is the FIRST thing you must do in order to obtain wisdom. It is the first step on the road to becoming a
wise man or woman.

Do you desire God's wisdom in your life? Do you really
want to be a wise person? The very first thing you must do
in order to obtain divine wisdom is to fear God. If you do
not fear God, nothing else in life will make any sense.

Conclusion

The reason why the first step to obtaining wisdom is to
fear God is that it is the chief part of wisdom. It is the soul
and substance of our relationship to God and the sweetest
part of walking with God. Without the fear of the Lord,
there can be no true wisdom. To become a wise person who
understands the ways of God and of man, the "first step" is
to fear the Lord. It is not only the first thing in life that you
should learn, but it is also the "choicest" aspect of your relationship to God. Without it, nothing in life will make any
sense. The fear of the Lord is thus the *chief aspect* of wisdom,
as well as the *first step* toward wisdom.

Part Three:

The Nature of Fearing God

Chapter 7: THE VOCABULARY OF FEARING GOD

In dealing with the nature of the fear of God, the very first problem we face is the poverty of the English word "fear." It does not tell us what *kind* of fear is in focus. It does not indicate any *specific* attributes. The English word "fear" is simply not precise enough to tell us how to relate to God.

Old Testament Vocabulary

This is in sharp contrast to the richness of the Hebrew language. One of the reasons why God chose Hebrew as a vehicle of divine revelation is its preciseness. The Old Testament uses seventeen different Hebrew words and one Aramaic word to describe different kinds of "fear." These words are not simple synonyms. They describe fear in different ways with different meanings. Nine of these eighteen words are used to describe man's fear of God. The following is a summary of how these words are used in reference to our walk with God.

1. Stand in Awe

The first Hebrew word that describes the fear that we should have of God is גּוּר (goor).

> *Stand in awe* of Him, all you descendants of Israel. (Psalm 22:23 [verse 24 in Hebrews text])

> Let all the inhabitants of the world *stand in awe* of Him. (Psalm 33:8)

51

In their respective contexts, this word means to turn aside from the normal pursuits of life and come into the presence of God. Once we are standing in His presence, our attitude should be one of wonder and reverential awe at the power and majesty of the Creator and Sovereign Ruler of the universe. It emphasizes that we must *stand* before God with the right attitudes.

Did you ever wonder why we *stand* so much during church services? Why do we *stand* to pray and *stand* to sing? The early Church understood that we needed to "stand in awe" of God and to worship Him with all our heart, soul, mind, and strength. The next time you stand in church, remind yourself that you are to stand in awe of the Great God whom you serve.

2. Tremble Before Him

The second Hebrew word is חוּל (chool). This word is very interesting. The original root meaning of the word means to whirl or writhe in pain. It is used to describe such painful situations as a woman giving birth. As the pregnant woman approaches the time to give birth, she *writhes* and cries out in her labor pains. (Isaiah 26:17) It also is used to describe the pain of the wounds inflicted by weapons of war such as arrows.

> The heaviest fighting was against Saul, and when the Philistine bowmen who were shooting located Saul, he was *severely wounded* by them. (1 Samuel 31:3)

It also described the inward dread, anxiety and terror that gripped the Cannanites when they heard the Israelites were coming.

When they hear the report of you, they *shall be in anguish* because of you. (Deuteronomy 2:25)

This word is used of man's fear of God five times and is translated as "tremble."

Tremble before Him, all the earth. (1 Chronicles 16:30)
Tremble before Him, all the earth. (Psalm 96:9)
Tremble, O earth, before the Lord! (Psalm 114:7)
You don't *tremble* before me, do you? (Jeremiah 5:22)

The one exception is Psalm 37:7. In this passage, the NIV mistranslates the word *chool* as "wait patiently." The NIV misses the point of the Psalmist. Just as a woman in childbirth endures the pain of labor because she looks forward to having her baby, even so we should patiently endure painful situations in life because we look forward to God's grace and mercy.

We all naturally want an easy life. But God sometimes leads us into paths of pain and suffering. In such circumstances, we must writhe in pain patiently before God without cursing or murmuring against Him. When a true child of God is crushed in the wine press of suffering, sweet wine comes forth. But this is not so with counterfeit Christians. When they are pressed down by pain and suffering, bitterness and cursing comes forth. Suffering reveals one's true character.

3. Be in Dread of Him

The third word is עָרַץ (*ah-ratz*) which means to be so terrified of or filled with dread of what is coming upon you that you physically shake or tremble. It emphasizes the external signs of fear such as trembling or shaking. It should be translated "tremble in dread of." This word is used of the fear of God three times.

> A God *greatly feared* in the council of the holy ones. (Psalm 89:7)

> It is the Lord of Hosts whom you should regard as holy. And He shall be your fear, and He shall be your *dread*. (Isaiah 8:13)

> Indeed, they will sanctify the Holy One of Jacob, and *will stand in awe* of the God of Israel. (Isaiah 29:23)

This word means that we ought to tremble at the very thought of coming under the condemnation of God. We should dread such an experience, "for our God is a consuming fire" (Hebrews 12:29).

Why is it mistranslated in Psalm 89:7 and Isaiah 29:23? We don't know why. Maybe the translator did not like the idea of "trembling in dread" of God. Thus the word is mistranslated as "greatly feared" and "stand in awe." But there are other Hebrew words which have those meanings. The Hebrew word means "to tremble in dread of" the Lord.

4. Living in Dread

The fourth word is פַּחַד (*pa-chad*) which usually means to live under a fearful apprehension of a distant danger which keeps the mind in suspense.

> So your life shall hang in doubt before you; and you *shall be in dread* night and day, and shall have no assurance of your life. (Deuteronomy 28:66)

It is used twelve times in reference to the fear of God. The word *pa-chad* implies a fear which is caused by an enemy or inflicted by God Himself.

> And the *dread* of God was on all the kingdoms of the lands when they heard that the Lord had fought against the enemies of Israel. (2 Chronicles 20:29)

It is used of things which come unexpectedly upon us and which startle us. The Hebrew word is also used as a name of God. The God of Isaac and the God of Jacob are both called by the name of "Fear" in Genesis 31:42, 53.

> "If the God of my father, the God of Abraham, and *the Fear* of Isaac, had not been for me, surely now you would have sent me away empty-handed. (Genesis 31:42)

> "The God of Abraham and the God of Nahor, the God of their father, judge between us." So Jacob swore by *the Fear* of his father Isaac. (Genesis 31:53)

The fear of the Lord was so central to Isaac's concept of God that one of his names for God was "Fear"!

5. To Be Frightened of God

The fifth word אֵימָה (*a-mah*) means to be frightened by something to the point of terror. It is used to describe the terror of darkness or death (Genesis 15:12; Psalm 55:4). It is used of the fear of God three times.

> *Terror* and dread fall upon them; By the greatness of Thine arm they are motionless as stone. (Exodus 15:16)

I will send My *terror* ahead of you, and throw into confusion all the people among whom you come, and I will make all your enemies turn their backs to you. (Exodus 23:27)

Let Him remove his rod from me, and let not *dread* of Him terrify me. (Job 9:34)

It is never used in the positive sense of reverential awe. It means that sinners should be in terror of what God will do to them in judgment for their sins.

One of the consequences of not preaching the doctrine of hell is that unbelievers get the idea that nothing bad will happen to them after death. Nature hates a vacuum. Since most Christians have been intimidated into keeping quiet about hell, false ideas on the afterlife have gained popularity. Many people believe that at death they will enter a tunnel of light and meet a being of light who will take them to the other side to join their loved ones who have gone on before them. Everything will be beautiful and happy. We wrote *Death and the Afterlife* (Bethany House) in order to refute such nonsense and to demonstrate that there is hell to shun as well as a heaven to gain.

6. The Terror of God

The Aramaic word דְּחַל (do-chal) is a word that always means stark terror. It is used of the terror that Nebuchadnezzar caused in the hearts of his enemies in Daniel 5:19. It is also used in the book of Daniel to speak of the terror of God.

I will make a decree that in all the dominion of my kingdom men are to fear and *tremble* before the God of Daniel. (Daniel 6:26)

When was the last time you heard a sermon on the "terror" of the Lord? Could it be that we have emphasized the love of God to the exclusion of His terror?

7. The Fear of God

Since the seventh word יָרֵא (*yah-re*) is the general word for fear in the Old Testament, it can have a positive or negative significance depending on the context. It is used for the "fear of God" 180 times. Please take note that we are not referring to how many times this Hebrew word is found in the Old Testament but to how many times it is specifically used in reference to God.

The Negative Sense

Abraham was afraid to let people know that Sara was his wife because he *feared* for his life (Genesis 26:7). To be afraid of burning to death is another example of this usage (Deuteronomy 5:5). It is in this sense that Moses was afraid to look upon God because he assumed that to see the essential glory of God meant instant death (Exodus 33:20).

> Then Moses hid his face, for he *was afraid* to look at God. (Exodus 3:6)

The word is *yah-re* translated as "trembling" in the presence of God.

> My flesh *trembles* for fear of You, and I am afraid of Thy judgments. (Psalm 119:120).

In this sense it means to be literally terrified of God.

> Lord, I have heard the report about You and I *fear*. (Habakkuk. 3:2).

Have you ever been so afraid of God that you literally trembled? It is often used where God terrifies the wicked with threats of judgment (Deuteronomy 2:25). It is the emotional response that sinners should have when God warns them,

> Now consider this, you who forget God, Lest I tear you in pieces, and there be none to deliver. (Psalm 50:22)

The Positive Sense

In the positive sense of worship and reverential awe, the word יָרֵא (*yah-re*) is used throughout the Psalms (Psalm 33:8; 34:9; 86:11; 112:1; 119:63). Indeed, Solomon tells us in Ecclesiastes 3:14,

> I know that everything God does will remain forever; there is nothing to add to it and there is nothing to take from it, for God has so worked *that men should fear Him.*

Political Respect

It also was used to describe the respect that people gave to political leaders such as Moses and Joshua (Joshua. 4:14).

Afraid of God More than Man

It is in this sense that the midwives feared God (Exodus 1:21). They did not obey Pharaoh's command to abort the Jewish babies because they feared God MORE than they feared him!

8. Terror and Fear

The eighth word is יָגֹר (*yah-goor*). It is used only once for the fear of God. Moses said that he was "horrified" by God's

58

plan to destroy the entire nation because of their wickedness.

> I *was afraid* of the anger and hot displeasure with which the Lord was wrathful against you in order to destroy you. (Deuteronomy 9:19)

9. Worship with Trembling

The last word is רְעָדָה (*re-ah-dah*). It is used in Psalm 2:11 in the command, "Worship the Lord with *trembling*." This is the only time it is used in the Bible. It means that in our worship of God we should be *trembling in awe* of His greatness.

New Testament Vocabulary

In the New Testament, all the different Hebrew words for "fear" are translated by the Greek verb φόβος (*phobos*) and the verb, adverbs and adjectives which modify that noun. The "fear" of God in the New Testament embraces all the emotions of the human heart.

The Christian and the Terror of God

Liberal theologians have taught for many years that "fearing" God was only valid in Old Testament times and thus it has no place in the life of a Christian. But the "terror" of the Lord also refers to the terrible judgments that God can bring upon His own people when they rebel against Him! We have so over emphasized the love of the Lamb that we have forgotten "the wrath of the Lamb."

> And the kings of the earth and the great men and the commanders and the rich and the strong and every slave and free man, hid themselves in the

caves and among the rocks of the mountains; and they said to the mountains and to the rocks, "Fall on us and hide us from the presence of Him who sits on the throne, and from *the wrath of the Lamb*; for the great day of their wrath has come; and who is able to stand?" (Revelation 6:15-17)

It was this "terror" of Christ's coming judgment upon sinners that motivated the Apostle Paul to evangelize the lost.

Knowing therefore the *terror* of the Lord, we persuade men. (2 Corinthians 5:11)

The coming judgment upon rebel sinners should likewise motivate us to share the Gospel with people.

Solemn Warnings

Many Christians today assume that they should never be afraid of God. The idea of divine chastisement for sin is foreign to thinking. They assume that once they have accepted Christ as their personal savior, God will look the other way as they sin. Becoming a child of God means freedom from divine chastisement in the Christian life.

This modern form of antinomianism is the exact opposite of what the Bible teaches. In Hebrews 12:4-13 we are told that one of the marks of being a child of God is divine chastisement. If you are His child, then He will punish you when you wander from the path of righteousness. There is no way to avoid the fact that the solemn warnings found in the Book of Hebrews are directed to professing Christians. We are told that we should be afraid of God if we fall away.

Therefore, as long as the promise of entering his rest remains valid, *let us be afraid* lest someone among you fails to reach it. (Hebrews 4:1)

> For if we choose to go on sinning after we have received the full knowledge of the truth, there is no more sacrifice for our sins. All that remains is a terrifying prospect of judgment and a raging fire that will consume God's enemies. It is a *terrifying* thing to fall into the hands of the living God! (Hebrews 10:26-27,31)

> Therefore, since we are receiving a kingdom that can't be shaken, we must be thankful and worship God in *reverence* and *fear* in a way that pleases him. For our God is an all-consuming fire. (Hebrews 12:28-29)

Apostates need to be warned that they are on their way to hell. The "Apostle of Love" called apostates "antichrists" and stated that when people fall away from the Faith through heresy or immorality, this only reveals that they were never saved to begin with (1 John 2:19). Their true unregenerate nature was revealed by their apostasy.

Jesus and The Fear of God

> The words of Jesus must be taken at face value.

> But I tell you, my friends, never be afraid of those who kill the body and after that can't do anything more. I'll show you the one you should be afraid of. Be afraid of the one who has the authority to throw you into hell after killing you. Yes, I tell you, *be afraid of him*! (Luke 12:4-5)

The New Testament clearly indicates that when we fall into sin, we should be afraid of the chastening hand of God. If we are not chastised by God, this is clear evidence that we are not the children of God (Hebrews 12:5-8).

Wonder, Awe, and Reverence

Fearing God in the New Testament also means to give God the reverence due to Him.

Your deeds are spectacular and amazing, Lord God Almighty.
    Your ways are just and true, King of the nations.
      Lord, who won't fear and praise your name?
For you alone are holy,
    and all the nations will come and worship you
      because your judgments have been revealed. (Revelation
      15:3-4)

The fact that the fear of God is taught in the Gospels (Matthew 10:28-29), the Acts (Acts 9:31), the Church Epistles (2 Corinthians 7:1), the General Epistles (1 Peter 2:17) and the Book of Revelation (Revelation 14:7) should convince us that it is an essential part of living a holy life before God.

Why So Much Shallowness Today?

Given the vast amount of Biblical material on the fear of the Lord, how can we justify our silence on and ignorance of the subject? Could it be that modern Christians are shallow in their lives and sloppy in their beliefs because they do not fear God? If we take the Bible seriously, the reason that most Christians today are weak, carnal, spineless, and mindless is rooted in the fact that they do not fear God!

Conclusion

The entire Bible is filled with exhortations to fear God. *Just as the presence of the fear of God is the surest sign of God's blessing, the absence of that fear is the surest sign of God's curse.*

Chapter 8: THE MEANINGS OF FEARING GOD

From our study of the various Hebrew and Greek words used by the authors of Scripture to speak of man's fear of God, it is obvious that the "fear" of God can mean different things to different people at different times. Most commentators have correctly distinguished reverential fear from slavish fear. But are these the only two distinctions that can be made?

More Than Two Distinctions

During a period of ten years, we closely examined all of the passages in the Bible which dealt with the fear of God. We discovered that the typical two-fold distinction of the fear of God was not adequate. During this time we not only exegeted each passage from the original text, but we also went thorough the standard commentaries on each passage. While this procedure took us years to complete, we were well rewarded for our labors.

As we went through the Bible examining each passage where the fear of God was mentioned, we kept certain questions in mind:

- **nature**: What was the nature of the fear in this passage?
- **origin**: What motivated this fear?
- **subjects**: Who is fearing God? Jew or Gentile? Individual or nation? Young or old? Believer or unbeliever?
- **attributes**: What was this fear like? Subjective v objective? Temporary or permanent? Positive or negative?

- **means**: How did this fear manifest itself?
- **consequences**: What happened to those who feared God? In what ways did their fear change their lives?

Since our purpose in this chapter is to give a broad overview of the many distinctions that must be made concerning the fear of God, we will not be giving a verse by verse exposition of all the hundreds of passages involved.

Objective/Subjective

The fear of the Lord may refer to something objective, that is, something which is outside of man and thus does not depend upon man's belief or feelings for its existence. On the other hand, the fear of God can refer to something subjective, that is, it may refer to the emotional state or inner feelings of man.

The Objective Fear of God

The objective fear of God has nothing to do with the emotions of man. It has nothing to do with man at all. It is something external to man that exists irrespective of whether man is there or not. In Scripture, the word "fear" is used to refer to objective things. What are they?

God's Name

Abraham, Isaac, and Jacob did not have a Bible that gave them the names of God. Instead, God revealed Himself directly to them and, at times, gave them names by which He was to be worshipped. They also developed other names for God which brought into view certain aspects of the person and work of God.

When the Patriarchs thought about God and their relationship to Him, they chose "Fear" as one of their name for

God because they feared Him above all things in this life and in the life to come.

> If the God of my father, the God of Abraham, the *Fear* of Isaac, had not been for me, surely now you would have sent me away empty-handed. (Genesis 31:42)

> "The God of Abraham, the God of Nahor, the God of their father, judge between us." So Jacob swore by the *Fear* of his father Isaac. (Genesis 31:53)

Jacob made an oath in the name of the "Fear" of Isaac. Why? Isaac's fear of God was so central in his life that it became a name for his God. Like Isaac, our greatest fear should be the frown of God and our greatest joy, the smile of God.

God's Word

The fear of God is used as a name for Scripture in Psalm 19:9. The entire Psalm is dedicated to the two-fold Revelation of God. In verses 1-6, the Psalmist celebrates General Revelation as given in the Creation. He states that no one can say that he is ignorant of God because God has not revealed Himself: "The heavens declare the glory of God and the skies proclaim the work of His hands" (Psalm 19:1).

General Revelation

General Revelation is the silent witness to the existence of God found in the creation around us and the conscience within us. It goes on twenty-four hours a day, seven days a week. The Apostle Paul pointed out that General Revelation means that all of humanity (including the heathen) is "without excuse" and thus under the just judgment of God (Romans 1:18-23).

While General Revelation is enough to condemn us, it is not enough to save us. This is why Psalm 19 does not leave us simply with General Revelation. The Palmist goes on to describe Special Revelation as given in Scripture. He refers to Scripture by such terms as "the law of the Lord;" "the statutes of the Lord;" "the precepts of the Lord;" "the commands of the Lord;" "*the fear of the Lord*" (Psalm 19:7-9)

In verse 9, David uses the phrase "the fear of the Lord," as a title for Scripture because it is the means by which we come to understand that there is a God to be feared and what this fear is all about.

God's Attributes

The word "fear" is also used in terms of God's attributes. Just as God is said to be loving or kind, he is also said to be terrible, terrifying, awesome and awful:

> You shall not dread them, for the LORD your God is in your midst, a great and *awesome* God. (Deuteronomy 7:21)

2 Samuel 7:23 tells us that not only is God in His nature "awesome," but God's works are "awesome" and "fearful" to behold.

The King James Version uses the word "terrible" instead of the word "awesome" (NASV). The KJV is actually closer to the original Hebrew on this point. Thus the God of the Bible is a "terrible" God who inspires terror in the hearts of rebel sinners.

Revealed Religion

The fear of the Lord is also used to refer to revealed religion, i.e., the true religion given to us by God. In Psalm

34:11, David said, "Come you children, listen to me and I will teach you *the fear of the Lord.*"

What is "the fear of the Lord" but to believe all that God has revealed in His Word. It means the religion revealed in the Bible. Thus throughout the Psalms, true believers are described as those who fear God. For example, in the Psalm 22:23, we are told, "All of *you who fear God,* praise Him."

In David's mind, fearing the Lord and believing in the Lord are one and the same thing. No one can truly believe in God without fearing Him. Those who fear God are referred to as true believers in general.

God-Fearers

Later during the inter-testamental period, those who "feared" God came to mean Gentile converts to Judaism. This is why Paul said in Acts 13:26,

My brothers, descendants of Abraham's family, and those among you who *fear God,* it is to us that the message of this salvation has been sent.

The expression "those among you who fear God" referred to those Gentiles who had abandoned their paganism and embraced the religion of Israel. They were called "God-fearers." The phrase no longer meant believers in general.

The Worship of God

Lastly, it is used for the public worship of God in both the Old and New Testament. In Psalm 2:11, the Psalmist commands us to, "*Worship the Lord with fear* and rejoice *with trembling.*"

In Revelation 15:3,4, we read,

Your deeds are spectacular and amazing, Lord God Almighty.

> *Your ways are just and true, King of the nations.*
>   *Lord, who won't fear and praise your name?*
> *For you alone are holy,*
>   *and all the nations will come and worship you*
>   *because your judgments have been revealed.* (Revelation
>   15:3-4)

The literary parallelism found in Revelation 15:4 equates "fearing" God with "bringing glory" to God. To fear God means, in this context, to worship the God who is there and who is not silent. Thus our worship of God should involve fearing Him in the sense of awe, reverence, wonder and praise.

Irreverent Behavior In Church

The lack of godly fear in public worship is the reason why there is very little reverence in many church services today. There is so much talking, laughing and carrying on before the service that it sounds more like a circus or a ball game than a worship service. We should be preparing our hearts for worship once the piano, organ or guitar begins to play. There is absolutely no excuse for people to be running around and making noise before church services.

All of us have been in church services where children are allowed to talk, play with toys, make faces at the people behind them, and, worst of all, make that irritating noise caused by rubbing a pencil up and down the cover of the hymnal.

Brethren, these things ought not to be. If you cannot control your children, then send them to junior church or to the nursery. Then ask your pastor for family counseling on how to raise your children in the fear and discipline of the Lord. If you do not train them in the fear of the Lord, who will?

Temporary/Permanent

The fear of God can be temporary or it can be permanent. We all know people who at one time attended church. There was a *temporary* fear of God in their lives. Then they turned away from the Lord and returned to the ways of wickedness. Today there is no fear of God before their eyes as they give full reign to their lusts.

There are always those people who "get religion" temporarily during some crisis in their life. The soldier in the fox hole is a good example of this. When the bullets are flying all around and the enemy is charging, it is easy to say, "God, if you get me out of this alive, I promise to serve you the rest of my life." Even when God delivers him, does he fear the Lord the next week? No, the vows he made to God are soon forgotten. The fear of God was only a temporary episode in an ungodly life. No true work of grace was done in his heart. He is more likely to found in the whorehouse than God's House.

What a contrast to those who walk in the fear of the Lord all their days! The permanent fear of God is one of the gracious provisions of the New Covenant.

> I will put *the fear of Me* in their hearts so *they will not turn away from me*. (Jeremiah 32:40)

When you come to know Jesus Christ in a true conversion experience, you cannot escape from it. The love of Christ is like the hymn, "O love that will not let me go." There is no one else to whom you can go for the words of eternal life (John 6:67-68). This is why in the New Covenant, God instills a permanent fear of Him into our hearts so that we will *never* fall away.

Positive/Negative

The fear of God can focus on the positive aspects of fear such as love, reverence and awe. Or, it can be focus on the negative aspects such as terror, horror and anxiety. The fear of the Lord contains both positive and negative elements.

It never ceases to amaze us to hear modern preachers telling people that once they are saved, they do not need to fear God. How even sadder it is to see the people going out and living in such a way that proves that they do not fear the Lord. We will have to answer to Christ when He returns (2 Corinthians 5:10).

Saving/Non-Saving

The fear of the Lord can be saving or it can be non-saving. The fear of God can motivate people to seek salvation. Thus John the Baptist, Jesus and the Apostles did not hesitate to *warn* people of the wrath to come (Matthew 3:7; Luke 12:5; Romans 1:18). They were saved *from* hell as well as to heaven (1 Thessalonians 1:10).

In times past, it was not strange to hear of sinners who turned to God in fear of hell and judgment. But this does not happen too often today. Why? The kind of God that is preached today is not the kind of deity that would really throw anyone into hell. He is all love and there is no wrath to escape.

It is possible, sadly, to fear God in a non-saving sense. Millions of religious people think they can earn their way to heaven by their own good works. How sad. They fear God's judgment and try to live a good life in the hope that their good deeds will outweigh their bad deeds.

Particular/General

The fear of God can be particular or it can be general. A person can fear the Lord in respect to one thing or it can be in general. For example, the Ninevites "feared" the coming judgment of God preached by Jonah. They fasted and prayed to remove that judgment (Jonah 3:5-10). But once the threat was gone, they went back to their wicked ways. Their fear was particular in that it focused on the specific judgment of God preached by Jonah.

In contrast, a true Christian seeks to apply the fear of the Lord to all of life. Whatever we do is to be done to the glory of God (1 Corinthians 10:31). Thus the fear of God should embrace all of life.

Individual/Group

An individual or a group can fear God. When God sends unusual judgments upon sinners, this can inspire corporate fear in the population of unbelievers and among the churches in general (Acts 5:5,11).

True heaven-sent revival comes to churches when the people are "walking in the fear of the Lord" (Acts 9:31 cf. 2:42-43). Reverence for the name of Jesus comes from a general fear of God (Acts 19:17).

This explains why people in general today—including far too many professing Christians—take the name of God and of Jesus in vain. When there is no general fear of God in the population at large, lawlessness, blasphemy and wickedness will abound (Genesis 20:21).

The fear of the Lord is also individual. Thus Joseph could truly say, "I fear God" (Genesis 42:18). Do *you* fear God?

Attitude/Action

The fear of God can be either an action or an attitude. It can refer to something that you do. Thus there are places in the Bible where it used in the sense of obedience. They "feared" God by doing what He said to do (Exodus 1:17). Or, it can refer to an attitude. Joseph was characterized by an attitude of fear toward God that enabled him to say "No!" to immorality.

Spiritual/Carnal

The fear of God can be either spiritual or carnal. That is, it can either come from the Holy Spirit or it can come from the natural heart of man.

The spiritual fear of God contains all the positive elements as well as all of the negative elements of fear. We rejoice with trembling. We worship in an attitude of awe and godly fear (Psalm 2:11).

A carnal fear of God usually contains only the negative aspects of fear. Those who only slavishly fear God have a carnal fear of God that is non-saving. The Ninevites would fall into this category.

Sincere/Hypocritical

The fear of God can be sincere or it can be hypocritical. Just because someone says that he fears God does not mean that he does in fact fear God. People can be quite hypocritical on this point.

The real question that must be asked is, "Do you fear God enough to depart from evil and to keep His commandments?" Obedience to God is where "the rubber meets the road."

Character Trait/Episode

The fear of God can refer to a character trait or simply to an episode in someone's life. Do you fear God? Is this fear part of your everyday life? Is the fear of the Lord a character trait of your life in general? Are you a "reverent" person?

Attractive/Repulsive

In some biblical contexts, the fear of God attracts people. People are actually drawn to God by their fear of Him (Psalm 5:7). In other passages, the fear of God made people run from Him (Revelation 6:15-17).

Mobilize/Paralyze

The fear of God can either mobilize or paralyze. In some cases, the fear of God mobilized people to do something positive. For example, Joseph was able to remain sexually pure because of his fear of God (Genesis 39:9). In other cases, the fear of God so paralyzed people that they could not do anything (Exodus 15:11-16).

Joy/Sadness

Sometimes, the fear of God refers to being caught up in the joyous awareness of God's greatness (Psalm 97:1). But then sometimes it also means to be in terror and anxiety because of His greatness (Psalm 99:1). The fear of God encompasses all the emotions found in the human heart.

Greater/Lesser

There are degrees of fearing God. In Psalm 89:7 we read that God is to be "greatly feared." Thus some people fear God *more* than other people do. Is your fear of the Lord great or small? Are increasing or decreasing in your fear of the Lord?

Caught and Taught

We are to teach our children the fear of the Lord (Psalm 34:11). They must learn to have reverence for God, His Word, His name and His Church. Please, don't put things on your Bible such as a coffee mug. Don't use God's name in vain. Don't ridicule the church which is the Bride of Christ. And don't have "roast preacher" every Sunday afternoon. Be reverent about the things of God (Psalm 46:10).

The Work of The Holy Spirit

Only the Holy Spirit can put a saving fear of God into the hearts of sinners. This is the goal of the Spirit's work in the New Covenant.

> They will be my people, and I will be their God. I will give them one heart and one way *so they will fear me always* for their own good and for the good of their descendants after them. I will make an everlasting covenant with them that I will not turn away from doing good for them. I will put *the fear of me* in their hearts so *they will not turn away from me.* (Jeremiah 32:38-40)

Each occurrence of the fear of the God in the Bible combines different aspects from the list above. For example, the "fear" of God that the Ninevites had was a temporary, negative, non-saving, corporate action which was a carnal, hypocritical, outward, false, terror of God's judgment. As soon as the judgment passed, they went back to their wickedness.

Conclusion

It is obvious by this time that the traditional two-fold division of the fear of God is not adequate. Our understanding of the fear of the Lord must go as deep as Scripture goes. *The deeper our understanding of what it means to fear God, the better able we are to fear Him as He ought to be feared.*

Part Four:

The Origins of Fearing God

Chapter 9: WHY WE SHOULD FEAR GOD

T he subject of the origins or causes of the fear of God is important because we are not born fearing God. It is something we must *learn* by instruction and by experience.

In Scripture, people did not just suddenly wake up one morning fearing God. There was always a *cause*, a *reason* or a *motivation* for that fear regardless of what kind of fear it was. Something or someone caused them to fear the Lord.

In many cases, the same doctrine, event or situation which caused a positive reverential awe in the people of God caused a negative terror in the hearts of unbelievers. The truth of God's absolute sovereignty is a good example of this phenomenon.

The Sovereignty of God

In Psalm 97 and 99, both Psalms begin with the glorious truth that "the LORD reigns" over all things. The response of the people of God is to rejoice (Psalm 97:1,8), be glad (Psalm 97:1,8,12), see His glory (Psalm 97:6), exalt the Lord (Psalm 97:9; Psalm 99:5,9), give thanks (Psalm 97:12), praise (Psalm 99:3), and worship (Psalm 99:5,9).

This is in stark contrast to how the wicked responded to the doctrine of God's sovereignty. After stating that God is enthroned in the heavens and is the Sovereign Ruler and Judge of all things, the Psalmist tells us how unbelievers responded to this doctrine: They are put to shame (Psalm 97:7) and tremble in fear (Psalm 99:1).

Indeed, they should fear! If God is Sovereign, then there is no way to escape His wrath on the day of Judgment. This is why so much hatred is directed against the doctrine of

God's sovereignty. If this doctrine is true, then there is no hope of escaping God's judgment.

Children and the Fear of God

Fearing God is something that parents should teach their children. As David stated, "Come you children, listen to me; I will teach you the fear of the LORD. (Psalm 34:11)"

Every parent should be vitally interested in how David did this. The entire Psalm is given over to a lesson in the fear of the Lord. David begins by giving his personal testimony of how the Lord was pleased to save him in vs. 1-6.

I will bless the Lord at all times; His praise shall continually be in my mouth. I sought the LORD, and He answered me, and delivered me from all my fears. This poor man cried unto the LORD and the LORD heard him; and saved him out of all his troubles.

David then sets forth WHY the Lord was pleased to deliver him in verse 7:

The angel of the LORD encamps around those who fear Him, and rescues them.

Having given his personal experience, David then gives an exhortation to fear the Lord:

O fear the LORD, you His saints; For to those who fear Him, there is no want.

A Long and Prosperous Life

David then sets forth a question which should encourage everyone to fear God.

Who is the man who desires life, and loves length of days that he may see good?

Obviously, everyone wants a long and happy life filled with goodness. But they must begin with the fear of God. This fear will lead them to live a righteous life (vs. 13-22).

Motives to Fear God

The hundreds of passages in the Bible which describe someone fearing the Lord usually also tell us the cause or motivation for that fear. The following is a breakdown of the major reasons why people fear God according to the Scriptures.

The Nature of God

The God who has revealed Himself in Scripture is a "terrible" and "awesome" God, i.e., He is the kind of God who inspires either reverence or terror in the hearts of men (Deuteronomy 7:21; 10:17; Psalm 47:2; 89:5-10). Thus the authors of Scripture single out various attributes of God as inspiring fear of Him. We should fear God for what He is, in and of Himself, in His own nature. For example:

1. The Greatness of God (Deuteronomy 7:21; Psalm 96:4).
2. The Sovereignty of God (Psalm 33:6-12; 97:1; 99:1; Daniel 6:26).
3. The Holiness of God (Revelation 15:4).
4. The Jealousy of God (Deuteronomy 6:13-15).
5. The Justice and Righteousness of God (2 Chronicles 19:6-9).
6. The Judgment of God against His enemies (Joshua 2:9-13).

The Names of God

We should fear God for His great and glorious names. It should even be a delight to fear God's name according to Nehemiah 1:11! No wonder the Psalmist prayed, "Unite my heart to fear Thy name." (Psalm 86:11)

Do you want God's blessings in your life? Moses said that you must "fear this honored and awesome name of God, the LORD your God" (Deuteronomy 28:58). If you want success in life, then you must "delight to fear Thy name" (Nehemiah 1:11).

We should glorify the name of God according to Psalm 86:12. The great and awesome name of God should be praised (Psalm 99:3). Because of the salvation of God's people, the nations will fear the name of the Lord (Psalm 102:15). God's name is holy and awesome (Psalm 111:9). Because God is a great King, His name is feared among the nations (Malachi 1:14). This is why all blasphemy will result in swift judgment (Exodus 20:7).

It should always shock us whenever someone takes the name of God or Jesus in vain. It is about time that we publicly protest against such blasphemy. The reason that people tolerate it on the TV and in the movies is that they no longer fear the *name* of the Lord.

The Word of God

The Scriptures are called "the fear of the Lord" in Psalm 19:9 in two senses. First, the Bible should be the object of our awe and reverence because it is the written Word of God and should be treated as such (Psalm 119:161; Isaiah 66:2,5). Second, the Bible is the source of our fear of God (Deuteronomy 17:18-20; 31:9-13). We learn what it means to fear God in the Bible.

The Works of God

God's mighty deeds in history should motivate us to fear Him all the days of our lives. His works are truly "awesome" (Psalm 66:3; 65:5,8). Heaven itself is filled with such praise.

Your deeds are spectacular and amazing, Lord God Almighty.
Your ways are just and true, King of the nations.
Lord, who won't fear and praise your name?
For you alone are holy,
and all the nations will come and worship you
because your judgments have been revealed. (Revelation 15:3-4)

We should be in awe of God's mighty acts because they are:

1. Many (Psalm 104:24)
2. Great (1 Chronicles 17:21)
3. Wonderful (1 Chronicles 16:9; Psalm 65:8)
4. Righteous (Psalm 145:17)
5. Marvelous, Righteous and True (Revelation 15:3)

The Mighty Works of God

Some of God's works are singled out in Scripture as especially promoting the fear of God.

- Creation: The fact that God made us means that we belong to Him and thus owe to Him our worship and obedience (Psalm 33:8-9).
- Sovereignty: Since He is working all things according to the counsel of His own Will (Ephesians 1:11), we should be in awe of His sovereignty (Psalm 33:11; Jeremiah 5:22-24).

- Judgment: We should fear the judgment of God more than the judgment of men. Man can kill the body but cannot kill the soul. But God can cast us body and soul into an eternal hell according to the Lord Jesus (Matthew 10:28).
- Forgiveness: God forgives our sins that we might fear Him (Psalm 130:4). The fear of God is not to be viewed as something which led to our conversion and then is dropped. The fear of God is the GOAL of God's plan of salvation!

Conclusion

God's wondrous nature, name, Word and works should motivate us to fear Him, for our God is an awesome God, a great and glorious God, mighty in judgment, compassionate in mercy, and working all things according to His sovereign will.

Chapter 10: THE TERROR OF THE LORD

The word "fear" as applied to God has over 20 different meanings in Scripture, as we have seen. When we analyzed how the word "fear" was used in Scripture, we found that we had to take into account the origin, attributes, nature, significance, situation, consequences, objects, and subjects of that fear.

A Broad Subject

The fear of the Lord is a very broad subject. Indeed, after spending many years researching this topic, we have only scratched the surface! The word "fear" has so many different meanings because we have to deal with such a wide range of human emotions and how human beings respond to God. People respond to God in many different ways, depending on the situation. Thus the fear of the Lord will have many different meanings corresponding to all the different kinds of emotions that are born in the hearts of sinners as they are forced to have dealings with God.

The Terror of the Lord

This applies most importantly to the subject of the terror of the Lord because it is so neglected today. The first reference in the Bible to the terror of the Lord is found in Genesis. When God asked Adam why he was hiding, Adam responded, "I heard your voice, *I was afraid*, so I hid himself." (Genesis 3:10)

The fear of God mentioned in this passage is the kind of fear that strikes terror and dread in the hearts of rebel sinners. This terror caused Adam and Eve to run from God;

to hide from His presence; to avoid confrontation with the living God. Adam and Eve experienced sheer, naked terror at the thought of being exposed to the all-seeing eye of God. Instead of running to God for the remedy to their sin and guilt, the terror of the Lord caused Adam and Eve to attempt, by any means whatsoever, to escape confrontation with the Righteous Judge of all the earth.

Running from the Light

The last thought in the mind of such sinners is to come into the presence of God where their sins can be exposed.

> For everyone who practices wickedness hates the light and does not come to the light, so that his actions may not be exposed. (John 3:20)

But just as there was no escape for Adam, there is no escape for modern day sinners.

> No creature can hide from him. Everything is naked and helpless before the eyes of the one to whom we must give an account. (Hebrews 4:13)

We find this terror expressed in those three little words, "I was afraid." The Hebrew word which is translated "afraid" refers to the kind of terror and dread that makes one physically tremble. Adam was literally trembling with terror at the very thought of coming into the presence of God.

Man's Fall into Sin and Guilt

When man sinned in the Garden, sin and guilt became part of the human condition. When we read in Genesis 3:7 that the eyes of Adam and Eve were "opened," this means that there was a new dimension in their lives. They were embarrassed because they saw that they were naked.

Before they sinned, Adam and Eve were naked because they lived in a garden where they did not need any clothing. There were no thorns or thistles. The weather was perfect. Thus there was no pain or shame. But once man sinned, they became embarrassed. They felt shame for the first time. This shame was rooted not in their naked bodies but in their sinful souls.

Fig Leaves

Guilt over their sin led to shame over their own bodies. While they could cover the shame of their nakedness with fig leaves, they had no way to cover their guilt and sin before God. Thus they tried to use fig leaves to hide from God. Up to that point, Adam and Eve had never experienced the dread or terror of the Lord. They had nothing to fear from the creation or the Creator. But now they were seized with fear, terror, dread, anxiety and worry.

Before the Fall

What are some of the lessons we can learn from the Fall of man into sin and guilt? First, before sin entered into the world, there was no terror of God; no negative fear of God; no anxiety and no dread of looking for certain judgment. Man had no reason to fear the wrath of God. Before the Fall, there was a positive awe, respect and love of God. The positive aspects of the fear of God could come to full bloom because they were rooted in the soil of sinless hearts.

After the Fall

After man sinned, the mere thought of being in the presence of God terrified him. He had only one thought in his heart: How to avoid a confrontation with the Almighty.

We Are All Hiding from God

Just like Adam and Eve, all of mankind is still running and hiding from God because of their sin and guilt before Him. When Adam heard the voice of God, he was forced to remember who God was and who he was. He had to think about the consequences of his accountability to God.

Adam's conscience was aroused with guilt and shame over his sin. Abject fear gripped him because he knew that God was a holy God; that he was accountable to God; that God would punish sin unto death and that there was absolutely no way to escape the judgment of God once the process began.

What was the outcome of man's attempt to hide from God and His judgment? First, the hiding failed! Did they remain hidden from God? No. There is always a day of Judgment. You may try to hide from God while you are alive, "But it is appointed unto man once to die, and after that, the judgment. (Hebrews 9:27)"

Second, the cover-up failed. The fig leaves did not fool anybody. And all the cover-ups that we do will end in judgment.

Third, their sin was exposed and there was nothing they could do about it. When God got through with Adam, he finally admitted in verse 12, "I ate it." In the same way, we will all be held accountable. Our sin will be exposed on the Day of Judgment. There will be no way to escape this exposure.

Fourth, the guilt was rightly placed. Adam, Eve and the devil all got the judgments they deserved. To each one, according to his deeds, a righteous judgment was levied.

Fifth, the punishment given was death. The process of physical death began the very day they sinned. They also spiritually died on that day because they were separated from God (Isaiah 59:2).

The Day of Doom

In the book of Revelation we find a description of what will happen at the end of human history when most of mankind will experience the dread, fright, and terror of God that leads them to attempt to hide from God.

> Then I saw the lamb open the sixth seal. There was a powerful earthquake. The sun turned as black as sackcloth made of hair, and the full moon turned as red as blood. The stars in the sky fell to the earth like a fig tree drops its fruit when it is shaken by a strong wind. The sky vanished like a scroll being rolling up, and every mountain and island was moved from its place. Then the kings of the earth, the important people, the generals, the rich, the powerful, and all the slaves and free people hid themselves in caves and among the rocks in the mountains. They said to the mountains and rocks, "Fall on us and hide us from the face of the one who sits on the throne and from the wrath of the lamb. For the great day of their wrath has come, and who is able to endure it?" (Revelation 6:12-17)

The reality of their sin and rebellion against God now finally dawns upon them. They now realize that the Bible was true after all. There IS a Judgment Day and God IS going to judge them!

As they feel the full weight of their guilt before God, they try to escape by calling upon the mountains to fall upon them. But this will fail in the end. The mountains, the rocks and the caves cannot hide them from the wrath of the Lamb. They are then assembled for the great Judgment Day and the books are opened and they are judged: "Anyone whose name was not found written in the Book of Life was thrown into the lake of fire (Revelation 20:15)." This is the kind of fear that causes sinners to flee the wrath of Almighty God. May this fear drive us to Mt. Calvary where we will find forgiveness and grace!

Conclusion

There are as many different ways to hide from God as there are sins. But none of these excuses will succeed anymore than Adam's fig leaf. People can hide in bomb shelters hollowed out deep inside of granite mountains to escape the great and terrible Day of God. But they will not escape.

"When the Son of Man comes in his glory and all the angels are with him, he will sit on his glorious throne. All the nations will be assembled in front of him, and he will separate them from each other like a shepherd separates the sheep from the goats. He will put the sheep on his right but the goats on his left. Then the king will say to those on his right, 'Come, you who have been blessed by my Father, inherit the kingdom prepared for you from the foundation of the world. "Then he will say to those on his left, 'Get away from me, you who are accursed, into the eternal fire that has been prepared for the devil and his angels!' These people will go away into eternal punishment, but the righteous will go into eternal life." (Matthew 25:31-34,41,46)

Part Five:

The Results of Fearing God

Chapter 11: THE BLESSINGS OF FEARING GOD

Whˑen we do what God commands, we are always blessed by Him. This is particularly true when we fear Him. In His Word God has promised special blessings to those individuals, families, churches, and nations who fear Him and keep His commandments.

The fear of the Lord should permeate every aspect of life. No part of our private or public life is to be left untouched by the fear of God. The benefits of fearing the Lord are stated in many passages throughout the Bible. The following is a small sample of the blessings which come to us as we fear Him with whom we have to do.

As Individuals

As believers, once we begin to practice the fear of God in all of life, we begin to experience a special anointing by the Holy Spirit. In Deuteronomy 6:4, we are told that we should "fear the LORD our God for our good always and for our survival."

For Our Own Good

Moses pleaded with the people of God to fear the Lord for their own good. Thus it was in their own best interest to fear God in all that they did and said. Not only was it for their own good that they should fear God, but it was necessary for their survival in this wicked world. The enemies of God and His people were all around them. In order to survive in such a hostile environment, they had to fear God.

The same is true for us today. If the only motivation to fear God that makes sense to the present self-centered generation is their own good and survival, then Moses' words are quite appropriate. It is in *our* own best interest to fear God and keep His commandments.

Divine Guidance

The Psalmist wrote, "Who is the man who fears the LORD? He will instruct him in the way that he should choose. The secret of the LORD is for those who fear Him, and He will make them know His covenant" (Psalm 25:12,14).

Those who fear the Lord will receive special divine guidance as they face the trials of life. God will reveal to them His secret will and make them understand what His covenant instructs them to do. What a comfort to know that as we fear Him, He will guide us according to His will in Christ Jesus.

Divine Protection

Behold, the eye of the LORD is on those who fear Him, on those who hope for His lovingkindness, to deliver their soul from death, and to keep them alive in famine. (Psalm 33:18-19)

After having misbehaved several times in a neighbor's home, a three year old child was told by his mother, "I will keep my eye on you for the next hour, and, if you get out of line again, I will take care of you when we get back to the house." The child did not have any problem whatsoever understanding what it meant for his mother to "keep an eye on him." It meant that she was going to take special notice of where he was and what he was doing at all times.

In the same way, the expression "the eye of the LORD" does not refer to the general attribute of omniscience. It means that God is taking special notice of and paying spe-

cial attention to those who fear Him. The big difference between the mother in our illustration and the Lord is that His
"eye" is on us to deliver us from death and from life-
threatening situations such as famine.

Our Guardian Angel

We are told that this divine protection will come to us
because,

the angel of the LORD encamps around those who
fear Him and rescues them.

The "angel of the LORD" is none other than the Lord Jesus
Christ. He will take special care of those who fear God.

Divine Wisdom

In Proverbs 1:7 we are told that, "The fear of the LORD
is the beginning of wisdom." The Hebrew concept of wisdom was not merely intellectual. It focused on the *application*
of divine wisdom to the every day problems of life. Wisdom
was thus a God-given *skill* for righteous living and not
merely knowledge or insight. As we fear the Lord, we will
be able to make the right decisions.

As Families

God not speaks to us as families as well as individuals.
His Word instructs us about the origin, nature, structure,
and inner workings of the family. Entire Psalms such as
Psalm 112 and Psalm 128 are devoted to the blessings which
will come upon our families as we fear the Lord.

The Brave Midwives

In Exodus 1:21 we are told that the midwives who disobeyed Pharaoh when he ordered them to kill all the male Jewish babies were rewarded by God in a special way.

And it came about that because the midwives feared God, that He established households for them.

The midwives were blessed with children of their own because they feared God more than they feared Pharaoh.

Honor for the Elderly

In Leviticus 19:32, we are told that when "the greyheaded" come into a room, we "shall rise up and honor the aged." Why? "You shall fear your God." Thus the respect we owe to our parents and the elderly is tied to the respect we have for God. *To the degree people no longer fear the Lord is to the degree they no longer respect their elders.*

As Churches

In the book of Acts the churches where blessed as they feared God. When the Holy Spirit was poured out at Pentecost, great fear came upon everyone including unbelievers (Acts 2:43). As a result, the church increased in numbers (Acts 2: 47).

After Ananias and Sapphira were struck dead for lying to the Holy Spirit, great fear came upon the whole church. (Acts 5:11) The judgment of God made people stop and think before they made promises to God which they did not intend to fulfill. One wonders how many people would die today if God judged them as He did Ananias and his wife?

As Nations

The level of immorality and injustice in a nation is directly related to the level of the fear of God in society. When a nation fears the Lord, justice is established throughout the land. This is why when Abraham saw that the Egyptians did not fear God, he was afraid for his life as well as for his wife (Genesis 20:11). Since they did not fear God, it was quite conceivable that they would simply kill him in order to get his wife.

Justice Hangs on It

Judges will be honest to the degree that they fear the Lord.

> And he (Jehoshaphat) appointed judges in the land in all the fortified cities of Judah, city by city. And he said to the judges, "Consider what you are doing, for you do not judge for man but for the LORD who is with you when you render judgment. Now then let the fear of the LORD be upon you; be very careful what you do, for the LORD our God will have no part in unrighteousness, or partiality, or the taking of a bribe." (2 Chronicles 19:5-7)

When judges no longer fear God, they will abuse their position and power to oppress the people of God. The wicked judges who presently sit on the Supreme Court have the blood of millions of butchered babies on their hands. They oppress the righteous and reward the wicked because they do not fear God.

Good Business Sense

The fear of God is even the key to business ethics (Leviticus 25:43; Colossians 3:22). If the fear of the Lord is dominant, employers will not take advantage of their employees and employees will not cheat their employers. Honesty and hard work abound when God is feared.

Sound Economic Policies

Such evils as high interest, high mortgages, and high taxes in Nehemiah's day were destroying the people. When they cried out for him to help them (Nehemiah 5:1-6), he said,

> The thing which you are doing is not good; should you not walk in the fear of our God because of the reproach of the nations, our enemies? (Nehemiah 5:9)

Nehemiah went on to tell them that if they feared God, such things as high taxes, high mortgages, and high interest had to stop (Nehemiah 5:10-13). Thus financial righteousness was established in the land through the fear of God.

Conclusion

The fear of God produces justice and righteousness in individuals, families, churches and nations. Society can only function for the good and with freedom for all its citizens to the degree that the people fear the Lord.

Blessed is that nation whose God is the Lord, the people whom He has chosen for His own inheritance. (Psalm 33:12)

CONCLUSION

We have examined the Biblical concept of the fear of God. Its importance is underscored by the hundreds of references to it in Scripture. Its various meanings are as broad as they are deep. It encompasses all of life and enables us to live the kind of life that pleases God. It is the fundamental and essential attitude toward God that we must develop and maintain in the Christian life.

The fear of the Lord will bring great blessings upon individuals, families, churches, and nations. Indeed, it is the key that unlocks the door to the treasure house of God. It is a fountain of life and the very soul and substance of true vital piety.

We see around us today what happens when people no longer fear God. Crimes and immorality abound on every hand. Divorce is destroying the family. Churches are destroyed by greed and power struggles. Judges oppress the righteous and reward the wicked. Politicians take bribes and make unjust laws.

What is the biblical remedy to the problems we face today? We need to return to the fear of God. This is the only way that we, our families, churches, and our nation can be delivered from the just wrath of Almighty God. The fear of the Lord is the beginning of wisdom and the fountain of all blessing.

SUPPLEMENT:

Selected Readings
on the
Fear of God
Throughout Church History

THE EARLY CHURCH FATHERS

The early church fought long and hard against various heresies that plagued the first believers. Various heretics such as the Marcionites taught that God was not to be feared because God is totally love. The early Fathers viewed the denial of the fear of God as a supreme heresy. They would be surprised to find that people are still denying the fear of God today.

Hermas the Shepherd

COMMANDMENT SEVENTH.

ON FEARING GOD, AND NOT FEARING THE DEVIL.

"Fear," said he, "the Lord, and keep His commandments. For if you keep the commandments of God, you will be powerful in every action, and every one of your actions will be incomparable. For fearing the Lord, you will do all things well. This is the fear which you ought to have, that you may be saved. But fear not the devil; for fearing the Lord, you will have dominion over the devil, for there is no power in him. But he in whom there is no power ought on no account to be an object of fear; but He in whom there is glorious power is truly to be feared. For every one that has power ought to be feared; but he who has not power is despised by all.

Fear, therefore, the deeds of the devil, since they are wicked. For fearing the Lord, you will not do these deeds, but will refrain from them. For fears are of two kinds: for if you do not wish to do that which is evil, fear the Lord, and you will not do it; but, again, if you wish to do that which is good, fear the Lord, and you will do it. Wherefore the fear of the Lord is strong, and great, and glorious. Fear, then, the Lord and you will live to Him, and as many as fear Him and keep His commandments will live to God." "Why," said I, "sir, did you say in regard to those that keep His commandments, that they will live to God?"

"Because," says he, "all creation fears the Lord, but all creation does not keep His commandments. They only who fear the Lord and keep His commandments have life with God; but as to those who keep not His commandments, there is no life in them."

THE APOLOGY

CHAPTER I.

They say that God is not to be feared; therefore all things are in their view free and unchecked. Where, however is God not feared, except where He is not? Where God is not, there truth also is not. Where there is no truth, then, naturally enough, there is also such a discipline as theirs. But where God is, there exists "the fear of God, which is the beginning of wisdom." Where the fear of God is, there is seriousness, an honorable and yet thoughtful diligence, as well as an anxious carefulness and a well-considered admission (to the sacred ministry) and a safely-guarded communion, and promotion after good service, and a scrupulous submission (to authority), and a devout attendance, and a modest gait, and a united church, and God in all things.

CHAPTER XXVII.

Listen, you sinners, and you who have not yet come to this; hear, that you may attain to such a pass! A better god has been discovered, who never takes offense, is never angry, never inflicts punishment, who has prepared no fire in hell, no gnashing of teeth in the outer darkness! He is purely and simply good. He indeed forbids all delinquency, but only in word. He is in you, if you are willing to pay him homage, for the sake of appearances, that you may seem to honor God; for your fear he does not want. And so satisfied are the Marcionites with such pretenses, that they have no fear of their god at all. They say it is only a bad man who will be feared, a good man will be loved.

Foolish man, do you say that he whom you call Lord ought not to be feared, whilst the very title you give him indicates a power which must itself be feared? But how are you going to love, without some fear that you do not love? Surely (such a god) is neither your Father, towards whom your love for duty's sake should be consistent with fear because of His power; nor your proper Lord, whom you should love for His humanity and fear as your teacher.

Kidnappers indeed are loved after this fashion, but they are not feared. For power will not be feared, except it be just and regular, although it may possibly be loved even when corrupt: for it is by allurement that it stands, not by authority; by flattery, not by proper influence. And what can be more direct flattery than not to punish sins? Come, then, if you do not fear God as being good, why do you not boil over into every kind of lust, and so realize that which is, I believe, the main enjoyment of life to all who fear not God? Why do you not frequent the customary pleasures of the maddening circus, the bloodthirsty arena, and the lascivious theater? Why in persecutions also do you not, when the censer is presented, at once redeem your life by the denial of your faith? God forbid, you say with redoubted emphasis.

So you do fear sin, and by your fear prove that He is an object of fear Who forbids the sin. This is quite a different matter from that obsequious homage you pay to the god whom you do not fear, which is identical in perversity indeed to is own conduct, in prohibiting a thing without annexing the sanction of punishment. Still more vainly do they act, who when asked, What is to become of every sinner in that great day? reply, that he is to be cast away out of sight. Is not even this a question of judicial determination?

He is adjudged to deserve rejection, and that by a sentence of condemnation; unless the sinner is cast away forsooth for his salvation, that even a leniency like this may fall in consistently with the character of your most good and excellent god! And what will it be to be cast away, but to lose that which a man was in the way of obtaining, were it not for his rejection—that is, his salvation? Therefore his being cast away will involve the forfeiture of salvation; and this sentence cannot possibly be passed upon him, except by an angry and offended authority, who is also the punisher of sin—that is, by a judge.

The Testaments of the Twelve Patriarchs

CHAPTER V—THE FEAR OF GOD.

"Therefore you shall be able to persuade yourselves with respect to the things that are profitable, if, like charmers, you say to the horrible serpent which lurks in your heart, 'The Lord God you shall fear, and Him alone you shall serve.' On every account it is advantageous to fear Him alone, not as an unjust, but as a righteous God. For one fears an unjust being, lest he be wrongfully destroyed, but a righteous one, lest he be caught in sin and punished. You can therefore, by fear towards Him, he freed from many hurtful fears. For if you do not fear the one Lord and Maker of all, you shall be the slaves of all evils to your own hurt, I mean of demons and diseases, and of everything that can in any way hurt you.

CHAPTER XII—THE FEAR AND LOVE OF GOD

"Thus, then, grateful service to Him who is truly Lord, renders us free from service to all other masters. If, then, it is possible for any one to be free from sin without fearing God, let him not fear; for under the influence of love to Him one cannot do what is displeasing to Him. For, on the one hand, it is written that we are to fear Him, and we have been commanded to love Him, in order that each of us may use that prescription which is suitable to his constitution. Fear Him, therefore, because He is just; but whether you fear Him or love Him, sin not. And may it be the case that any one who fears Him shall be able to gain the victory over unlawful desires, shall not lust after what belongs to others, shall practice kindness, shall be sober, and act justly! For I see some who are imperfect in their fear of Him sinning very much. Let us therefore fear God, not only because He is just; for it is through pity for those who have received injustice that He inflicts punishment on those who have done the injustice. As water therefore quenches fire, so does fear extinguish the desire for evil practices. He who teaches fearlessness does not himself fear; but he who does not fear, does not believe that there will be a judgment, strengthens his lusts, acts as a magician, and accuses others of the deeds which be himself does."

The Reformers had to refute the denial of the fear of God in their own day. In this light, Calvin's comments are worth repeating.

John Calvin: Commentary on Psalm 25:12

Moreover, the interrogatory style of speaking, which he here employs, seems designed to show how few there are who fear God: for, although all men in general pray, and manifest some appearance of piety, yet where is there one among so many who is really in earnest? Instead of this, almost all men indulge themselves in their own drowsiness. The fear of God, therefore, is very rare; and on this account it is that the world, for the most part, continues destitute of the Spirit of counsel and wisdom.

John Calvin: Commentary on Psalm 22:23

But as the chief and most essential part of this harmony proceeds from a sincere and pure affection of heart, none will ever, in a right manner, celebrate the glory of God, except the man who worships him under the influence of holy fear.

The fear which he recommends is not, however, such as would frighten the faithful from approaching God, but that which will bring them truly humbled into his sanctuary, as has been stated in the fifth psalm. Some may be surprised to find David addressing an exhortation to praise God, to those whom he had previously commended for doing so. But this is easily explained, for even the holiest men in the world are never so thoroughly imbued with the fear of God as not to have need of being continually incited to its exercise. Accordingly, the exhortation is not at all superfluous when, speaking of those who fear God, he exhorts them to stand in awe of him, and to prostrate themselves humbly before him.

The Puritans not only taught the fear of the Lord but they practiced it every day.

Charles Bridges: Commentary on Proverbs

The fear of the Lord is the beginning of knowledge; but fools despise wisdom and instruction.

The preface has stated the object of this Book of Wisdom. The book itself now opens with a noble sentence. 'There is not'—as Bishop Patrick observes—'such a wise instruction to be found in all their books (speaking of Heathen ethics), as the very first of all in Solomon's, which he lays as the ground of all wisdom.' *The fear of the Lord is the beginning of knowledge.* So had the wise man's father. (Psalm 111:10.) Such is the weight of this saying, that Solomon again repeats it. Nay—after having gone round the whole circuit; after having weighed exactly all the sources of knowledge; his conclusion of the whole matter is this, that *the fear of God* in its practical exercise "is the whole of man" (Ecclesiastes 12:13. Comp. Job, 28:12-14, with 28)—all his duty; all his happiness; his first lesson and his last. Thus, when about to instruct us from the mouth of God, he begins at *the beginning, the principal part.* All heathen wisdom is but folly. Of all knowledge, the knowledge of God is the *principal.* There is no true knowledge without godliness (Comp. Deuteronomy 4:6, 7).

But what is this *fear of the Lord?* It is that affectionate reverence; by which the child of God bends himself humbly and carefully to his Father's law. His wrath is so bitter, and his love so sweet; that hence springs an earnest desire to please him, and—because of the danger of coming short from his own weakness and temptations—a holy watchfulness and *fear,* "that he might not sin against him" (Hebrews 12:28, 29). This enters into every exercise of the mind, every object of life (Hebrews 13:17). The oldest proficient in the Divine school seeks a more complete molding into its spirit. The godly parent trains up his family under its influence (Genesis 18:19; Ephesians 6:4). The Christ scholar honors it

as *the beginning*, the head, *of all his knowledge*; at once sanctifying its end, and preserving him from its most subtle
temptations.

Why then do multitudes around us *despise wisdom and
instruction?* Because *the beginning of wisdom*—"*the fear of
God*—is not before their eyes" (Psalm 36:1). They know not
its value. They scorn its obligation. Wise they may be in
their own sight. But surely God here gives them their right
name. For *fools* they must be, to *despise* such a blessing
(Jeremiah 8:9); to rush into willful ruin (Verses 22, 24-32;
comp. 1 Samuel 2:25; 1 Kings 12:13; Jeremiah 36:22-32); to
treasure up work for despairing repentance (Chap. 5:12, 13;
29:1). Good Lord! May your childlike *fear* be my *wisdom*, my
security, my happiness!

The "Prince of Preachers" spoke often of the fear of God
as the main root of holiness.

Charles Spurgeon

The Treasury of David on Psalm 111

"The fear of the Lord is the beginning of wisdom," etc. The
text shows us the first step to true wisdom, and the test of
common sense. It is so frequently repeated, that it may pass
for a Scripture maxim, and we may be sure it is of singular
importance. Job starts the question, "Where shall wisdom be
found? and where is the place of understanding?" He
searches nature through in quest of it, but cannot find it: he
cannot purchase it with the gold of Ophir, and its price is
above rubies. At length he recollects the primitive instruction of God to man, and there he finds it: "To man he said,
Behold, the fear of the Lord, that is wisdom; and to depart
from evil is understanding."—Job 28:28. Solomon, the wisest

of men, begins his Proverbs with this maxim, "The fear of the Lord is the beginning of knowledge" (Proverbs 1:7). And he repeats it again: "The fear of the Lord is the beginning of wisdom; and the knowledge of the holy," (the knowledge of those that may be called *saints* with a sneer), "is understanding" (Proverbs 9:10). *"The fear of the Lord"* in Scripture signifies not only that pious passion or filial reverence of our adorable Father who is in heaven, but it is frequently put for the whole of practical religion; hence it is explained in the last part of the verse by *"doing his commandments,"* The fear of the Lord, in this latitude, implies all the graces and all the virtues of Christianity' in short, all that holiness of heart and life which is necessary to the enjoyment of everlasting happiness. So that the sense of the text is this: To practice religion and virtue, to take that way which leads to everlasting happiness, is *wisdom*, true wisdom, the *beginning* of wisdom, the first step towards it: unless you begin here you can never attain it; all your wisdom without this does not deserve the name; it is madness and nonsense. *"To do his commandments"* is the best test of a *"good understanding"*: a *"good"* sound *"understanding"* have *"all they"* that do this, *"all"* of them without exception: however weak some of them may be in other things, they are wise in the most important respect; but without this, however cunning they are in other things, they have lost their understandings; they contradict common sense; they are beside themselves. In short, to pursue everlasting happiness as the end, in the way of holiness as the mean, this is *"wisdom"* this is common sense, and there can be none without this.—Samuel Davies, A.M. (1724-1761) President of Princeton College, New Jersey

It is not only the beginning of wisdom, but the middle and the end. It is indeed the Alpha and Omega, the essence, the body and the soul, the sum and substance. He that has the fear of God is truly wise... It is surely wisdom to love that which is most lovable, and to occupy our hearts with that which is most worthy of our attachment, and the most capable of satisfying us.—From the French of Daniel de Superville, 1700.

Verse 10 (first clause).—Fear is not all then; no, for it is but the beginning. God will have us begin, but not end there. We have begun with *qui timet Eum*, "who fears him;" we must end with *et operatur justitiam*, "and does justice," and then comes *acceptus est Illi*, and not before. For neither fear, if it be fear alone; nor faith, if it be faith alone, is accepted of Him. If it be true fear, if such as God will accept, it is not *timor piger*, "a dull lazy fear"; his fear that feared his lord and "went and digged his talent into the ground," and did nothing with it. Away with his fear and him "into outer darkness."—Lancelot Andrewes.

Verse 10 (second clause).—Where the fear of the Lord rules in the heart, there will be constant conscientious care to keep his commandments: not to talk them, but to do them; and such *"have a good understanding,"* i.e., First, They are well understood, their obedience is graciously accepted as a plain indication of their mind, that they do indeed fear God.

Secondly, They understand well.

1. It is a sign they do understand well: the most obedient are accepted as the most intelligent. They are wise that make God's law their rule, and are in everything ruled by it.

2. It is the way to understand better. "A good understanding are they to all that do them"; i.e., the fear of the Lord, and the laws of God give men a good understanding, and are able to make them wise unto salvation.—Condensed from Matthew Henry.

Modern commentators have not abandoned the fear of God. The great Lutheran commentator Lenski speaks out on this issue throughout his works.

R. C. H. Lenski: Commentary on 2 Corinthians 7:1

"In God's fear" (see 5:11) = in this ethical sphere. The objective genitive names God as the one who is feared.

Although it is called a low motive, one that is no longer used by Christians today, it is not only found throughout Scripture but belongs to the highest Christian motivation even as Paul uses it here. It goes hand in hand with love: love is the positive side, fear the negative; love prompts one to do what pleases God, fear prompts one to refrain from what displeases God. Neither can dispense with the other; neither functions alone. Fear in the sense of "terror" is quite another matter. This could not be called the beginning of wisdom, Proverbs 9:10; Psalm 111:10; it is the deadly dismay which the wicked experience when God's judgment finds them out.

A FEAR TO BE DESIRED
BY CHARLES SPURGEON

A Sermon from the Metropolitan Tabernacle Pulpit

"And shall fear the LORD and his goodness in the latter days."—Hosea 3:5

This passage refers in the first place to the Jews. If we read the whole verse, and the preceding one, we shall see that they describe the present sad condition of God's ancient people, and inspire us with hope concerning their future: "For the children of Israel shall abide many days without a king, and without a prince, and without a sacrifice, and without an image, and without an ephod, and without teraphim: after shall the children of Israel return and week the Lord their God, and David their king; and shall fear the Lord and his goodness in the latter days."

From this, and many other texts of Scripture, we may conclude, without the shadow of a doubt, that the Jews shall, one day, acknowledge Jesus to be their King. The Son of David—who is here, doubtless, called by the name of David, and who, when he died upon the cross, had Pilate's declaration inscribed over his head, "This is Jesus the King of the Jews,"—will then be owned by them as their King, and then shall they be restored to more than their former joy and glory. God has great things in store for the seed of Abraham in the latter days. He has not finally cast them away, and he will be true to that covenant which he made with their fathers, and on Judea's plains shall roam a happy people, who shall lift up their songs of praise unto Jehovah in the name of Jesus Christ their Lord and Savior. Whenever that shall happen, we, or those who will then be living, may know that the latter days have fully come, because it is foretold here, and in other passages, that this is what will occur in the latter days.

I am not going to attempt any explanation of the prophetic intimations concerning the future, but this one fact is plain enough: when the end of the world is approaching, and the fullness of the Gentiles is gathered in, and all the splendor of the latter days has really commenced, then "shall the children of Israel return, and seek the Lord their God, and David their king; and shall fear the Lord and his goodness."

On this occasion I intend only to call your attention to this expression "They shall fear the Lord and his goodness;" for what Israel will do, in a state of grace, is precisely what all spiritual Israelites do when the grace of God rests upon them. The fear of the Lord, which is the beginning of wisdom, fills the heart, and the goodness of the Lord becomes the source and fountain of that fear in the hearts of all those whom the Lord has blessed with his grace. So I shall, first of all, ask you to notice *a distinction which is to be observed*; secondly, *a grace which is to be cultivated*; and then thirdly, *a sin which is to be repented of in the case of many*.

I. First, then here IS A DISTINCTION TO BE OBSERVED.

Human language is necessarily imperfect. Since man's fall, and especially since the confusion of tongues at Babel, there has not only been a difference in speech between one nation and another, but also between one individual and another. Probably, we do not all mean exactly the same thing by any one word that we use; there is just a shade of difference between your meaning and my. The confusion of tongues went much further than we sometimes realize; and so completely did it confuse our language that we can not, on all occasions, mean quite the same thing to ourselves even when we use the same word.

Hence, "fear" is a word which has a very wide range of meaning. There is a kind of fear which is to be shunned and avoided,—that fear which perfect love casts out—because it has torment. But there is another sort of fear which has in it the very essence of love, and without which there would be no joy even in the presence of God. Instead of perfect love casting out this fear, perfect love nourishes and cherishes it, and, by communion with it, itself derives strength from it. Between the fear of a slave and the fear of a child, we can all perceive a great distinction. Between the fear of God's great power and justice which the devils have, and that fear which a child of God has when he walks in the light with his God, there is as much difference, surely as between hell and heaven.

In the verse from which our text is taken, that difference is clearly indicated: "Afterward shall the children of Israel return and seek the Lord their God, and David their king; and shall fear the Lord;" so that *this fear is connected with seeking the Lord*. It is a fear which draws them towards God, and makes them search for him. You know how the fear of the ungodly influences them. It makes them afraid of God so they say, "Whither shall we flee from his presence?" They would take the wings of the morning if they could, and fly to the uttermost parts of the earth, if they had any hope that God could not reach them there; at the last, when this fear will take full possession of them, they will call upon the rocks and the hills to hide them from the face of him who will then sit upon the throne, whose wrath they will have such cause to dread.

The fear of God, as it exits in unrenewed men, is a force which ever drives them further and yet further away from God. They never get any rest of mind until they have ceased to think of him; if a thought of God should, perchance, steal into their mind, fear at once lays hold of them again, and that fear urges them to flee from God.

But the fear mentioned in our text draws to God. The man who has this fear in his heart cannot live without seeking God's face, confessing his guilt before him, and receiving pardon from him. He seeks God because of this fear. Just as Noah, "moved with fear," built the ark wherein he and his household were saved, so do these men, "moved with fear," draw nigh unto God, and seek to find salvation through his love and grace. Always notice this distinction, and observe that the fear which drives anyone away from God is a vice and a sin, but the fear that draws us towards God, as with silken bonds, is a virtue to be cultivated.

This appears even more clearly in the Hebrew, for they who best understand that language tell us that this passage should be read thus, "They shall fear *toward* the Lord, and *toward* his goodness." *This fear leans toward the Lord.* When you really know God, you will be thrice happy if you do run toward him, falling down before him, worshipping him with bowed head yet glad heart, all the while fearing toward him, and not away from him. Blessed is the man whose heart is filled with that holy fear which inclines his steps in the way of God's commandments, inclines his heart to seek after God, and inclines his whole soul to enter into fellowship with God, that he may be acquainted with him, and be at peace.

It is also worthy of notice that *this fear is connected with the Messiah*: "They shall seek the Lord their God, and David their King,"—who stands here as the type of Jesus the Messiah, the King of Israel; and further on it is said, "They shall fear the Lord and his goodness." I should not do wrong if I were to say that Christ is Jehovah's goodness—that, in his blessed person you have all the goodness and mercy and grace of God condensed and concentrated. "In him dwells all the fullness of the Godhead bodily." So, that fear which is a sign of grace in the heart—that fear which we ought all to seek after—always links itself on to Christ Jesus. If you fear God, and do not know that there is a Mediator between God and men, you will never think of approaching him. God is a consuming fire, then how can you draw near to him apart from Christ? If you fear God, and do not know of Christ's atonement, how can you approach him? Without faith, it is impossible to please God, and without the blood of Jesus there is no way of access to the divine mercy-seat.

If you do not know Christ, you will never come unto God. Your fear must link itself with the goodness of God as displayed in the person of his dear Son, or else it cannot be that seeking fear, that fear toward the Lord, of which our text speaks. It will be a fleeing fear—a fear that will drive you further and yet further away from God, into greater and deeper darkness—into dire destruction—in fact, into that pit whose bottomless abyss swallows up all hope, all rest, and all joy forever.

II. Let this distinction be kept in mind, and then we may safely go on to consider, in the second place, THE GRACE WHICH IS TO BE CULTIVATED: "they shall fear the Lord and his goodness."

We will divide the one thought into two; and, first, I will speak about that fear of God which is the work of the Holy Spirit, a token a grace, a sign of salvation, and a precious treasure to be ever kept in the heart.

What is this fear of God? I answer, first, *it is a sense of awe of his greatness.* Have you never felt this sacred awe stealing insensibly over your spirit, hushing, and calming you, and bowing you down before the Lord? It will come, sometimes, in the consideration of the great works of nature. Gazing upon the vast expanse of waters,—looking up to the innumerable stars, examining the wing of an insect, and seeing there the matchless skill of God displayed in the minute; or standing in a thunderstorm, watching, as best you can, the flashes of lightning, and listening to the thunder of Jehovah's voice, have you not often shrunk into yourself, and said, "Great God, how terrible you are but full of delight, like a child who rejoices to see his father's wealth, his father's wisdom, his father's power—happy, and at home, but feeling oh, so little! We are less than nothing, we are all but annihilated in the presence of the great eternal, infinite, invisible All-in-all. Gracious men often come into this state of mind and heart by watching the words of God; so they do when they observe what he does in providence. Dr. Watts truly sings:

> "Here he exalts neglected worms
> To scepters and a crown;
> Anon the following page he turns,
> And treads the monarch down."

The mightiest kings and princes are but as grasshopper in his sight. "The nations are as a drop of a bucket, and are counted as the small dust of the balance," that has not weight enough to turn the scale. We talk about the greatness of mankind; but "all nations before him are as nothing; and they are counted to him less than nothing, and vanity." Again Dr. Watts wisely sings:

> "Great God! how infinite are you!
> What worthless worms are we!"

When we realize this, we are filled with a holy awe as we think of God's greatness, and the result of that is that we are moved to fall before him in reverent adoration. We turn to the Word of God, and there we see further proofs of his greatness in all his merciful arrangements for the salvation of sinners—and especially in the matchless redemption wrought out by his well-beloved Son, every part of which is full of the divine glory; and as we gaze upon that glory with exceeding joy, we shrink to nothing before the Eternal, and the result again is lowly adoration. We bow down, and adore and worship the living God, with a joyful, tender fear, which both lays us low, and lifts us very high, for never do we seem to be nearer to heaven's golden throne than when our spirit gives itself up to worship him whom it does not see, but in whose realized presence it trembles with sacred delight.

It is the same fear, but looked at from another point of view, which has regard *to the holiness of God*. What a holy being is the great Jehovah of hosts! There is in him no fault, no deficiency, no redundancy; he is whole, and therefore holy; there is nothing there but himself, the wholly perfect God. "Holy! holy! holy!" is a fit note for the mysterious living creatures to sound out before his throne above; for, all along, he has acted according to the principle of unsullied holiness. Though blasphemers have tried, many times, to:

"Snatch from his hand the balance and the rod,
     Rejudge his judgments, be the god of God,"

they have always failed, and still he sits on the lonely majesty of his absolute perfection, while they, like brute beasts, crouch far beneath him, and despise what they cannot comprehend. But to a believing heart, God is all purity. His light is "as the color of the terrible crystal," of which Ezekiel writes; his brightness is so great that no man can approach unto it. We are so sinful that, when we get even a glimpse of the divine holiness, we are filled with fear, and we cry, with Job, "I have heard of you by the hearing of the ear: but now my eye sees you. Wherefore I abhor myself, and repent in dust and ashes." This is a kind of fear which we have need to cultivate, for it leads to repentance, and confession of sin, to aspirations after holiness, and to the utter rejection

122

of all self-complacency and self-conceit. God grant that we may be completely delivered from all those forms of pride and evil.

The fear of God also takes another form, that is, *the fear of his Fatherhood which leads us to reverence him.* When divine grace has given us the new birth, we recognize that we have entered into a fresh relationship towards God; namely, that we have received "the Spirit of adoption, whereby we cry, Abba, Father." Now, we cannot truly cry unto God, "Abba, Father" without at the same time feeling, "Behold, what manner of love the Father has bestowed upon us, that we should be called the sons of God." When we recognize that we are "heirs of God, and joint-heirs with Christ," children of the Highest, adopted into the family of the Eternal himself, we feel at once, as the spirit of childhood works within us, that we both love and fear our great Father in heaven, who has loved us with an everlasting love, and has "begotten us again unto a lively hope by the resurrection of Jesus Christ from the dead, to an inheritance incorruptible, and undefiled, and that fades now away."

In this childlike fear, there is not an atom of that fear which signifies being afraid. We, who believe in Jesus, are not afraid of our Father; God forbid that we ever should be. The nearer we can get to him ,the happier we are. Our highest wish is to be for ever with him, and to be lost in him; but, still, we pray that we may not grieve him; we beseech him to keep us from turning aside from him; we ask for his tender pity towards our infirmities, and plead with him to forgive us and to deal graciously with us for his dear Son's sake. As loving children, we feel a holy awe and reverence as we realize our relationship to him who is our Father in heaven—a dear, loving, tender, pitiful Father, yet our Heavenly Father, who "is greatly to be feared in the assembly of the saints, and to be had in reverence of all them that are about him."

This holy fear takes a further form when *our fear of God's sovereignty leads us to obey him as our King;* for he, to whom we pray, and in whom we trust, is King of kings, and Lord of lords, and we gladly own his sovereignty. We see him sitting upon a throne which is dependent upon no human or angelic power to sustain it. The kings of the earth must ask their fellow-men to march in their ranks in order to sustain their rulers, but our King "sits on no precarious throne, nor borrows leave to be" a king. As the Creator of all things, and all beings, he has a right to the obedience of all the creatures he has made. Again I say that we, who believe in Jesus, are not afraid of God even as our King, for he has made us also to be kings and priests, and we are to reign with him, through Jesus Christ, for ever and ever. Yet we tremble before him lest we should be rebellious against him the slightest degree. With a childlike fear, we are afraid lest one revolting thought or one treacherous wish should ever come into our mind or heart to stain our absolute loyalty to him. Horror takes hold upon us when we hear others deny that "the Lord reigns" but even the thought that we should ever do this grieves us exceedingly, and we are filled with that holy fear, which moves us to obey every command of our gracious King so far as we knot it to be his command. Having this fear of God before our eyes, we cry to those who would tempt us to sin, "How then can I do this great wickedness, and sin against God?" It is not because we are afraid of him, but because we delight in him, that we fear before him with an obedient reverential fear; and, beloved, I do firmly believe that, when this kind of fear of God works itself out to the full, it crystallizes into love. So excellent, so glorious, so altogether everything that could be desired, so far above our highest thought or wish, are you, O Jehovah, that we lie before you, and shrink into nothing; yet, even as we do so, we feel another sensation springing up without us. We feel that we love you; and, as we decrease in our own estimation of ourselves, we feel that we love you more and more. As we realize our own nothingness, we are more than ever conscious of the greatness of our God. "Your heart shall fear, and be enlarged," says the prophet Isaiah, and so it comes to pass with us. The more we fear the Lord, the more we love him, until this becomes to us the true fear of God, to love him with all our heart, and mind, and soul, and strength. May he bring us to this blessed climax by the effectual working of his Holy Spirit!

Now I want to dwell, with somewhat of emphasis, upon the second part of this fear: "They shall fear the Lord *and his goodness.*" It may at first seem, to some people, a strange thing that we should fear God's goodness; but there are some of us who know exactly what this expression means, for we have often experienced just what it describes. How can we fear God's goodness? I speak what I have often felt, and I believe many of you can do the same as you look back upon the goodness of God to you—saving you from sin, and making you to be his child; and as you think of all his goodness to you in the dispensations of his providence. You may, perhaps, be like Jacob, who left his Father's house with his wallet and his staff; and when he came back with a family that formed two bands, and with abundance of all that he could desire, he must have been astonished at what God had done for him. And when David sat upon his throne in Jerusalem, surrounded by wealth and splendor, as he recollected how he had fed his flock in the wilderness, and afterwards had been hunted, by Saul, like a partridge upon the mountains, he might well say, "Is this the manner of man, O Lord God?"

In this way, *God's goodness often fills us with amazement*, and amazement has in it an element of fear. We are astonished at the Lord's gracious dealings with us, and we say to him, "Why have you been so good to me, for so many years, and in such multitudes of forms? Why have you manifested so much mercy and tenderness toward me? You have treated me as if I had never grieved or offended you. You have been as good to me as if I had deserved great blessings at your hands. Had you paid me wages, like a hired servant, you would never have given me such sweetness and such love as you have now lavished upon me, though I was once a prodigal, and wandered far from you. O God, your love is like the sun; I cannot gaze upon it, its brightness would blind my eyes! I fear, because of your goodness." Do you know, dear friends, what this expression means? If a sense of God's goodness comes upon you in all its force, you will feel that God is wonderfully great to have been so good to you. Most of us have had friends who have become tired of us after a while. Possibly, we have had some very kind friends, who are not yet tired of us; but, still, they have failed us every now and then at some points; either their power could not meet our necessity, or they were not willing to do what we needed. But our God has poured out his mercy for us like a river; it has flowed on without a break. These many years he has continued to bless us, and has heaped up his mercies, mountain upon mountain, until it has seemed as though he would reach the very stars with the lofty pinnacles of his love. What shall we say to all this? Shall we not fear him, and adore him, and bless him for all the goodness that he has made to pass before us; and, all the while, feel that, even to kiss the hem of his garment, or to lie beneath his footstool, is too great an honor for us?

Then there will come upon us, when we are truly grateful to God for his goodness toward us, *a sense of our own responsibility*; and we shall say, "What shall I render unto the Lord for all his benefits toward me?" We shall feel that we cannot render t him anything compared with what we ought to render; and there will come upon us this fear—that we shall never be able to live at all consistently with the high position which his grace has given to us. As God said concerning his ancient people, we shall fear and tremble for all the goodness and for all the prosperity that he has procured for us. It will seem as though he had set us on the top of a high mountain, and had bidden us walk along that lofty ridge; it is a ridge of favor and privilege, but it is so elevated that we fear lest our brain should reel, and our feet should slip, because of the height of God's mercy to us. Have you never felt like that, beloved? If God has greatly exalted you with his favor and love, I am sure you must have felt like that many a time.

Then, next, *this holy fear is near akin to gratitude.* The fear of a man, who really knows the love and goodness of God, will be somewhat of this kind. He will fear lest he should really be, or should seem to be, ungrateful. "What," he asks, "can I do? I am drowned in mercy. It is not as though my ship were sailing in a sea of mercy; I have been so loaded with the favor of the Lord that my vessel has gone right down, and the ocean of God's love and mercy has rolled right over the masthead. What can I do, O Lord? If you had given me only a little mercy, I might have done something, in return, to express my gratitude. But, oh! your great mercy in electing me, in redeeming me, in converting me, and in preserving me, and in all the goodness of your providence toward me—what can I do in return for all these favors? I feel struck dumb; and I am afraid lest I should have a dumb heart as well as a dumb tongue; I fear lest I should grieve you by anything that looks like ingratitude."

Then the child of God begins, next, *to fear lest he should become proud*; "for," says he, "I have noticed that, when God thus favors some men, they begin to exalt themselves, and to think that they are persons of great importance; so, if the Lord makes the stream of my life flow very joyously, I may imagine that it is because there is some good thing in me, and be foolish enough to being to ascribe the glory of it to myself." A true saint often trembles concerning this matter;

he sometimes gets even afraid of his mercies. He knows that his trials and troubles never did him any hurt; but he perceives that, sometimes, God's goodness has intoxicated him as with sweet wine, so he begins to be almost afraid of the goodness of his God to him. He thinks to himself, "Shall I be unworthy of all this favor, and walk in a way that is inconsistent with it?" He looks a little ahead, and he knows that the flesh is frail, and that good men have often been found in very slippery places, and he says, "What if, after all this, I should be a backslider? You, O Lord, have brought me into the banqueting house, and your banner over me is love; you have stayed me with flagons, and comforted me with apples; you have laid bare they very heart to me, and made me know that I am a man greatly beloved. Shall I, after all this, ever turn aside from you? Will the ungodly ever point at me, and say, 'Aha! Aha! Is this the man after God's own heart? Is this the disciple who said he would die rather than deny his Master?'" Such a fear as that very properly comes over us at times, and then we tremble because of all the goodness which God has made to pass before us.

I think you can see, dear friends, without my needing to enlarge further upon this point, that, while a time of sorrow and suffering is often, to the Christian, a time of confidence in his God; on the other hand, a time of prosperity is, to the wise man, a time of holy fear. Not that he is ungrateful, but he is afraid that he may be. Not that he is proud; he is truly humble because he is afraid lest he should become proud. Not that he loves the things of the world, but he is afraid lest his heart should get away from God, so he fears because of all the Lord's goodness to him. May the Lord always keep us in that state of fear, for it is a healthy condition for us to be in. Those who walk so very proudly, and with too great confidence, are generally the ones who first tumble down. My observation and experience have taught me this; when I have met with anyone who knew that he was a very good man—he has generally proved to be like some of those pears that we sometimes see in the shop—very handsome to look at, but sleepy and rotten all through. Then, on the other hand, I have noticed a great many other people, who have always been afraid that they would go wrong, and who have trembled and feared at almost every step they took. They have feared lest they should grieve the Lord, and they have cried unto him day and night, "Lord, uphold us" and he has done so, and they have been enabled to keep their garments unspotted to their life's end. So my prayer is that I may never cease to feel this holy fear before God, and that I may never get to fancy for a moment that there is or ever can be anything in me to cause me to boast or to glory in myself. May God save all of us from that evil; and the more we receive of his goodness, the more may we fear with childlike fear in his presence?

III. Now I must close with just a few words upon the last point; which is, A SIN TO BE REPENTED OF.

I cannot help fearing that I am addressing some to whom my text does not apply except by way of contrast. Are there not some of you, who are unsaved, and yet who do not fear God? O sirs, may the Holy Spirit make you to fear and tremble before him! You have cause enough to fear. If you live all day lone without even thinking of God, or if when you do think of him you try to smother the thought at once—if you say that you can get on very well without him, and that life is happy enough without religion—I could weep for you because you do not weep for yourselves.

You say, "We are rich;" yet, all the while, you are wretched, and miserable, and poor. Your poverty is all the worst because you fancy that you are rich. You are also blind. That is bad enough, yet you say, "We can see." It is doubly sad when the spiritually blind declare that they can see, for they will never ask for the sacred eye-salve, or go to the great Oculist who can open blind eyes, so long as they are satisfied with their present condition. It is a great pity that many unconverted men do not fear God even with a servile fear. If they would only begin with that, it might prove to be the lowest rung of the heavenly ladder and lead on to the blessed fear which is the portion of the children of God.

There are other of you, I am afraid, who never fear either God or his goodness. How I wish you would do so, for the Lord has been very good to you. You were saved at sea after you had been wrecked. You were raised up from fever when others died. You have been prospered in business, on the whole, though you have had some struggles. Blessed with children, and made happy in your home—all this you owe to the God whom you have never acknowledged. The goodness of God to some ungodly men is truly wonderful. I think when they sit down at night, when everybody else has gone to bed, and remember how they began life with scarcely a shilling to bless themselves with, yet God has multiplied their substance and given them much to rejoice in, their hearts ought to be full of gratitude towards their Benefactor.

I would like all such people to recollect what God said by the mouth of the prophet Hosea: "She did not know that I gave her corn, and wine, and oil, and multiplied her silver and gold, which they prepared for Baal. Therefore will I return, and take away my corn in the time thereto, and my wine in the season thereof, and will recover my wool and my flax given to cover he nakedness."

Take care, O you ungrateful souls, that the Lord does not begin to strip you of the mercies which you have failed to appreciate! I pray that you may be led to confess whence all these blessings came, and to cry, "My Father, you will be my Guide, henceforth and for ever. Since you have dealt so lovingly and tenderly with me, I will come and confess my sin unto you, and trust in your dear Son as my Savior and

Friend, that I may henceforth be led and commanded by you alone, and may fear before you all the days of my life."

My God grant to every one of us the grace to believe in Jesus, and to rest in him, and then to walk in the fear of the Lord all our days, for Christ's sake, Amen.

THE FEAR OF GOD BY JOHN BUNYAN

WHAT THE FEAR OF GOD IS, AND HOW TO DISTINGUISH IT FROM THAT WHICH IS NOT A GODLY FEAR

"Blessed is everyone that fears the Lord."—Psalm 128:1

This exhortation is not only found here in the text, but is in several other places of the Scripture pressed, and that with much vehemence, upon the children of men, as in Ecclesiastes 12:13 and 1 Peter 1:17, etc. I shall not trouble you with long preambles, or fore-speech as to the matter, nor shall I here so much as meddle with the context, but shall immediately fall upon the words themselves, and briefly treat of the fear of God.

The text, you see, presents us with matter of greatest moment, to wit, with God, and with the fear of him.

First. They present us with God, the true and living God, maker of the worlds, and upholder of all things by the word of his power; that incomprehensible Majesty, in comparison of whom all nations are less than the drop of a bucket, and than the small dust of the balance. This is he that fills heaven and earth, and is everywhere present with the children of men, beholding the evil and the good; for he has set his eyes upon all their ways.

So that, considering that by the text we have presented to our souls the Lord God and Maker of us all, who also will be either our Saviour or Judge, we are in reason and duty bound to give the more earnest heed to the things that shall be spoken, and be the more careful to receive them, and put them in practice; for, as I said, as they present us with the mighty God, so they exhort us to the highest duty towards him, to wit, to fear him; I call it the highest duty, because it is, as I may call it, not only a duty in itself, but, as it were, the salt that seasons every duty. For there is no duty performed by us that can by any means be accepted of God, if it be not seasoned with godly fear. Wherefore the Apostle says, "Let us have grace, whereby we may serve God acceptably with reverence and godly fear." Of this fear, I say, I would discourse at this time; but because this word fear is variously taken in the Scripture, and because it may be profitable to us to see it in its variety, I shall therefore choose this method for the managing of my discourse, even to show you the nature of the word in its several, especially of the chiefest, acceptations.

I. Then by this word "fear" we are to understand even God himself, who is the object of our fear.

II. By this word "fear" we are to understand the word of God, the rule and director of our fear.

Now to speak to this word, "fear," as it is thus taken.

I. Of this word "fear," as it respects God himself, who is the object of our fear.

By this word "fear," as I said, we are to understand God himself, who is the object of our fear; for the divine Majesty goes often under this very name himself. This name Jacob called him by, when he and Laban hid together on Mount Gilead, after that Jacob had made his escape to his father's house: "Except," said he, "the God of Abraham, and the fear of Isaac had been with me, surely now you would have sent me away empty." So again, a little after, when Jacob and Laban agree to make a covenant of peace each with other, though Laban, after the jumbling way of the heathen by his oath, puts the true God and the false together, yet "Jacob swore by the fear of his father Isaac." (Genesis 31:42, 53).

By the fear, that is, by the God of his father Isaac. And, indeed, God may well be called the fear of his people, not only because they have by his grace made him the object of their fear, but because of the dread and terrible majesty that is in him. "He is a might God, and terrible, and with God is terrible majesty." (Daniel 7:28; 10:17. Hebrews 1:5; 4:14; 9:32; Job 37:22)

Who knows the power of his anger? "The mountains quake at him, the hills melt, and the earth is burnt at his presence; yea, the world, and all that dwell therein. Who can stand before his indignation? who can abide the fierceness of his anger? His fury is poured out like fire, and the rocks are thrown down by him." (Nahum 1:5, 6)

His people know him, and have his dread upon them, by virtue whereof there is begot and maintained in them that godly awe and reverence of his majesty which is agreeable to their profession of him. "Let him be your fear, and let him be your dread." Set his majesty before the eyes of your souls, and let his excellency make you afraid with godly fear. (Isaiah 8:12, 13)

There are these things that make God to be the fear of his people:

First. His presence is dreadful, and that not only his presence in common, but his special, yea, his most comfortable and joyous presence. When God comes to bring a soul news of mercy and salvation, even that visit, that presence of God is fearful. When Jacob went from Beersheba towards Haran, he met with God in the way by a dream, in the which he apprehended a ladder set upon the earth, whose top reached to heaven. Now in this dream, from the top of this ladder he saw the Lord, and heard him speak unto him, not threateningly—not as having his fury come up into his face—but in the most sweet and gracious manner, saluting him with promise of goodness after promise of goodness, to the number of eight or nine; as will appear, if you read the place (Genesis 28:16, 17). Yet I saw, when he awoke, all the grace that discovered itself in this heavenly vision to him could not keep him from dread and fear of God's majesty. "And Jacob awoke out of his sleep, and said, Surely the Lord was in this place, and I knew it not; and he was afraid, and said, How dreadful is this place! this is none other but the house of God, and this is the gate of heaven."

At another time, to wit, when Jacob had that memorable visit from God, in which he gave him power as a prince to prevail with him—yea, and gave him a name, that by his remembering it he might call God's favor the better to his mind, yet even then and there such dread of the majesty of God was upon him, that "he went away wondering that his life was preserved." (Genesis 32:30) Man crumbles to dust at the presence of God; yea, though he shows himself to us in his robes of salvation.

We have read how dreadful and how terrible even the presence of angels have been unto men, and that when they have brought them good tidings from heaven. (Judges 13:22; Matthew 28:4; Mark 16:5,6) Now if angels, which are but creatures are, through the glory that God has put upon them, so fearful and terrible in their appearance to men, how much more dreadful and terrible must God himself be to us, who are but dust and ashes? When Daniel had the vision of his salvation sent him from heaven—for so it was, "O Daniel," said the messenger, "a man greatly beloved;"— yet behold the dread and terror of the person speaking fell with that weight upon this good man's soul, that he could not stand, nor bear up under it. He stood trembling, and cries out, "Oh, my Lord, by the vision my sorrows are turned upon me, and I have retained no strength! And how can the servant of this my lord talk with this my lord! for as for me straightway there remains no strength in me." (Daniel 10:16) See you here if the presence of God is not a dreadful and a fearful thing; yea, his most gracious and merciful appearances; how much more then when he shows himself to us as one that dislikes our ways, as one that is offended with us for our sins!

And there are three things that in an eminent manner make his presence dreadful to us.

1. The first is God's own greatness and majesty; the discovery of this, or of himself thus, even as no poor mortals are able to conceive of him, is altogether unsupportable. The man dies to whom he thus discovers himself. "And when I saw him" says John, "I fell at his feet as dead." (Revelation 1:17) It was this, therefore, that Job would have avoided in the day that he would have approached unto him. "Let not your dread," says he, "make me afraid. Then call you, and I will answer; or let me speak, and answer me." (Job 13:21,22) But why does Job after this manner thus speak to God? Why, it was from a sense that he had of the dreadful majesty of God, even the great and dreadful God that keeps covenant with his people. The presence of a king is dreadful to the subject, yea, though he carried it never so condescendingly; if then there be so much glory and dread in the presence of the king, what fear and dread must there be, think you, in the presence of the eternal God!

2. When God gives his presence to his people, that his presence causes them to appear to themselves more what they are than at other times, by all other light, they can see. "Oh, my Lord," said he, "by the vision my sorrows are turned upon me;" and why was that, but because by the glory of that vision he saw his own vileness more than at other times? So again: "I alone," says he, "saw this great vision;" and what follows? why, "and my comeliness was turned in me into corruption, and I retained no strength." (Daniel 10:8) By the presence of God, when we have it indeed, even our best things, our comeliness, our sanctity and righteousness, all do immediately turn to corruption, and polluted rags. The brightness of his glory dims them, as the

clear light of the shining sun puts out the glory of the fire or candle, and covers them with the shadow of death.

See also the truth of this in that vision of the prophet Isaiah. "Woe is me," said he, "for I am undone, for I am a man of polluted lips, and I dwell among a people of unclean lips." Why? what is the matter? how came the prophet by this sight? "Why," says he, "my eyes have seen the King, the Lord of hosts." (Isaiah 6:5) But do you think that this outcry was caused by unbelief? no, nor yet begotten by slavish fear. This was to him the vision of his Saviour, with whom also he had communion before (chap. 1:2-5), it was the glory of that God with whom he had now to do, that turned, as was noted before of Daniel, his comeliness in him into corruption, and that gave him yet greater sense of the disproportion that was betwixt his God and him, and so a greater sight of his defiled and polluted nature.

3. Add to this the revelation of God's goodness, and it must needs make his presence dreadful to us; for when a poor defiled creature shall see that this great God has, notwithstanding his greatness, goodness in his heart, and mercy to bestow upon him; this makes his presence yet the more dreadful. "They shall fear the Lord and his goodness" (Hosea 3:5). The goodness as well as the greatness of God does beget in the heart of his elect an awful reverence of his majesty. "Fear you not me" says the Lord, "will you not tremble at my presence?" And then to engage us in our soul to the duty, he adds one of his wonderful mercies to the world, for a motive, "Fear you not me?" why, who are you? He answers, "Even I, which have" set, or placed "the sand for the bound of the sea by a perpetual decree that it cannot pass; and though the waves thereof toss themselves, yet can they not prevail, though they roar, yet can they not pass over it." (Jeremiah 5:22)

Also when Job had God present with him, making manifest the goodness of his great heart to him, what does he say? How does he behave himself in his presence? "I have heard of you," says he, "by the hearing of the ear, but now my eyes see you; wherefore I abhor myself, and repent in dust and ashes." (Job 42:5,6)

And what mean the tremblings, the tears, those breakings and shakings of heart that attend the people of God, when in an eminent manner they receive the pronunciation of the forgiveness of sins at his mouth, but that the dread of the majesty of God is in their sight mixed therewith? God must appear like himself, speak to the soul like himself; nor can the sinner, when under these glorious discoveries of its Lord and Saviour, keep out the beams of his majesty from the eyes of its understanding. "I will cleanse them," says he, "from all their iniquity, whereby they have sinned against me, and I will pardon all their iniquities whereby they have sinned, whereby they have transgressed against me." And what then? "And they shall fear and tremble for all the goodness, and for all the prosperity that I procure unto it." (Jeremiah 33:8,9)

Alas! there is a company of poor, light, frothy professors in the world that carry it under that which they called the presence of God, more like to antics, than sober, sensible Christians; yea, more like to a fool of a play, than those that have the presence of God. They would not carry it so in the presence of a king, nor yet of the lord of their land, were they but receivers of mercy at his hand. They carry it, even in their most eminent seasons, as if the sense and sight of God, and his blessed grace to their souls in Christ, had a tendency in it to make men wanton. But, indeed, it is the most humbling and heart-breaking sight in the world; it is fearful.

Objection: But would you now have us rejoice at the sight and sense of the forgiveness of our sins?

Answer: Yes; but yet I would have you, and indeed you shall, when God shall tell you that your sins are pardoned indeed, "rejoice with trembling," (Psalm 2:11) for then you have solid and godly joy. A joyful heart and wet eyes, in this will stand very well together, and it will be so, more or less. For if God shall come to you indeed, and visit you with the forgiveness of sins, that visit removes the guilt, but increases the sense of your filth; and the sense of this, that God has forgiven a filthy sinner, will make these both rejoice and tremble. Oh, the blessed confusion that will then cover your face while you, even you so vile a wretch, will stand before God to receive at his hand your pardon, and so the first-fruits of your eternal salvation! "That you may remember, and be confounded, and never open your mouth any more, because of your shame," you filth, "when I am pacified towards you for all that you have done," says the Lord God. (Ezekiel 16:63)

Second. But, as the presence, so the name of God, is dreadful and fearful; wherefore his name does rightly go under the same title, "That you may fear that glorious and fearful name, The Lord your God." (Deuteronomy 28:58) The name of God, what is that, but that by which he is distinguished and known from all others? Names are to distinguish by; so man is distinguished from beasts, and angels from men; so heaven from earth, and darkness from light; especially when by the name the nature of the thing is signified and expressed; and so it was in their original, for then names expressed the nature of the things so named. And, therefore, it is that the name of God is the object of our fear, because by his name his nature is expressed: "Holy and reverend is his name." (Psalm 111:9) And again; "He proclaimed the name of the Lord, The Lord, the Lord God, gracious and merciful, long-suffering, and abundant in goodness and truth; keeping mercy for thousands, pardoning iniquity, transgression and sins, and that will by no means clear the guilty." (Exodus 34:6,7)

Also, his name, I am, Jah, Jehovah, with several others, what is by them intended but his nature, as his power, wisdom, eternity, goodness and omnipotence, etc. might be expressed and declared. The name of God is therefore the object of a Christian's fear. David prayed to God that he would unite his heart to fear his name. (Psalm 136:11) Indeed, the name of God is a fearful name, and should always be reverenced by his people; yea, his name is to be feared for ever and ever, and that not only in his church, and among his saints, but even in the world and among the heathen. "So the heathen shall fear the name of the Lord, and all kings your glory." (Psalm 102:15) God tells us that his name is dreadful, and that he is pleased to see men be afraid before his name. Yea, one reason why he executes so many judgments upon men as he does, is that others might see and fear his name. "So shall they fear the name of the Lord from the west, and his glory from the rising of the sun." (See Malachi 4:2; Revelation 11:18; Malachi 1:4; 2:5; Isaiah 59:18,19)

The name of a king is a name of fear: "And I am a great king, says the Lord of hosts." The name of master is a name of fear: "And if I be a master, where is my fear, says the Lord?" yea, rightly to fear the Lord is a sign of a gracious heart. And again, "To them that fear your name," says he, "shall the Son of righteousness arise with healing in his wings;" yea, when Christ comes to judge the world, he will give reward to his servants the prophets, and to his saints, and to them that fear his name, small and great. Now, I saw, since the name of God is that by which his nature is expressed, and since he naturally is so glorious and incomprehensible, his name must needs be the object of our fear, and we ought always to have a reverent awe of God upon our hearts at whatsoever time we think of, or hear his name, but most of all, when we ourselves do take his holy and fearful name into our mouths, especially in a religious

140

manner, that is, in preaching, praying, or holy conference. I do not by thus saying intend, as if it was lawful to make mention of his name in light and vain discourses; for we ought always to speak of it with reverence and godly fear, but I speak it to put Christians in mind that they should not in religious duties show lightness of mind, or be vain in their words when yet they are making mention of the name of the Lord, "And let every one that names the name of our Lord Jesus Christ depart from iniquity." (2 Timothy 2:19)

Make mention, then, of the name of the Lord at all times with great dread of his Majesty upon your hearts, and in great soberness and truth. To do otherwise is to profane the name of the Lord, and to take his name in vain; "And the Lord will not hold him guiltless that takes his name in vain." Yea, God says, that he will cut off the man that does it; so jealous is he of the honor due unto his name. (Exodus 20:7. Leviticus 20:3.) This therefore shows you the dreadful state of those that lightly, vainly, lyingly, and profanely make use the name, this fearful name of God, either by their blasphemous cursing and oaths, or by their fraudulent dealing with their neighbors; for some men have no way to prevail with their neighbor to bow under a cheat, but by calling falsely upon the name of the Lord to be witness that the wickedness is good and honest; but how these men will escape, when they shall be judged, devouring fire and everlasting burnings for their profaning and blaspheming of the name of the Lord, becomes them betimes to consider of. (Jeremiah 14:14,15; Ezekiel 20:39; Exodus 20:7)

Third. But as the presence and name of God are dreadful and fearful in the church, so are his worship and service. I say his worship, or the works of service, to which we are by him enjoined while we are in this world, are dreadful and fearful; things. This David conceives, when he says, "But as for me, I will come into your house in the multitude of your mercies, and in your fear will I worship towards your holy temple." (Psalm 5:7) And again, says he, "Serve the Lord with fear." To praise God is a part of his worship. But says Moses, "Who is a God like unto you, glorious in holiness, fearful in praises, doing wonders?" (Exodus 15:11) To rejoice before him is a part of his worship; but David bids us "rejoice with trembling." (Psalm 2:11) Yea, the whole of our service to God, and every part thereof, ought to be done by us with reverence and godly fear. And therefore let us, as Paul says again, "cleanse ourselves from all filthiness of flesh and spirit, perfecting holiness in the fear of God." (Hebrews 13; 2 Corinthians 7:1)

1. That which makes the worship of God so fearful a thing, is, for that it is the worship of God. Al manner of service carries more or less dread and fear along with it, according as the quality or condition of the person is, to whom the worship and service is done. This is seen in the service of subjects to their princes, the service of servants to their lords, and the service of children to their parents. Divine worship then, being due to God—for it is now of Divine worship we speak—and this God so great and dreadful in himself and name, his worship must therefore be a fearful thing.

2. Besides, this glorious Majesty is himself present to behold his worshippers in their worshipping him. "When two or three of you are gathered together in my name, I am there;" that is, gathered together to worship him, "I am there," says he. And so, again, he is said to "walk in the midst of the seven golden candlesticks," (Revelation 1:13) that is, in the churches, and that with a countenance like the sun, with a head and hair as white as snow, and with eyes like a flame of fire. This puts dread and fear into his service; and therefore his servants should serve him with fear.

3. Above all things, God is jealous of his worship and service. In all the ten words, he tells us not anything of his being a jealous God, but in the second which respects his

worship. (Exodus 20) Look to yourselves, therefore, both as to the matter and manner of your worship; "for I the Lord your God," says he, "am a jealous God, visiting the sins of the fathers upon the children." This therefore does also put dread and fear into the worship and service of God.

4. The judgments that sometimes God has executed upon men for their want of godly fear, while they have been in his worship and service, put fear and dread upon his holy appointments.

(1) Nadab and Abihu were burned to death with fire from heaven, because they attempted to offer false fire upon God's altar, (Leviticus 10:1-3); and the reason rendered why they were so served, was, because God will be sanctified in them that come nigh him. To sanctify his name is to let him be your dread and your fear, and to do nothing in his worship but what is well-pleasing to him. But because these men had not grace to do this, therefore they died before the Lord.

(2) Eli's sons, for want of this fear, when they ministered in the holy worship of God, were both slain in one day by the sword of the uncircumcised Philistines. (See 1 Samuel 2.)

(3) Uzzah was smitten, and died before the Lord, for but an unadvised touching of the ark, when the men forsook it. (1 Chronicles 13:9,10.)

(4) Ananias, and Sapphira his wife, for telling of a lie in church, when they were before God, were both stricken dead upon the place before them all, because they wanted the fear and dread of God's majesty, name, and service, when they came before him. (Acts 5)

This, therefore, should teach us to conclude, that, next of God's nature and name, his service, his instituted worship, is the most dreadful thing under heaven. His name is upon his ordinances, his eye is upon the worshippers, and his wrath and judgment upon those that worship not in his fear. For this cause some of those at Corinth were by God himself cut off, (1 Corinthians 11:27-32;) and to others he has given the back, and will again be with them no more.

This also rebukes three sorts of people:

1. Such as regard not to worship God at all; be sure they have no reverence of his service, nor fear of his majesty before their eyes. Sinner, you do not come before the Lord to worship him; you do not bow before the high God; you neither worship him in your closet nor in the congregation of saints. The fury of the Lord and his indignation must in short time be poured out upon you, and upon the families that call not upon his name. (Psalm 129:6; Jeremiah 10:25.)

2. This rebukes such as count it enough to present their body in the place where God is worshipped, not minding with what heart or with what spirit they come thither. Some come into the worship of God to sleep there; some come thither to meet with their chapmen, and to get into the wicked fellowship of their vain companions. Some come thither to fee their lustful and adulterous eyes with the flattering beauty of their fellow-sinners. Oh what a sad account will these worshippers give, when they shall count for all this, and be damned for it, because they come not to worship the Lord with that fear of his name that became them to come in, when they presented themselves before him!

3. This also rebukes those that care not, so they worship, how they worship; how, where, or after what manner they worship God. Those, I mean, "whose fear towards God" is taught by the precepts of men.

They are hypocrites; their worship also in vain, and a stink in the nostrils of God. Wherefore the Lord said, Forasmuch as this people draw near me with their mouth, and honor me with their lips, but have removed their heart far from me, and their fear towards me is taught by the precepts of men: therefore, behold, I will proceed to do a marvelous work among this people, even a marvelous work, and a wonder: for the wisdom of their wise men shall per-

ish, and the understanding of their prudent shall be hid."
(Isaiah 29:13. Matthew 15:7-9. Mark 7:6,7.)

Thus I conclude this first thing, namely, that God is
called our dread and fear. I shall now come to the second
thing, to wit, to the rule and director of our fear.

II. Of this word "fear," as it is taken for the word of
God.

But again, this word "fear" is sometimes to be taken for
the word, the written word of God; for that also is and
ought to be the rule and director of our fear. So David calls
it in the 19th Psalm. "The fear of the Lord," says he, "is
clean, enduring for ever." The fear of the Lord, that is, the
word of the Lord, the written word; for that which he calls
in this place the fear of the Lord, even in the same place he
calls the law, statutes, commandments, and judgments of
God. "The law of the Lord is perfect, converting the soul:
the testimony of the Lord is sure, making wise the simple:
the statutes of the Lord are right, rejoicing the heart: the
commencement of the Lord is pure, enlightening the eyes:
the fear of the Lord is clean, enduring for ever: the judgments of the Lord are true and righteous altogether." All
these words have respect to the same thing, to wit, to the
word of God, jointly designing the glory of it. Among which
phrases, as you see, this is one, "The fear of the Lord is
clean, enduring for ever." This written word is therefore the
object of a Christian's fear. This is that also which David intended when he said, "Come, you children, hearken to me; I
will teach you the fear of the Lord." (Psalm 34:11.) I will
teach you the fear, that is, I will teach you the commandments, statutes, and judgments of the Lord, even as Moses
commanded the children of Israel: "You shall teach them
diligently unto your children, and shall talk of them when
you sit in your house, and when you walk by the way, and
when you lie down, and when you rise up." (Deuteronomy
6:4-7.)

That also in the 11th of Isaiah intends the same; where the Father says of the Son, that "he shall be of a quick understanding in the fear of the Lord; that he may judge and smite the earth with the rod of his mouth." This rod in the text is none other but the fear, the word of the Lord; for he was to be of a quick understanding, that he might smite, that is, execute it according to the will of his Father, upon and among the children of men. Now this, as I said, is called the fear of the Lord, because it is called the rule and director of our fear; for we know now how to fear the Lord in a saving way without its guidance and direction. As it is said of the priest that was sent back from the captivity to Samaria, to teach the people to fear the Lord, so it is said concerning the written word; it is given to us, and left among us that we may read therein all the days of our life, and learn to fear the Lord. (Deuteronomy 6:1-3, 24; 10:12; 17:19.) And he it is that, trembling at the word of God, is even by God himself not only taken notice of, but counted as laudable and praiseworthy, as is evident in the case of Josiah. (2 Chronicles 34:26,27.) Such also are the approved of God, let them be condemned by whomsoever: "Hear the word of the Lord, you that tremble at his word; your brethren that hated you, and cast you out for my name's sake, said, Let the Lord be glorified; but he shall appear to your joy, and they shall be ashamed." (Isaiah 66:5.)

Further; such shall be looked to, by God himself cared for and watched over, that no distress, temptation, or affliction, may overcome them and destroy them. "To this man will I look," says God, "even to him that is poor and of a contrite spirit, and that trembles at my word.: It is the same in substance with that in the same prophet in chap. 57: "For thus says the high and holy One that inhabits eternity, whose name is Holy: I dwell in the high and holy place, with him also that is of a contrite and humble spirit, to revive the spirit of the humble, and to revive the heart of the contrite ones." Yea, the way to escape dangers foretold, is to hearken to, understand, and fear the word of God. "He that feared the word of the Lord amongst the servants of Pharaoh, made his servants and cattle flee into houses, and they were secured. But he that regarded not the word of the Lord, left his servants and cattle in the field, and they were destroyed of the hail." (Exodus 9:20-25.)

If at any time the sins of a nation or church are discovered and bewailed, it is by them that know and tremble at the word of God. When Ezra heard of the wickedness of his brethren, and had a desire to humble himself before God for the same, who were they that would assist him in that matter, but they that trembled at the word of God? "Then," says he, "were assembled to me every one that trembled at the word of the God of Israel, because of the transgression of those that had been carried away." (Ezra 9:4.) They are such also that tremble at the word that are best able to give counsel in the matters of God, for their judgment best suits with his mind and will. "Now, therefore," says he, "let us make a covenant with our God to put away all the (strange) wives, according to the counsel of my Lord, and of those that tremble at the commandment of our God, and let it be done according to the law." (Ezra 10:3.) Now, something of the dread and terror of the word lies in these things.

First. As I have already hinted, from the Author of them, they are the words of God. Therefore you have Moses and the prophets, when they came to deliver their errand, their message to the people, still saying: "Hear the word of the Lord," "Thus says the Lord," and the like. So when Ezekiel was sent to the house of Israel, in their state of religion, thus was he bid to say unto them, "Thus says the Lord God," "Thus says the Lord God." (Ezekiel 2:4; 3:11.) This is the honor and majesty, then, that God has put upon his written word; and thus he has done even of purpose, that we might make them the rule and directory of our fear, and that we

might stand in awe of and tremble at them. When Habakkuk heard the word of the Lord, his belly trembled, and
rottenness entered into his bones. "I trembled in myself,"
said he, "that I might have rest in the day of trouble."
(Habakkuk 3:16.) The word of a king is as the roaring of a
lion; where the word of a king is, there is power; what is it
then when God, the great God, shall roar out of Zion, and
utter his voice from Jerusalem, whose voice shakes not only
the earth, but also heaven! How does holy David set it forth:
"The voice of the Lord is powerful, the voice of the Lord is
full of majesty," etc. (Psalm 29.)

Second. It is a word that is fearful, and may well be
called the fear of the Lord, because of the subject matter of
it, to wit, the state of sinners in another world, for that is it
unto which the whole Bible bends itself, either more immediately or more mediately; all its doctrines, counsels,
encouragements, threatenings, and judgments, have a look,
one way or other, upon us with respect to the next world,
which will be our last state, because it will be to us a state
eternal. This word, this law, these judgments, are they that
we shall be disposed of by. "The word that I have spoken,"
says Christ, "it shall judge you," and so consequently dispose of you, "at the last day." (John 12:48.) Now, if we
consider that our next state must be eternal, either eternal
glory or this eternal fire must be our portion according as
the words of God revealed in the Holy Scriptures shall de-
termine, who will not but conclude that therefore the words
of God are they at which we should tremble, and they by
which we should have our fear of God guided and directed,
for by them we are taught how to please him in everything?

Third. It is to be called a fearful word, because of the
truth and faithfulness of it. The Scripture cannot be broken.
Here they are called the Scriptures of truth, the true sayings
of God, and also the fear of the Lord, for that every jot and
tittle thereof is for ever settled in heaven, and stands more

148

steadfast than does the world. "Heaven and earth," said Christ, "shall pass away, but my word shall not pass away." (Matthew 24.) Those, therefore, that are favored by the word of God, those are favored indeed, and that with the favor that no man can turn away; but those that by the word of the Scriptures are condemned, those can no man justify and set quit in the sight of God. Therefore what is bound by the text is bound, and what is released by the text is release; also the bond and release is unalterable. (Daniel 10:21; Revelation 19:9; Matthew 24:35; Psalm 119:89; John 10:35.) This, therefore, calls upon God's people to stand more in fear of the word of God than of all the terrors of the world.

There wants even in the hearts of God's people a greater reverence of the word of God than to this day appears among us; and this let me say, that want of reverence of the word is the ground of all disorders that are in the heart, life, conversation, and in Christian communion. Besides, the want of reverence of the word lays men open to the fearful displeasure of God. "Whoever despises the word shall be destroyed, but he that fears the word shall be rewarded." (Proverbs 13:13.)

All transgression begins at wandering from the word of God; but, on the other side, David says, "Concerning the works of men, by the word of your lips I have kept me from the paths of the destroyer." (Psalm 17:4.) Therefore Solomon says, "My son, attend to my words; incline your ear unto my sayings; let them not depart from your eyes; keep them in the midst of your heart, for they are life to them that find them, and health to all their flesh." (Proverbs 4:20,21.) Now, if indeed you would reverence the word of the Lord, and make it your rule and director in all things, believe that the word is the fear of the Lord; the word that stands fast for ever, without and against which God will do nothing, either in saving or damning of the souls of sinners.

But to conclude this:

1. Know, that those that have not due regard to the word of the Lord, and that make it not their dread and their fear; but the rule of their life is the lust of their flesh, the desire of their eyes, and the pride of life; are sorely rebuked by this doctrine, and are counted the fools of the world; for "Lo, they have rejected the word of the Lord, and what wisdom is in them?" (Jeremiah 8:9.) That there are such a people is evident, not only by their irregular lives, but by the manifest testimony of the word. "As for the word of the Lord," said they to Jeremiah, "which you have spoken to us in the name of the Lord, we will not hearken unto you, but will certainly do whatsoever thing goes out of our own mouth." (Jeremiah 44:16.) Was this only the temper of wicked men, then? is not the same spirit of rebellion amongst us in our days? Doubtless there is, for there is no new thing: "The thing that has been done, is that that shall be, and that which is done, is that which shall be done; and there is no new thing under the sun." (Ecclesiastes 1:9.) Therefore as it was then, so it is with many in this day. As for the word of the Lord, it is nothing at all to them; their lusts, and whatsoever proceeds out of their own mouths, that they will do, that they will follow. Now, such will certainly perish in their own rebellion; for this is as the sin of witchcraft; it was the sin of Corah and his company, and that which brought upon them such heavy judgments; yea, and they are made a sign that you should not do as they, for they perished, because they rejected the word, the fear of the Lord, from among the congregation of the Lord, "and they became a sign." The word which you despise still abides to denounce its woe and judgment upon you; and unless God will save such with the breath of his word—and it is hard trusting to that—they must never see his face with comfort. (1 Samuel 15:22, 23; Numbers 26:9,10.)

2.. Are the words of God called by the name of the fear of the Lord? Are they so dreadful in their receipt and sentence? then this rebukes them that esteem the words and things of men more than the words of God, as those do who are drawn from their respect of, and obedience to, the word of God, by the pleasures or threats of men. Some there be who verily will acknowledge the authority of the word, yet will not stoop their souls thereto: such, whatever they think of themselves, are judged by Christ to be ashamed of the word; wherefore their state is damnable as the other. "Whosoever," says he, "shall be ashamed of me and of my words in this sinful and adulterous nation, of him also shall the Son of Man be ashamed, when he comes in the glory of the Father, with the holy angels." (Mark 8:38.)

3. And if these things be so, what will become of those that mock at, and professedly contemn the words of God, making them as a thing ridiculous, and not to be regarded? Shall they prosper that do such things? From the promises, it is concluded that their judgment now of a long time slumbers not, and when it comes it will devour them without remedy. (2 Corinthians 34:15.) If God, I say, has put that reverence upon his word as to call it the fear of the Lord, what will become of them that do what they can to overthrow its authority, by denying it to be his word, and by raising cavils against its authority? Such stumble indeed at the word, being appointed thereunto, but it shall judge them in the last day. (1 Peter 2:8; John 12:48.) But thus much for this.

Having thus spoken of the object and rule of our fear, I should come now to speak of fear as it is a grace of the Spirit of God in the hearts of his people; but before I do that, I shall show you that there are divers sorts of fear besides. For man being a reasonable creature, and having even by nature a certain knowledge of God, has also naturally something of some kind of fear of God at times, which, although it be not that which is intended in the text, yet

151

ought to be spoken to, that that which is not right may be distinguished from that that is.

Of several sorts of Fear of God in the heart of the children of men.

There are, I say, several sorts or kinds of fear in the hearts of the sons of men, I mean, besides that fear of God that is intended in the text, and that accompanies eternal life.

I shall here make mention of three of them:

First. There is a fear of God that flows even from the light of nature. Second. There is a fear of God that flows from some of his dispensations to men, which yet is neither universal nor saving. Third. There is a fear of God in the heart of some men that is good and godly, but does nor for ever abide so. To speak a little to all these, before I come to speak of fear as it is a grace of God in the hearts of his children.

First. And to the first, to wit, that there is a fear of God that flows even from the light of nature.

A people may be said to do things in a fear of God, when they act one towards another in things reasonable and honest betwixt man and man, not doing that to others they would not have done to themselves. This is that fear of God which Abraham though the Philistines had destroyed in themselves, when he said of his wife to Abimelech, "She is my sister." For when Abimelech asked Abraham why he said of his wife, She is my sister, he replied saying, "I thought verify that the fear of God is not in this place, and they will slay me for my wife's sake." (Genesis 20:11.) I thought verify that in this place men had stifled and choked that light of nature that is in them, at least so far forth as not to suffer it to put them in fear, when their lusts were powerful in them to accomplish their ends on the object that was present before them. But this I will pass by, and come to the second thing; namely, to show that there is a fear of God that flows from some of his dispensations to men, which yet is neither universal nor savings. This fear, when opposed to that which is saving, may be called as ungodly fear of God; I shall describe it by these several particulars that follow.

1. There is a fear of God that causes a continual grudging, discontent, and heart-risings against God under the hand of God; and that is, when the dread of God in his coming upon men, to deal with them for their sins, is apprehended by them, and yet by this dispensation they have no change of heart to submit to God thereunder. The sinners under this dispensation cannot shake God out of their mind, nor yet graciously tremble before him, but through the unsanctified frame that they now are in they are afraid with ungodly fear, and so in their minds let fly against him. This fear oftentimes took hold of the children of Israel when they were in the wilderness in their journey to the promised land; still they feared that God in this place would destroy them, but not with that fear that made them willing to submit, for their sins, to the judgment which they fear, but with that fear that made them let fly against God. This fear showed itself in them, even at the beginning of their voyage, and was rebuked by Moses at the Red Sea, but it was not there, nor yet at any other place, so subdued, but that it would rise again in them at times, to the dishonor of God, and the anew making of them guilty of sin before him. (Exodus 14:11-13; Numbers 14:1-9.) This fear is that which God said he would send before them, in the day of Joshua, even a fear that should possess the inhabitants of the land, to wit, a fear that should arise for that faintness of heart that they should be swallowed up of, at their apprehending of Joshua in his approaches toward them to destroy them. "I will send my fear before you, and will destroy all the people to whom you shall come, and I will make all your enemies turn their backs unto you." "This day, says God, "will I begin to put the dread of you and the fear of you upon the

nations that are under the whole heavens who shall hear report of you, and shall tremble, and be in anguish because of you." (Deuteronomy 2:25; 11:25.)

Now this fear is also, as you here see, called anguish, and in another place an hornet, for it, and the soul that it falls upon, do greet each other as boys and bees do. The honey puts men in fear, nor so as to bring the heart into a sweet compliance with his terror, but so as to stir up the spirit into acts of opposition and resistance, yet withal they flee before it. "I will send hornets before you, which shall drive out the Hivite," (Exodus 23:28.) Now this is fear, whether it be wrought by a misapprehending of the judgments of God, as in the Israelites, or otherwise as in the Cannanites, yet ungodliness is the effect thereof, and therefore I call it an ungodly fear of God, for it stirs up murmurings, discontents, and heart-risings against God, while he with his dispensations is dealing with them.

2. There is a fear of God that drives a man away from God (I speak not now of the Atheist, nor of the pleasurable sinner, nor yet of these, and that fear that I spoke of just now), I speak now of such who, through a sense of sin and of God's justice, fly from him of a slavish, ungodly fear. This ungodly fear was that which possessed Adam's heart in the day that he did eat of the tree concerning which the Lord had said unto him, "In the day you eat thereof, you shall surely die." For then was he possessed with such a fear of God as made him seek to hide himself from his presence. "I heard," said he, "your voice in the garden, and I was afraid, because I was naked, and I hid myself." (Genesis 3:10.) Mind it, he had a fear of God, but it was not godly; it was not that that made him afterwards submit himself unto him; for that would have kept him from not departing from him, or else have brought him to him again, with bowed, broken, and contrite spirit. But this fear, as the rest of his sin, managed his departing from his God, and pursued him to provoke

him still so to do; by it he kept himself from God, by it his whole man was carried away from him. I call it ungodly fear because it began in his ungodly apprehensions of his Maker; because it confined Adam's conscience to the sense of justice only, and consequently to despair.

The same fear also possessed the children of Israel when they heard the law delivered to them on Mount Sinai; as is evident, for it made them that they could neither abide his presence, nor hear his word. It drove them back from the mountain. It made them, says the Apostle to the Hebrews, "that they could not endure that which was commanded." (Hebrews 12.) Wherefore this fear Moses rebukes, and forbids their giving way thereto. "Fear not," said he, but had that fear been godly, he would have encouraged it, and not forbid and rebuke it as he did. "Fear not," said he, "for God is come to prove you;" they thought otherwise. "God," said he, "is come to prove you, and that his fear may be before your faces." Therefore that fear that already had taken possession of them was not the fear of God, but a fear that was of Satan, of their own misjudging hearts, and so a fear that was ungodly. (Exodus 20:18,19.) Mark you, here is a fear and a fear, a fear forbidden and a fear commended; a fear forbidden because it engendered their hearts to bondage, and to ungodly thoughts of God and of his word; it made them that they could not desire to hear God speak to them anymore. (ver. 19-21.)

Many also at this day are possessed with this ungodly fear; and you may know them by this. They cannot abide conviction for sin, and if at any time the word of the law, by the preaching of the word, comes near them, they will not abide that preacher, nor such kind of sermons any more. They are, as they deem, best at east when furthest off of God, and of the power of his word. The word preached brings God nearer to them than they desire he should come, because whenever God comes near, their sins by him are manifest, and so is the judgment too that to them is due. Now these not having faith in the mercy of God through Christ, nor that grace that tends to bring them to him, they cannot but think of God amiss, and their so thinking of him makes them say unto him, "Depart from us, for we desire not the knowledge of your ways." Wherefore their wrong thoughts of God beget in them this ungodly fear; and again, this ungodly fear does maintain in them the continuance of these wrong and unworthy thoughts of God, and therefore, through that devilish service wherewith they strengthen one another, the sinner, without a miracle of grace prevents him, is drowned in destruction and perdition.

It was this ungodly fear of God that carried Cain from the presence of God into the land of Nod, and that put him there upon any carnal worldly business, if perhaps he might by so doing stifle convictions of the majesty and justice of God against his sin, and so live the rest of his vain life in the more sinful security and fleshly ease.

This ungodly fear is that also which Samuel perceived at the people's apprehension of their sin to begin to get hold of their hearts; wherefore he, as Moses before him, quickly forbids their entertaining of it. "Fear not," said he, "you have done all this wickedness, yet turn not aside from following the Lord." For to turn them aside from following of him was the natural tendency of this fear. "But fear not," said he, that is, with that fear that tends to turn you aside. Now, I say, the matter that this fear works upon (as in Adam, and the Israelites mentioned before) was their sin. "You have sinned," says he, that is true, "yet turn not aside; yet fear not with that fear that would make you so do." (1 Samuel 12:20.) Note by the way, sinner, that when the greatness of your sins, being apprehended by you, shall work in you that fear of God as shall incline your heart to fly from him, you are possessed with a fear of God that is ungodly, yea, so ungodly, that not any of your sins for heinousness may be compared therewith, as might be made manifest in many particulars; but Samuel having rebuked this fear, presently sets before the people another, to wit, the true fear of God; "Fear the Lord," says he, "serve him with all your heart." (ver. 24.) And he gives them this encouragement so to do, "for the Lord will not forsake his people." This ungodly fear is that which you read of in Isaiah 2, and in many other places, and God's people should shun it as they would shun the devil, because its natural tendency is to forward the destruction of the soul in which it has taken possession.

3. There is a fear of God which, although it has not in it that power as to make men flee from God's presence, yet it is ungodly, because, even while they are in the outward way of God's ordinances, their hearts are by it quite discouraged from attempting to exercise themselves in the power of religion. Of this sort are they which dare not cast off the hearing, reading, and discourse of the word as others; no, nor the assembly of God's children for the exercise of other religious duties, for their conscience is convinced this is the way and worship of God. But yet their heart, as I said, by this ungodly fear, is kept from a powerful gracious falling in with God. This fear takes away their heart from all holy and godly zeal for his name in public; and there by many professors whose hearts are possessed with this ungodly fear of God; and they are intended by the slothful one. He was a servant, a servant among the servants of God, and had gifts and abilities given him therewith to serve Christ, as well as his fellows, yea, and was commanded too, as well as the rest, to occupy till his Master came. But what does he? why, he takes his talent, the gift that he was to lay out for his master's profit, and puts it in a napkin, digs a hole in the earth, and hides his Lord's money; and lies in a lazy manner at to-elbow all his days, not out of, but in his Lord's vineyard; for he came among the servants also at last. By which it is manifest that he had not cast off his profes-

sion, but was slothful and negligent while he was in it. But what was it that made him thus slothful? what was it that took away his heart while he was in the way, and that discouraged him from falling in with the power and holy practice of religion according to the talent he received? Why, it was this; he gave way to an ungodly fear of God, and that took away his heart from the power of religious duties. "Lord," said he, "behold here is your pound, which I have kept, laid up in a napkin, for I feared you." Why, man does, the fear of God make a man idle and slothful? No, no; that is, if it be right and godly. This fear was therefore evil fear; it was that ungodly fear of God which I have here been speaking of. For I feared you, or, as Matthew has it, "for I was afraid." Afraid of what? Of Christ, "that he was an hard man, reaping where he sowed not, and gathering where he had not sown." this his fear being ungodly, make him apprehend of Christ contrary to the goodness of his nature, and so took away his heart from all endeavors to be doing of that which was pleasing in his sight. (Luke 19:20; Matthew 25:24,25.) And thus do all those that retain the name and show of religion, but are neglecters as to the power and godly practice of it. These will live like dogs and swine in the house; they pray not, they watch not their hearts, they pull not their hands out of their bosoms to work; they do not strive against their lusts, nor will they ever resist unto blood, striving against sin; they cannot take up their cross, or improve what they have to God's glory.

Let all men, therefore, take heed of this ungodly fear, and shun it as they shun the devil, for it will make them afraid where no fear is. It will tell them that there is a lion in the street, the unlikeliest place in the world for such a beast to be in; it will put a vizard upon the face of God most dreadful and fearful to behold, and then quite discourage the soul as to his service; so it served the slothful servant, and so it will serve you, poor sinner, if you entertain it, and give way thereto. But,

4. This ungodly fear of God shows itself also in this. It will not suffer the soul that is governed thereby to trust only to Christ for justification of life, but will bend the powers of the soul to trust partly to the works of the law. Many of the Jews were, in the time of Christ and his apostles, possessed with this ungodly fear of God, for they were not as the former, to wit, as the slothful servant, to receive a talent and hide it in the earth in a napkin, but they were an industrious people, they followed after the law of righteousness, they had a zeal of God and of the religion of their fathers; but how then did they come to miscarry? Why, their fear of God was ungodly, it would not suffer them wholly to trust to the righteousness of faith, which is the imputed righteousness of Christ. They followed after the law of righteousness, but attained not to the law of righteousness. Wherefore? because they sought it not by faith, but, as it were, by the works of the law. But what was it that made the join their works of the law with Christ but their unbelief, whose foundation was ignorance and fear? They were afraid to venture all in one bottom, they thought two strings to one bow would be best, and thus betwixt two stools they came to the grounds. And hence, to fear and to doubt are put together as being the cause one of another, yea, they are put ofttimes the one for the other; thus, ungodly fear for unbelief: "Be not afraid, only believe," and therefore he that is overruled and carried away with this fear, is coupled with the unbeliever that is thrust out from the holy city among the dogs. But the fearful, and unbelievers, and murderers, are without. (Revelation 21:8.) The fearful and unbelieving, you see, are put together, for, indeed, fear, that is, this ungodly fear, is the ground of unbelief, or, if you will, unbelief is the ground of fear, this fear; but I stand not upon nice distinctions. This ungodly fear has a great hand in keeping of

the soul from trusting only to Christ's righteousness for justification of life.

5. This ungodly fear of God is that which will put men upon adding to the revealed will of God their own inventions, and their own performances of them as a means to pacify the anger of God. For the truth is, where this ungodly fear reigns, there is no end of law and duty. When those that you read of in the book of Kings (2 Kings 17) were destroyed by the lions, because they had set up idolatry in the land of Israel, they sent for a priest from Babylon that might teach them the manner of the God of the land; but behold when they knew it, being taught it by the priest, yet their fear would not suffer them to be content with that worship only. "They feared the Lord," says the text, "and served their own gods." And again, "So these nations feared the Lord, and served their graven images." It was this fear also that put the Pharisees upon inventing so many traditions, as the washing of cups, and beds, and tables, and basins, with abundance of such other like gear. (Mark 7.) None knows the many dangers that an ungodly fear of God will drive a man into. How has it racked and tortured the Papists for hundreds of years together! For what else is the cause but this ungodly fear, at least in the most simple and harmless of them, of their penances, as creeping to the cross, going barefoot on pilgrimage, whipping themselves, wearing of sackcloth, saying so many paternosters, so many avemaries, making so many confessions to the priest, giving so much money for pardons and abundance of other the like, but this ungodly fear of God? for could they be brought to believe this doctrine, that Christ was delivered for our offences, and raised again for our justification, and to apply it by faith with godly boldness to their own souls, this fear would vanish, and so consequently all those things with which they so needlessly and unprofitably afflicted themselves, offend God, and grieve his people.

Therefore, gentle reader, although my text does bid that indeed you should fear God, yet it includes not, nor accepts of any fear; no, not of any fear of God. For there is, as you see, a fear of God that is ungodly, and that is to be shunned as their sin. Wherefore, the wisdom and your care should be, to see and prove your fear to be godly, which shall be the next thing that I shall take in hand.

Third. The third thing that I am to speak to is, that there is a fear of God in the heart of some men that is good and godly, but yet does not for ever abide so.

Or you may take it thus: "There is a fear of God that is godly but for a time."

In my speaking to and opening of this to you, I shall observe this method:

1. I shall show you what this fear is.

2. I shall show you by whom or what this fear is brought in the heart.

3. I shall show you what this fear does in the soul. And,

4. I shall show you when this fear is to have an end.

1. For the first. This fear is an effect of sound awakenings by the word of wrath, which begets in the soul a sense of its right to eternal damnation; for this fear is not in every sinner; he that is blinded by the devil, and that is not able to see that his state is damnable, he has not this fear in his heart; but he that is under the powerful workings of the word of wrath, as God's elect are at first conversion, he has this godly fear in his heart; that is, he fears that that damnation will come upon him which by the justice of God is due unto him, because he has broken his holy law. This is the fear that made the three thousand cry out, "Men and brethren, what shall we do?" and that made the jailer cry out, and that with great trembling of soul, "Sirs, what must I do to be saved?" (Acts 16:3.)

The method of God is to kill and make alive, to smite and then heal: when the commandment came to Paul, sin

161

revived, and he died, and that law which was ordained to life he found to be unto death, That is, it passed a sentence of death upon him for his sins, and slew his conscience with that sentence. Therefore, from that time that he heard that word, "Why do you persecute me?" which is all one as if he had said, "Why do you commit murder?" he lay under the sentence of condemnation by the law, and under this fear of that sentence in his conscience. He lay, I say, under it until that Ananias came to him to comfort him, and to preach unto him the forgiveness of sins. (Acts 9.) The fear, therefore, that now I call godly, it is that fear which is properly called the fear of eternal damnation for sin, and this fear, at first awakening, is good and godly, because it arises in the soul from a true sense of its very state. Its state by nature is damnable, because it is sinful, and because he is not one that as yet believes in Christ for remission of sins. "He that believes not shall be damned." "He that believes not is condemned already, and the wrath of God abides on him." (Mark 16:16; John 3:18,36.) The which, when the sinner at first begins to see, he justly fears it; I say, he fears it justly, and therefore godly, because by this fear he subscribes to the sentence that is gone out against him for sin.

2. By whom or by what is this fear wrought in the heart?

To this I shall answer in brief. It is wrought in the heart by the Spirit of God, working there at first as a spirit of bondage on purpose to put us in fear. This Paul insinuates in Romans 8:15; saying, "You have not received the spirit of bondage again to fear,": He does not say, "You have not received the spirit of bondage;" for that they had received, and that to put them in fear, which was at their first conversion, as by the instances made mention of before is manifest; all that he says is, that they had not received it again, that is, after the Spirit, as a spirit of adoption, is come; for then as a spirit of bondage it comes no more. It is then the Spirit of

God, even the Holy Ghost, that convinces us of sin, and so of our damnable state because of sin. (John 16:8.) For it cannot be that the Spirit of God should convince us of sin, but it must also show us our state to be damnable because of it, especially if it so convinces us before we believe, and that is the intent of our Lord in that place, "of sin," and so of their damnable state by sin, because they believe not on me. Therefore the Spirit of God, when he works in the heart as a spirit of bondage, he does it by working in us by the law, for by the law is the knowledge of sin. (Romans 3:20.) And he, in this his working, is properly called a spirit of bondage.

(1.) Because by the law he shows us, that indeed we are in bondage to the law, the devil, and death, and damnation; for this is our proper state by nature, though we see it not until the Spirit of God shall come to reveal this our state of bondage unto our own senses by revealing to us our sins by the law.

(2.) He is called, in this his working, the spirit of bondage, because he here also holds us; to wit, in this sight and sense of our bondage-state, so long as is meet we should be so held, which to some of the saints is a longer, and to some a shorter time. Paul was held in its three days and three nights, but the jailer and the three thousand, so far as can be gathered, not above an hour; but some in these later times are so held for days and months, if not years. But I say, let the time be longer or shorter, it is the Spirit of God that holds him under this yoke, and it is good that a man should be in his time held under it: as is that saying of the Lamentation, "It is good that a man bear the yoke in his youth" (Lamentations 3:27), that is, at his first awakening; so long as seems good to this Holy Spirit to work in this manner by the law. Now, as I said, the sinner at first is by the Spirit of God held in this bondage, that is, has such a discovery of his sin, and of his damnation for sin made to him, and also is held so fast under the sense thereof, that it is not in the power of any man, not yet of the very angels in heaven, to release him, or set him free until the Holy Spirit changes his ministration, and comes in the sweet and peaceable tidings of salvation by Christ in the gospel, to his poor, dejected, and afflicted conscience.

3.. I now come to show you what this fear does in the soul. Now, although this godly fear is not to last always with us, as I shall further show you anon, yet it greatly differs from that which is wholly ungodly of itself, both because of the author, and also of the effects of it. Of the author I have told you before, I now shall tell you what it does.

(1.) This fear makes a man judge himself for sin, and to fall down before God with a broken mind under this judgment; the which is pleasing to God, because the sinner by so doing justifies God in his saying, and clears him in his judgment. (Psalm 51:14.)

(2.) As this fear makes a man judge himself, and cast himself down at God's foot, so it makes him condole and bewail his misery before him, which is also well-pleasing in his sight. "I have surely heard Ephraim bemoaning himself, saying, You have chastised me, and I was chastised, as a bullock unaccustomed to the yoke," etc. (Jeremiah 31:18,19.)

(3.) This fear makes a man lie at God's foot, and puts his mouth in the dust, if so be there may be hope. This also is well-pleasing to God, because now is the sinner as nothing, and in his own eyes less than nothing, as to any good or desert. "He sits alone, and keeps silence because he has now this yoke upon him. He puts his mouth in the dust, if so be there may be hope." (Lamentations 3:28,29).

(4.) This fear puts a man upon crying to God for mercy, and that in most humble manner; now he sensibly cries, now he dejectedly cries, now he feels and cries, now he smarts and cries out, "God be merciful to me a sinner." (Luke 18:13.)

(5.) This fear make a man that he cannot accept of that for support and succor which others that are destitute thereof will take up and be contended with. This man must be washed by God himself, and cleansed from his sin by God himself. (Psalm 51.)

(6.) Therefore this fear goes not away until the Spirit of God does change his ministration as to this particular, in leaving off to work now by the law, as afore, and coming to the soul with the sweet word of promise of life and salvation by Jesus Christ.

Thus far this fear is godly, that is, until Christ by the Spirit in the gospel is revealed and made over unto us, and no longer. Thus far this fear is godly, and the reason why it is godly is, because the groundwork of it is good. I told you before what this fear is, namely, "It is the fear of damnation." Now the ground for this fear is good, as is manifest by these particulars. 1. The soul fears damnation, and that rightly, because it is in its sins. 2. The soul fears damnation rightly, because it has not faith in Christ, but is at present under the law. 3. The soul fears damnation rightly now, because by sin, the law, and for want of faith, the wrath of God abides on it. But now, although thus far this fear of God is good and godly, yet after Christ by the Spirit in the word of the gospel is revealed to us, and we made to accept of him as so revealed and offered to us by a true and living faith; this fear, to wit, of damnation, is no longer good, but ungodly. Nor does the Spirit of God ever work it in us again. Now we do not receive the spirit of bondage again to fear, that is to say, to fear damnation, but we have received the spirit of adoption whereby we cry, Father, Father. But I would not be mistaken, when I say, that this fear is no longer godly. I do not mean with reference to the essence and habit of it, for I believe it is the same in the seed which shall afterwards grow up to a higher degree, and into a more sweet and gospel current and manner of working, but

I mean reference to this act of fearing damnation; I say, it shall never by the Spirit be managed to that work, it shall never bring forth that fruit more. And my reasons are,

1. Because that the soul by closing through the promise, by the Spirit, with Jesus Christ, is removed off of that foundation upon which it stood when it justly feared damnation. It has received now forgiveness of sin, it is now no more under the law, but in Jesus Christ by faith; there is therefore now "no condemnation to it." (Acts 26:18; Romans 6:14; 8:1.) The groundwork, therefore, being now taken away, the Spirit works that fear no more.

2. He cannot, after he has come to the soul as a spirit of adoption, come again as a spirit of bondage to put the soul into his first fear; to wit, a fear of eternal damnation, because he cannot say and unsay, do and undo. As a spirit of adoption he told me that my sins were forgiven me, that I was included in the covenant of grace, that God was my Father through Christ, that I was under the promise of salvation, and that this calling and gift of God to me is permanent, and without repentance. And do you think that after he has told me this, and sealed up the truth of it to my precious soul, that he will come to me, and tell me that I am yet in my sins, under the curse of the law and the eternal wrath of God? No, no, the word of the gospel is not year, yea; nay, nay: it is only yea, and amen; it is so, "as God is true." (2 Corinthians 1:17-20.)

3. The state, therefore, of the sinner being changed, and that too by the Spirit's changing his dispensation, leaving off to be now as a spirit of bondage to put us in fear, and coming to our heart as the spirit of adoption to make us cry Father, Father, he cannot go back to his first work again; for it so, then he must gratify, yea, and also ratify, that profane and popish doctrine, forgiven today, unforgiven tomorrow, a child of God today, a child of hell tomorrow; but what says the Scriptures? "Now, therefore, such as no more

Supplement: *The Fear of God* by John Bunyan

strangers and foreigners, but fellow-citizens with the saints, and of the household of God; and are built upon the foundation of the apostles and prophets, Christ Jesus himself being the chief corner-stone; in whom all the building, fitly framed together, grows into an holy temple in the Lord, in whom you also are builded together for an habitation of God through the Spirit." (Ephesians 2.)

Objection: But this is contrary to my experience.

Why, Christian, what is your experience?

Why, I was at first, as you have said, possessed with a fear of damnation, and so under the power of the spirit of bondage.

Well said, and how was it then?

Why, after some time of continuance in these fears I had the spirit of adoption sent to me, to seal up to my soul the forgiveness of sins, and so he did; and was also helped by the same spirit, as you have said, to call God, Father, Father.

Well said, and what after that?

Why, after that I fell into as great fears as ever I was in before.

Answer: All this may be granted, and yet, nevertheless, what I have said will abide a truth, for I have not said that after the spirit of adoption is come, a Christian shall not again be in as great fears, for he may have worse than he had at first; but I say, that after the spirit of adoption is come, the spirit of bondage, as such, is sent of God no more to put us into those fears. For, mark, "for we have not received the spirit of bondage again to fear." Let the word be true, whatever they experience is. Do you not understand me?

After the Spirit of God has told me, and also helped me to believe it, that the Lord for Christ's sake has forgiven my iniquities; he tells me no more than they are not forgiven. After the Spirit of God has helped me, by Christ, to call God my Father, he tells me no more than the devil is my father.

167

After he has told me that I am not under the law, but under grace, he tells me no more than I am not under grace, but under the law, and bound over by it, for my sins, to the wrath and judgment of God; but this is the fear that the Spirit, as a spirit of bondage, works in the soul at first.

Question: Can you give me further reason yet to convict me of the truth of what you say?

Answer: Yes. 1. Because as the Spirit cannot give himself the lie, so he cannot overthrow his own order of working, nor yet contradict that testimony that his servants by his inspiration have given to his order of working with them. But he must do the first, if he says to us (and that after we have received his own testimony, that we are under grace) that yet we are under sin, the law, and wrath.

And he must do the second, if (after he has gone through the first work on us, as a spirit of bondage, to the second as a spirit of adoption) he should overthrow as a spirit of bondage again, what before he had built as a spirit of adoption.

And the third must therefore needs follow, that is, he overthrows the testimony of his servants; for they have said, that now we received the spirit of bondage again to fear no more; that is, after that we by the Holy Ghost are enabled to call God Father, Father.

2. This is evidence, also, because the covenant in which now the soul is interested, abides, and is everlasting, not upon the supposition of my obedience, but upon the unchangeable purposes of God, and the efficacy of the obedience of Christ, whose blood also has confirmed it. It is ordered in all things, and sure, said David; and this, said he, is all my salvation (2 Samuel 23:5.) The covenant then is everlasting in itself, being established upon so good a foundation, and therefore stands in itself everlastingly bend for the good of them that are involved in it. Hear the tenor of the covenant, and God's attesting of the truth thereof.

"This is the covenant that I will make with the house of Israel, after those days, says the Lord: I will put my laws into their mind, and write them in their hearts, and I will be to them a God, and they shall be to me a people; and they shall not teach every man his neighbor, and every man his brother, saying, Know the Lord, for they shall all know me, from the least to the greatest; for I will be merciful t their unrighteousness, and their sins and iniquities I will remember no more." (Hebrews 8:10-12.) No if God will do thus unto those that he has comprised in his everlasting covenant of grace, then he will remember their sins no more, that is, unto condemnation—for so it is that he does forget them; then cannot the Holy Ghost, who also is one with the Father and the Son, come to us again, even after we are possessed with these glorious fruits of this covenant, as a spirit of bondage, to put us in fear of damnation.

3. The Spirit of God, after it is come to me as a spirit of adoption, can come to me no more as a spirit of bondage, to put me in fear, that is, with my first fears, because by that faith that he, even he himself, has wrought in me to believe and call God Father, Father, I am united to Christ, and stand no more upon my own legs, in my own sins or performances; but in his glorious righteousness before him, and before his Father; but he will not cast away a member of his body, of his flesh, and of his bones; nor will he that the Spirit of God should come as a spirit of bondage to put him into a grounded fear of damnation, that stands complete before God in the righteousness of Christ; for that is an apparent contradiction.

Question: But may it not come again as a spirit of bondage, to put me into my first fears for my good?

Answer: The text says the contrary: :for we have not received the spirit of bondage again to fear." Nor is God put to it for want of wisdom, to say and unsay, do and undo, or else he cannot do good. When we are sons, and have received the adoption of children, he does not use to send the Spirit after that to tell us we are slaves and heirs of damnation, also that we are without Christ, without the promise, without grace, and without God in the world; and yet this he must do if it comes to use after we have received him as a spirit of adoption, and put us, as a spirit of bondage, in fear as before.

Question: But by what spirit is it then that I am brought again into fears, even into the fears of damnation, and so into bondage?

Answer: By the spirit of the devil, who always labors to frustrate the faith, and hope, and comfort of the godly.

Question: How does that appear?

Answer: 1. By the groundlessness of such fears. 2. By the unseasonableness of them. 3. By the effects of them.

1. By the groundlessness of such fears. The ground is removed; for the grounded fear of damnation is this, I am yet in my sins, in a state of nature, under the law, without faith, and so under the wrath of God; this, I say, is the ground of the fear of damnation, the true ground to fear it; but now the man that we are talking of is one that has the ground of this fear taken away by the testimony and seal of the spirit of adoption: he is called, justified, and has, for the truth of this his condition, received the evidence of the spirit of adoption, and has been thereby enabled to call God, Father, Father. Now he that has received this, has the ground of the fear of damnation taken from him; therefore his fear, I say, being without ground, is false, and so no work of the Spirit of God.

2. By the unseasonableness of them. This spirit always comes too late. It comes after the spirit of adoption is come. Satan is always for being too soon, or too late. If he would have men believe they are children, he would have them believe it while they are slaves, slaves to him and their lusts. If he would have them believe they are slaves, it is when

they are sons, and have received the spirit of adoption, and the testimony, by that, of their sonship before. And this evil is rooted even in his nature; "He is a liar, and the father of it," (John 8) and his lies are not known to saints more than in this, that he labors always to contradict the work and order of the Spirit of truth.

3. It also appears by the effects of such fears. For there is a great deal of difference betwixt the natural effects of these fears which are wrought indeed by the spirit of bondage, and those which are wrought by the spirit of the devil afterwards. The one, to wit, the fears that are wrought by the spirit of bondage, causes us to confess the truth, to wit, that we are Christless, graceless, faithless, and so at present, that is, while he is so working, in a sinful and damnable case; but the other, to wit, the spirit of the devil when he comes, which is after the spirit of adoption is come, he causes us to make a lie, that is to say, we are Christless, graceless, and faithless. Now this, I say, is wholly and in all the parts of it a lie, and he is the father of it.

Besides, the direct tendency of the fear that the Spirit of God, as a spirit of bondage, works in the soul, is to cause us to come repenting home to God by Jesus Christ, but these latter fears tend directly to make a man, he having first denied the work of God, as he will, if he falls in with them, to run quite away from God, and from his grace to him in Christ, as will evidently appear if you give but a plain and honest answer to these questions following.

Question 1: Do not these fears make you question whether there was ever a work of grace wrought in your soul?

Answer: Yes, verily, that they do.

Question 2: Do not these fears make you questions whether ever your first fears were wrought by the Holy Spirit of God?

Answer: Yes, verily, that they do.

171

Question 3: Do not these fears make you question whether ever you have had, indeed, any true comfort from the word and Spirit of God?

Answer: Yes, verily, that they do.

Question 4: Do you not find intermixed with these fears plain assertions that your first comforts were either from your fancy, or from the devil, and a fruit of his delusions?

Answer: Yes, verily, that I do.

Question 5: Do not these fears weaken your heart in prayer?

Answer: Yes, that they do.

Question 6: Do not these fears keep you back from laying hold of the promise of salvation by Jesus Christ?

Answer: Yes, for I think if I were deceived before, if I were comforted by a spirit of delusion before, why may it not be so again; so I am afraid to take hold of the promise.

Question 7: Do not these fears tend to the hardening of your heart, and to the making of you desperate?

Answer: Yes, verily, that they do.

Question 8: Do not these fears hinder you from profiting in hearing or reading of the word?

Answer: Yes, verily, for still whatever I hear or read, I think nothing that is good belongs to me.

Question 9: Do not these fears tend to the stirring up of blasphemies in your heart against God?

Answer: Yes, to the almost distracting of me.

Question 10: Do not these fears make you sometimes think, that it is in vain for you to wait upon the Lord any longer?

Answer: Yes, verily, and I have many times almost come to this conclusion, that I will read, pray, hear, company with God's people, or the like, no longer.

Well, poor Christian, I am glad that you have so plainly answered me, but I pray that you look back upon your answer; how much of God do you think if in these things, how much of his Spirit, and the grace of his word? Just none at all, for it cannot be that these things can be the true and natural effects of the workings of the Spirit of God. No, not as a spirit of bondage. These are not his doings; do you not see the very paw of the devil in them, yea in every one of your ten confessions; is there not palpably high wickedness in every one of the effects of this fear?

I conclude, then, as I began, that the fear that the Spirit of God, as a spirit of bondage, works, is good and godly; not only because of the author, but also because of the ground and effects; but yet it can last no longer as such, as producing the aforesaid conclusion, than till the Spirit, as the spirit of adoption, comes, because that then the soul is manifestly taken out of the state and condition into which it had brought itself by nature and sin, and is put into Christ, and so by him into a state of life and blessedness by grace. Therefore, if first fears come again into your soul after that the spirit of adoption has been with you, know they come not from the Spirit of God, but apparently from the spirit of the devil, for they are a lie in themselves, and their effects are sinful and devilish.

Objection: But I had also such wickedness as those in my heart at my first awakening, and therefore by your argument neither should that be but from the devil.

Answer: So far forth as such wickedness was in your heart, so far did the devil and your own heart seek to drive you to despair, and drown you there. But you have forgot the question; the question is not whether then you were troubled with such iniquities, but whether your fears of damnation at that time were not just and good, because grounded upon your present condition, which was, for that you were out of Christ, in your sins, and under the curse of the law; and whether now, since the spirit of adoption is come unto you and has you, and has done that for you as has been mentioned; I say, whether you ought for anything whatsoever to give way to the same fear, from the same ground of damnation; it is evident you ought not, because the ground, the cause, is removed.

Objection: But since I was sealed to the day of redemption, I have grievously sinned against God; have not I therefore cause to fear as before? May not, therefore, the spirit of bondage be sent again to put me in fear as at first? Sin was the first cause, and I have sinned now.

Answer: No, by no means, for we have not received the spirit of bondage again to fear. That is, God has not given it us, "for God has not given us the spirit of fear, but of power, of love, and of a sound mind." (2 Timothy 1:7.) If, therefore, our first fears come upon us again, after that we have received at God's hands the spirit of love, of power, and of a sound mind, it is to be refused though we have grievously sinned against our God. This is manifest from 1 Samuel 12: "Fear not; you have done all this wickedness." That is, not with that fear which would have made them fly from God as concluding that they were not now his people. And the reason is, because sin cannot dissolve the covenant into which the sons of God, by his grace, are taken. "If his children forsake my law, and walk not in my judgments; if they break my statutes, and keep not my commandments; then will I visit their transgressions with a rod, and their iniquities with stripes; nevertheless, my loving-kindness I will not utterly take away from him, nor suffer my faithfulness to fail." (Psalm 139:30-33.) Now, if sin does not dissolve the covenant—if sin does not cast me out of this covenant, which is made personally with the Son of God, and into the hands of which by the grace of God I am put, then ought I not, though I have sinned, to fear with my first fears.

Sin, after that the spirit of adoption is come, cannot dissolve the relation of father and son, of father and child. And this the church did rightly assert, and that when her heart was under great hardness, and when she had the guilt of erring from his ways; says she, "Doubtless you are our Father." (Isaiah 63:16,17.) Doubtless you are, though this be our case, and though Israel should not acknowledge us for such.

That sin dissolves not the relation of father and son is further evident (Galatians 4:4): "When the fullness of the time was come, God sent forth his Son, made of a woman, made under the law, to redeem them that were under the law, that we might receive the adoption of sons. And because you are sons, God has sent forth the Spirit of his Son into your hearts, crying, Father, Father." Now mark, "wherefore you are no more a servant"—that is, no more under the law of death and damnation, but a son, and if a son, then an heir of God through Christ.

Suppose a child does grievously transgress against and offend his father, is the relation between them therefore dissolved? Again, suppose the father should scourge and chasten the son for such offense, is the relation between them therefore dissolved? Yea, suppose the child should now through ignorance cry, and say, This man is now no more my father; is he therefore now no more his father? does not everybody see the folly of such arguings? Why, of the same nature is that doctrine that says, that after we have received the spirit of adoption, that the spirit of bondage is sent to us again to put us in fear of eternal damnation.

Know, then, that your sin, after you have received the spirit of adoption to cry unto God, Father, Father, is counted the transgression of a child, not of a slave, and that all that happens to you for that transgression is but the chastisement of a father. "And what son is he whom the father chastens not?" It is worth your observation, that the Holy Ghost checks those who, under their chastisements for sin, forget to call God their Father. "You have," says Paul, "forgotten the exhortation that speaks unto you as unto children; My son, despise not the chastening of the Lord, nor faint when you are rebuked of him." Yea, observe yet further, that God's chastening of his children for their sin is a sign of grace and love, and not of his wrath and your damnation; therefore, now there is no ground for the afore-said fear. "For whom the Lord loves he chastens, and scourges every son whom he receives." (Hebrews 12.) Now, if God would not have those that have received the Spirit of the Son, however he chastises them, to forget the relation that by the adoption of sons they stand in to God, if he checks them that do forget it, when his rod is upon their backs for sin; then it is evident that those fears that you have under a color of the coming again of the spirit as a spirit of bondage to put you in fear of eternal damnation, is nothing else but Satan disguised, the better to play his pranks upon you.

I will yet give you two or three instances more, wherein it will be manifest that whatever happens to you, I mean as a chastisement for sin, after the spirit of adoption is come, you ought to hold fast by faith the relation of Father and son.

1. The people spoken of by Moses are said to have lightly esteemed the rock of their salvation, which rock is Jesus Christ, and that is a grievous sin indeed; yet says he, "Is not God your Father that has bought you?" and then puts them upon considering the days of old. (Deuteronomy 32:6.)

2. They, in the prophet Jeremiah, had played the harlot with many lovers, and done evil things as they could: and as another scripture has it, gone a whoring from under their God, yet God calls to them by the prophet, saying "Wilt though not from this time cry unto me, My Father, you are the guide of my youth?" (Jeremiah 3:4.)

3. Remember also that eminent text made mention of in I Sam. xii, "Fear not, you have done all this wickedness," and labor to maintain faith in your soul, of your being a child, it being true that you have received the spirit of adop-

tion before, and so that you ought not to fall under your first fears, because the ground is taken away of your eternal damnation.

Now, let not any, from what has been said, take courage to live loose lives, under a supposition that once in Christ, and ever in Christ, and the covenant cannot be broken, nor the relation of father and child dissolved; for they that do so, it is evident have not known what it is to receive the spirit of adoption. It is the spirit of the devil in his own hue that suggests this unto them, and that prevails with them to do so; shall we do evil that good may come? shall we sin that grace may abound? or shall we be base in life because God by grace has secured us from wrath to come? God forbid; these conclusions betoken one void of the fear of God indeed, and of the spirit of adoption too. For what son is he, that because the father cannot break the relation, nor suffer sin to do it—that is, betwixt the father and him—that will therefore say, I will live altogether after my own lusts, I will labor to be a continued grief to my father?

Yet lest the devil, for some are not ignorant of his devices, should get an advantage against some of the sons, to draw them away from the filial fear of their father, let me here, to prevent such temptations, present such with these following considerations.

1. Though God cannot, will not dissolve the relation which the spirit of adoption has made betwixt the father and the son, for any sins that such do commit, yet he can, and often does, take away from them the comfort of their adoption, not suffering children, while sinning, to have the sweet and comfortable sense thereof on their hearts. "He can tell how to let snares be round about them, and sudden fear trouble them. He can tell how to send darkness that they may not see, and to let abundance of waters cover them." (Job 22:10,11.)

2. God can tell how to hide his face from them, and so to afflict them with that dispensation, that it shall not be in the power of all the world to comfort them. "When he hides his face, who can behold him?" (Job 23:8,9; 34:29.)

3. God can tell how to make you again to possess the sins that he long since has pardoned, and that in such wise that things shall be bitter to your soul. "You write things against me," says Job, "and make me to possess the iniquities of my youth." By this also he made once David groan, and pray against it as an insupportable affliction. (Job 13:26; Psalm 25:7.)

4. God can lay you in the dungeon in chains, and roll a stone upon you; he can make your feet fast in the stocks, and make you a gazing-stock to men and angels. (Lamentations 3:7,53,55. Job 13:27.)

5. God can tell how to cause to cease the sweet operations and blessed influences of his grace in your soul, and to make those gospel showers that formerly you have enjoyed, to become now to you nothing but powder and dust. (Psalm 51; Deuteronomy 28:24.)

6. God can tell how to fight against you with the sword of his mouth, and to make you a butt for his arrows; and this is a dispensation most dreadful. (Revelation 2:16; Job 6:4; Psalm 38:2-5.)

7. God can tell how so to bow you down with guilt and distress, that you shall in no wise be able to lift up your head. (Psalm 40:12.)

8. God can tell how to break your bones, and to make you by reason of that to live in continual anguish of spirit: yea, he can send a fire into your bones that shall burn, and none shall quench it. (Psalm 51:8; Lamentations 3:4; 1:13. Psalm 102:3; Job 30:30.)

9. God can tell how to lay you aside, and make no use of you as to any work for him in your generation. He can

throw you aside as a broken vessel. (Psalm 31:12; Ezekiel 44:10-13.)

10. God can tell how to kill you, and to take you away from the earth for your sins. (1 Corinthians 11:29-32.)

11. God can tell how to plague you in your death, with great plagues, and of long continuance. (Psalm 78:45; Deuteronomy 28.)

12. What shall I say? God can tell how to let Satan loose upon you; when you lie dying, he can license him then to assault you with great temptations, he can tell how to make you possess the guilt of all your unkindness towards him, and that when you, as I said, are going out of the world, he can cause that your life shall be in continual doubt before you, and not suffer you to take any comfort day or night; yea, he can drive you even to a madness with his chastisements for your folly, and yet all shall be done by him to you as a father chastises his son. (Deuteronomy 28:65-67.)

13. Further; God can tell how to tumble you from off your death-bed in a cloud, he can let you die in the dark; when you are dying, you shall not know whither you are going, to wit, whether to heaven or to hell. Yea, he can tell how to let you seem to come short of life, both in your own eyes, and also in the eyes of them that behold you. "Let us therefore fear," says the Apostle, though not with slavish, yet with filial fear, "lest a promise being left us of entering into rest, any of us should seem to come short of it." (Hebrews 4:1.)

Now all this, and much more can God do to his as a Father by his rod and fatherly rebukes: ah, who know, but those that are under them, what terrors, fears, distresses and amazements God can bring his people into! He can put them into a furnace, a fire, and no tongue can tell what, so unsearchable and fearful are his fatherly chastisements, and yet never give them the spirit of bondage again to fear.

Therefore, if you are a son, take heed of sin, lest all these things overtake you, and come upon you,.

Objection: But I have sinned, and am under this high and mighty hand of God.

Answer: Then you know what I say is true, but yet take heed of hearkening unto such temptations as would make you believe you are out of Christ, under the law, and in a state of damnation; and take heed also that you do not conclude that the author of these fears in the Spirit of God come to you again as a spirit of bondage to put you into such fears, lest unawares to yourself though you do defy the devil; dishonor your Father, overthrow good doctrine, and bring yourself into a double temptation.

Objection: But if God deals thus with a man, how can he otherwise think, but that he is a reprobate, a graceless, Christless, and faithless one?

Answer: Nay, but why do you tempt the Lord your God? why do you sin and provoke the eyes of his glory? "why does the living man complain, a man for the punishment of his sins?" (Lamentations 3:39.) He does not willingly afflict, nor grieve the children of men; but if you sin, though God should save your soul, as he will if you are an adopted son of God, yet he will make you know that sin is sin; and his rod that he will chastise you with, if need be, shall be made of scorpions. Read the whole book of Lamentations; read Job's and David's complaints; yea, read what happened to his Son, his well-beloved, and that when he did but stand in the room of sinners, being in himself altogether innocent; and then consider, O you sinning child of God, if it is any injustice in God; yea, if it be not, necessary that you should be chastised for your sin.

But then, I say, when the hand of God is upon you, how grievous it may be, take heed, and beware that you give not way to your first fears, lest, as I said before, you add to your affliction. And to help you here, let me give you a few instances of the carriages of some of the saints under some of the most heavy afflictions that they have met with for sin.

1. Job was in great affliction, and that, as he confessed, for sin, (Job 7:20,) inasmuch that he said, God had set him for his mark to shoot at, and that he ran upon him like a giant; that he took him by the neck, and shook him to pieces, and counted him for his enemy; that he hid his face from him, and that he could not tell where to find him; yet he counted not all this as a sign of a damnable state, but as a trial and chastisement, and said, when he was in the hottest of the battle, "When I am tried, I shall come forth like gold." And again, when he was pressed upon by the tempter to think that God would kill him, he answers with greatest confidence, "Though he slay me, yet will I trust in him." (Job 16; 14:12; 19:11; 23:8-10; 13:15.)

2. David complained that God had broken his bones; that he had set his face against his sins, and had taken from him the joy of his salvation; yet even at this time he says, "God of my salvation." (Psalm 51:8,9,12,14.)

3. Heman complained that his soul was full of troubles; that God had laid him the lowest pit; that he had put his acquaintance far from him, and casting off his soul, and had hid his face from him; that he was afflicted from his youth up, and ready to die with trouble. He says, moreover, that the fierce wrath of God went over him; that his terrors had cut him off; yea, that by reason of them he was distracted; and yet, even before he makes any of these complaints, he takes fast hold of God, as his saying, "O Lord God of my salvation." (Psalm 88.)

4. The church in the Lamentations complains that the Lord had afflicted her for her transgressions, and that in the day of his fierce anger; also that he had trodden under foot her mighty men, and that he had called the heathen against her: she says that he had covered her with a cloud in his anger; that he was an enemy, and that he had hung a chain

upon her: she adds, moreover, that he had shut out her prayer, broken her teeth with gravel-stones, and covered her with ashes; and in conclusion, that he had utterly rejected her. But what does she do under all this trial? Does she give up her faith and hope, and return to that fear that begot the first bondage? No: "The Lord is my portion, says my soul, therefore will I hope in him;" yea, she adds, "O Lord, you have pleaded the cause of my soul, you have redeemed my life." (Lamentations 1:5; 2:1,2,5; 3:7,8,16; 5:22; 3:24,31,58.)

These things show that God's people, even after they have received the spirit of adoption, have fell foully into sin, and have been bitterly chastised for it; and also, that when the rod was most smart upon them, they made great conscience of giving way to their first fears, wherewith they were made afraid by the Spirit as it wrought as a spirit of bondage; for indeed there is no such thing as the coming of the spirit of bondage to put us in fear the second time, as such, that is, after he is come as the spirit of adoption to the soul.

I conclude, then, that that fear that is wrought by the spirit of bondage is good and godly; because the ground for it is sound; and I also conclude that he comes to the soul as a spirit of bondage but once, and that once is before he comes as a spirit of adoption; and if, therefore, the same fear does again take hold of your heart, that is, if after you have received the spirit of adoption you fear again the damnation of your soul, that you are out of Christ and under the law, that fear is bad and of the devil, and ought by no means to be admitted by you.

Question: But since it is as you say, how does the devil, after the spirit of adoption is come, work the child of God into those fears of being out of Christ, not forgiven, and so an heir of damnation again?

Answer:

1. By giving the lie, and by prevailing with us to give it too, to the work of grace wrought in our hearts, and to the testimony of the Holy Spirit of adoption. Or,

2. By abusing of our ignorance of the everlasting love of God to his in Christ, and the duration of the covenant of grace. Or,

3. By abusing some scripture that seems to look that way, but does not. Or,

4. By abusing our senses and reason. Or,

5. By strengthening of our unbelief. Or,

6. By overshadowing of our judgment with horrid darkness. Or,

7. By giving of us counterfeit representations of God. Or,

8. By stirring up, and setting in a rage, our inward corruptions. Or,

9. By pouring into our hearts abundance of horrid blasphemies. Or,

10. By putting of wrong constructions on the rod and chastening hand of God. Or,

11. By charging upon us that our ill behaviors under the rod and chastening hand of God is a sign that we indeed have no grace, but are downright damned graceless reprobates.

By these things, and others like these, Satan, I say, Satan brings the child of God, not only to the borders, but even into the bowels of the fears of damnation, after it has received a blessed testimony of eternal life, and that by the Holy Spirit of adoption.

Question: But would you not have the people of God stand in fear of his rod, and be afraid of his judgments?

Answer: Yes; and the more they are rightly afraid of them, the less they will come under them; for it is want of fear that brings us into sin, and it is sin that brings us into these afflictions. But I would not have them fear with the fear of slaves, for that will add no strength against sin; but I would have them fear with the reverential fear of sons, and that is the way to depart from evil.

Question: How is that?

Answer: Why, having before received the spirit of adoption, still to believe that he is our Father, and so to fear with the fear of children, not as slaves fear a tyrant. I would, therefore, have them to look upon his rod, rebukes, chidings, and chastisements, and also upon the wrath wherewith he does inflict, to be but the dispensations of their Father. This believe, maintains, or at least helps to maintain in the heart a son-like bowing under the rod. It also maintains in the soul a son-like confession of sin, and a justifying of God under all the rebukes that he grieves us with. It also engages us to come to him, to claim and lay hold of former mercies, to expect more, and to hope a good end shall be made of all God's present dispensations towards us. (Micah 7:9; Lamentations 1:18; Psalm 77:10-12; Lamentations 3:31-34.) Now God would have us thus fear his rod, because he is resolved to chastise us therewith, if so be we sin against him, as I have already showed; for although God's bowels turn within him, even while he is threatening his people, yet if we sin, he will lay on the rod so hard as to make us cry, "Woe unto us that we have sinned!" (Lamentations 5:16); and therefore, as I said, we should be afraid of his judgments, yet only as afore is provided as of the rod, wrath and judgment of a Father.

Question: But have you yet any other considerations to move us to fear God with child-like fear?

Answer: I will in this place give you five.

1. Consider that God thinks meet to have it so, and he is wiser in heart than you; he knows best how to secure his people from sin, and to that end has given them law and commandments to read, that they

may learn to fear him as a Father. (Job 37:24; Ecclesiastes 3:14; Deuteronomy 17:1,19.)

2. Consider, he is mighty in power; if he touch but with a fatherly touch, man nor angel cannot bear it; yea, Christ makes use of that argument, He "has power to cost into hell, fear him." (Luke 12:4,5.)

3. Consider that he is everywhere; you cannot be out of his sight or presence, nor out of the reach of his hand. "Fear you not me?" says the Lord. "Can any hide himself in secret places that I should not see him, says the Lord? Do not I fill heaven and earth, says the Lord?" (Jeremiah 5:22; 23:24.)

4. Consider that he is holy, and cannot look with liking upon the sins of his own people. Therefore, says Peter, "Be as obedient children, not fashioning yourselves according to your former lusts in your ignorance, but as he that has called you is holy, so be you holy in all manner of conversation, because it is written, Be you holy, for I am holy. And if you call on the Father, who without respect of persons judges according to every man's work, pass the time of your sojourning here in fear."

5. Consider that he is good, and has been good to you, good in that he has singled you out from others, and saved you from their death and hell, though you perhaps were worse in your life than those that he left when he laid hold on you. Oh this should engage your heart to fear the Lord all the days of your life: "They shall fear the Lord, and his goodness in the latter days." (Hosea 3:5.) And now for the present: I have done with that fear, I mean as to its first workings, to wit, to put me in fear of damnation, and shall come in the next place to treat of the grace of fear, more immediately intended in the text.

Of the grace of Fear more immediately intended in the text.

I shall now speak to this fear, which I call a lasting godly fear; first, by way of explication; by which I shall show:

I.   How by the Scripture it is described.
II.   I shall show you what this fear flows from. And then,
III.   I shall also show you what does flow from it.

I. For the first of these, to wit, how by the Scripture this fear is described, and that, First. More generally. Second. More particularly.

First. More generally.

1. It is called a grace, that is, a sweet and blessed work of the Spirit of grace, as he is given to the elect by God. Hence the Apostle says, "Let us have grace, whereby we may serve God acceptably, with reverence and godly fear," (Hebrews xii.;) for as that fear that brings bondage is wrought in the soul by the Spirit as a spirit of bondage; so that fear, which is a fear that we have while we are in the liberty of sons, is wrought by him as he manifests to us our liberty; "where the Spirit of the Lord is, there is liberty," that is, where he is as a spirit of adoption, setting the soul free from that bondage under which it was held by the same Spirit while he wrought as a spirit of bondage. Hence as he is called a spirit working bondage to fear, so he, as the Spirit of the Son and of adoption, is called, "the Spirit of the fear of the Lord." (Isaiah 11:2.) Because it is that Spirit of grace that is the author, animater, and maintainer of our filial fear, or of that fear that is son-like, and that subjects the elect unto God, his word, and ways; unto him, his word and ways as a Father.

2. This fear is called also the fear of God, not as that which is ungodly is, nor yet as that may be which is

wrought by the Spirit as a spirit of bondage; but by way of eminency, to wit, as a dispensation of the grace of the gospel, and as a fruit of eternal love. "I will put my fear in their hearts, and they shall not depart from me." (Jeremiah 32:38-41.)

3. This fear of God is called God's treasure, for it is one of his choice jewels, it is one of the rarities of heaven. "The fear of the Lord is his treasure." (Isaiah 33:6.) And it may well go under such a title; for as treasure, so the fear of the Lord is not found in every corner. It is said, all men have not faith, because that also is more precious than gold; the same is said about this fear, "There is no fear of God before their eyes: that is, the greatest part of men are utterly destitute of this goodly jewel, this treasure, the fear of the Lord. Poor vagrants, when they come straggling to a lord's house, may perhaps obtain some scraps and fragments, they may also obtain old shoes, and some sorry cast-off rags, but they get not any of his jewels; they may not touch his choicest treasure, that is kept for the children, and those that shall be his heirs. We may say the same also of this blessed grace of fear, which is called here God's treasure. it is only bestowed upon the elect, the heirs, and children of the promise; all others are destitute of it, and so continue to death and judgment.

4. This grace of fear is that which makes men excel and go beyond all men in the account of God' it is that which beautifies a man, and prefers him above all other; "Have you," says God to Satan, "considered my servant Job, that there is none like him in all the earth, a perfect and an upright man, one that fears God and eschews evil?" (Job 1:8; 2:3.) Mind it, "There is none like him, none like him in all the earth." I suppose he means either in those parts, or else he was the man that abounded in the fear of the Lord: none like him to fear the Lord; he only excelled others with respect to his reverencing of God, bowing before him, and

sincerely complying with his will, and therefore is counted the excellent man. It is not the knowledge of the will of God, but our sincere complying therewith, that proves we fear the Lord; and it is our so doing that puts upon us the note of excelling; hereby appears our perfection, herein is manifest our uprightness. A perfect and an upright man is one that fears God, and that because he eschews evil. Therefore this grace of fear is that without which no part or piece of service which we do to God can be accepted of him. It is, as I may call it, the salt of the covenant, which seasons the heart, and therefore must not be lacking there; it is also that which salts or seasons all our doings, and therefore must not be lacking in any of them. (Leviticus 2:13.) For,

5. I take this grace of fear to be that which softens and mollifies the heart, and that makes it stand in awe both of the mercies and judgments of God. This is that that retains in the heart that due dread and reverence of the heavenly Majesty that is meet should be both in, and kept in the heart of poor sinners. Wherefore, when David described this fear, in the exercise of it, he calls it an awe of God. "Stand in awe," says he, "and sin not;" and again, "My heart stands in awe of your word;" and again, "Let all the earth fear the Lord." What is that? or how is that? why? "Let all the inhabitants of the world stand in awe of him." (Psalm 4:4; 33:8.) This is that, therefore, that is, as I said before, so excellent a thing in the eyes of God, to wit, a grace of the Spirit, the fear of God, his treasure, the salt of the covenant, that which makes men excel all others; for it is that which makes the sinner to stand in awe of God, which posture is the most comely thing in us, throughout all ages. But,

Second, And more particularly.

1. This grace is called "the beginning of knowledge," (Proverbs 1:7) because by the first gracious discovery of God to the soul this grace is begot: and again, because the first time that the soul does apprehend God in Christ to be good

unto it, this grace is animated, by which the soul is put into an holy awe of God, which causes it with reverence and due attention to hearken to him, and tremble before him. It is also by virtue of this fear that the soul does inquire yet more after the blessed knowledge of God. This is the more evident, because, where this fear of God is wanting, or where the discovery of God is not attended with it, the heart still abides rebellious, obstinate, and unwilling to know more, that it might comply therewith; nay, for want of it, such sinners say rather, As for God, let him depart from us, and for the Almighty, We desire not the knowledge of his ways.

2. This fear is called "the beginning of wisdom," (Job 28:28; Psalm 111:10) because then, and not till then, a man begins to be truly spiritually wise; what wisdom is there where the fear of God is not? Therefore the fools are described thus, "For that they hated knowledge, and did not choose the fear of the Lord." (Proverbs 1:29.) The word of God is the fountain of knowledge, into which a man will not with godly reverence look until he is endued with the fear of the Lord: therefore it is rightly called "the beginning of wisdom: but fools despise wisdom and instruction." (Proverbs 1:7.) It is therefore this fear of the Lord that makes a man wise for his soul, for life, and for another world. It is this that teaches him how he should do to escape those spiritual and eternal ruins that the fool is overtaken with, and swallowed up of for ever. A man void of this fear of God, wherever he is wise, or in whatever he excels, yet about the matters of his soul there is none more foolish than himself; for through the want of the fear of the Lord he leaves the best things at sixes and sevens, and only pursues with all his heart those that will leave him in the snare when he dies.

3. This fear of the Lord is to hate evil. To hate sin and vanity; sin and vanity, they are "the sweet morsels of the fool," (Job 20:12) and such which the carnal appetite of the

flesh runs after; and it is only the virtue that is in the fear of the Lord that makes the sinner have an antipathy against it. "By the fear of the Lord men depart from evil." (Proverbs 16:6.) That is, men shun, separate themselves from, and eschew it in its appearances. Wherefore it is plain that those that love evil are not possessed with the fear of God. There is a generation that will pursue evil, that will take it in, nourish it, lay it up in their hearts, hide it, and plead for it, and rejoice to do it. These cannot have in them the fear of the Lord, for that is to hate it, and to make men depart from it; where the fear of God and sin is, it will be with the soul as it was with Israel when Omri and Tibni strove to reign among them both at once, one of them must be put to death, they cannot live together. Sin must down, for the fear of the Lord begs in the soul a hatred against it, an abhorrence of it; therefore sin must die, that is, as to the affections and lusts of it; for as Solomon says in another case, where no wood is, the fire goes out. So we may say, where there is a hatred of sin, and where men depart from it, there it loses much of its power, waxes feeble, and decays. Therefore Solomon says again, "Fear the Lord and depart from evil," (Proverbs 3:7) as who should say, Fear the Lord, and it will follow that you shall depart from evil; departing from evil is a natural consequence, a proper effect of the fear of the Lord sin is annihilated, or has lost its being in the soul; there still will those Canaanites be, but they are hated, loathed, abominated, fought against, prayed against, watched against, strove against, and mortified by the soul. (Romans 7.)

4. This fear is called a fountain of life. "The fear of the Lord is a fountain of life, to depart from the snares of death." (Proverbs 14:27.) It is a fountain, or spring, which so continually supplies the soul with variety of considerations of sin, of God, of death, and life eternal, as to keep the soul in continual exercise of virtue, and in holy contemplation. It

is a function of life; every operation thereof, every act and exercise thereof, has a true and natural tendency to spiritual and eternal felicity. Wherefore the wise man says in another place, "The fear of the Lord tends to life, and he that has it shall abide satisfied, he shall not be visited with evil." (Proverbs 19:23.) It tends to life, even as of nature everything has a tendency to that which is most natural to itself, the fire to burn, the water to wet, the stone to fall, the sun to shine, sin to defile, etc. Thus, I say, the fear of the Lord tends to life; the nature of it is to put the soul upon fearing of God, of closing with Christ, and of walking humbly before him. "It is a foundation of life, to depart from the snares of death." What are the snares of death, but sin, the wiles of the devil, etc., from which the fear of God has a natural tendency to deliver you, and to keep you in the way that tends to life?

5. This fear of the Lord, it is called "the instruction of wisdom." (Proverbs 15:33.) You heard before that it is the beginning of wisdom; but here you find it called the instruction of wisdom; for indeed it is not only that which makes a man begin to be wise, but to improve, and make advantage of all those helps and means to life which God has afforded to that end; that is, both to his own and his neighbor's salvation also. It is the instruction of wisdom; it will make a man capable to use all his natural parts, all his natural wisdom to God's glory, and his own good. There lies, even in many natural things, that, into which if we were instructed, would yield us a great deal of help to the understanding of spiritual matters: "For in wisdom has God made all the world;" nor is there any thing that God has made, whether in heaven above or on earth beneath, but there is couched some spiritual mystery in it. The which men matter no more, than they do the ground they tread on, or than the stones that are under their feet, and all because they have not this fear of the Lord; for had they that, that would teach them to think, even from that knowledge of God, that has

by the fear of him put into their hearts, that he being so great and so good, there must needs be abundance of wisdom in the things he has made; that fear would also endeavor to find out what that wisdom is, yea, and give to the soul the instruction of it. In that it is called the instruction of wisdom, it intimates to us that its tendency is to keep all even, and in good order in the soul. when Job perceived that his friends did not deal with him in an even spirit and orderly manner, he said that "they forsook the fear of the Almighty." (Job 6:14.) For this fear keeps a man even in his words and judgment of things. It may be compared to the ballast of the ship, and to the poise of the balance of the scales, it keeps all even, and also makes us steer our course right with respect to the things that pertain to God and man.

What this Fear of God flows from.

II. I come now to the second thing, to wit, to show you what this fear of God flows from.

First, this fear, this grace of fear, this son-like fear of God, it flows from the distinguishing love of God to his elect. "I will be their God," says he, "and I will put my fear in their hearts." None other obtain it but those that are enclosed and bound up in that bundle. Therefore they in the same place are said to be those that are wrapped up in the eternal or everlasting covenant of God, and so designed to be the people that should be blessed with this fear. "I will make an everlasting covenant with them," says God, "that I will not turn away from them to do them good, but I will put my fear in their hearts, and they shall not depart from me." (Jeremiah 32:40.) This covenant declares unto men, that God has, in his heart, distinguishing love for some of the children of men, for he says he will be their God, that he will not leave them, nor yet suffer them to depart, to wit, finally from him. Into these men's hearts he does put his fear, this blessed grace, and this rare and effectual sign of his love, and of their eternal salvation.

Second, this fear flows from a new heart. This fear is not in men by nature; the fear of devils they may have, as also an ungodly fear of God; but this fear is not in any, but where there dwells a new heart, another fruit and effect of this everlasting covenant, and of this distinguishing love of God. "A new heart also will I give them." A new heart, what a one is that? why, the same prophet says in another place, "A heart to fear me," a circumcised one, a sanctified one. (Jeremiah 32:39; Ezekiel 11:19; 36:26.) So then, until a man receive a heart from God, a heart from heaven, a new heart, he has not this fear of God in him. New wine must not be put into old bottles, lest the one, to wit, the bottles, mar the wine, or the wine the bottles; but new wine must have new bottles, and then both shall be preserved. (Matthew 9:17.) This fear of God must not be, cannot be found in old hearts; old hearts are not bottles out of which this fear of God proceeds, but is it from an honest and good heart, from a new one, from such an one that is also an effect of the everlasting covenant, and love of God to men.

I will give them a heart to fear me. There must in all actions be heart, and without heart no action is good; nor can there be faith, love, or fear, from every kind of heart; these must flow from such an one whose nature is to produce and bring forth such fruit: "Do men gather grapes of thorns, or figs of thistles?" so from a corrupt heart there cannot proceed such fruit as the fear of God, as to believe in God, and love God. (Luke 6:43-45.) The heart naturally is deceitful above all things, and desperately wicked, how then should there flow from such an one the fear of God? It cannot be. He therefore that has not received at the hands of God a new heart, cannot fear the Lord.

Third, this fear of God flows from an impression, a sound impression that the word of God makes on our souls;

for without an impress of the word, there is no fear of God. Hence it is said that God gave to Israel good laws, statutes, and judgments, that they might learn them, and in learning them, learn to fear the Lord their God. Therefore, says God in another place, "Gather the people together, men, women, and children, and the stranger that is within your gates, that they may hear, and that they may learn to fear the Lord your God." (Deuteronomy 6:1,2; 31:12.) For as a man drinks good doctrine into his soul, so he fears God. If he drinks it in much, he fears him greatly; if he drinks it in but little, he fears him but little; if he drinks it no in at all, he fears him not at all. This, therefore, teaches us how to judge who fears the Lord; they are those that learn, and that stand in awe of the word; those that have by the holy word of God the very form of itself engraved upon the face of their souls, they fear God. (Romans 6:17.) But, on the contrary, those that do not love good doctrine, that give not place to the wholesome truths of the God of heaven revealed in his testament to take place in their souls, but rather despise it, and the true possessors of it, they fear not God. For, as I said before, this fear of God, it flows from a sound impression that the word of God makes upon the soul; and therefore,

Fourth, this godly fear flows from faith, for where the word makes sound impression on the soul, by that impression is faith begotten, whence also this fear does flow; therefore, right hearing of the word is called "the hearing of faith." (Galatians 3:2.) Hence it is said again, "By faith Noah being warned of God of things not seen as yet, moved with fear, prepared an ark to the saving of his house, by which he condemned the world, and became heir of the righteousness which is by faith." (Hebrews 11:7.) The word, the warning that he had from God of things not seen as yet, wrought, through faith therein, that fear of God in his heart that made him prepare against unseen dangers, and that he might be an inheritor of unseen happiness. Where, therefore, there is not faith in the world of God, there can be none of this fear; and where the word does not make sound impression on the soul, there can be none of this faith. So that as vices hang together, and have the links of a chain, dependence one upon another, even so the graces of the Spirit also are the fruits of one another, and have such dependence on each other, that the one cannot be without the other. No faith, no fear of God; devil's faith, devil's fear; saint's faith, saint's fear.

Fifth, this godly fear also flows from sound repentance for and from sin: godly sorrow works repentance, and godly repentance produces this fear. "For behold," says Paul, "this self-same thing, that you sorrowed after a godly sort, what carefulness it wrought in you, what clearing of yourselves, yea what indignation, yea what fear!" (2 Corinthians 7:10, 11.) Repentance is the effect of sorrow, and sorrow is the effect of smart, and smart the effect of faith. Now, therefore, fear must needs be an effect of and flow from repentance. Sinner, do not deceive yourself; if you are a stranger to sound repentance, which stands in sorrow and shame before God for sin, as also in turning from it, you have no fear of God; I mean, none of this godly fear, for that is the fruit of and flows from sound repentance.

Sixth, this godly fear also flows from a sense of the love and kindness of God to the soul. Where there is no sense or hope of the kindness and mercy of God by Jesus Christ, there can be none of this fear, but rather wrath and despair, which produces that fear that is either devilish, or else that which is only wrought in us by the Spirit, as a spirit of bondage; but these we do not discourse of now; wherefore the godly fear that now I treat of, it flows from some sense or hope of mercy from God by Jesus Christ. "If you, Lord" says David, "should mark iniquity, Oh Lord, who should stand? but there is forgiveness with you that you may be feared." (Psalm 130:3,4.) "There is mercy with you," this the soul has sense of, and hope in, and therefore fears God. Indeed, nothing can lay a stronger obligation upon the heart to fear God, than sense of or hope in mercy. (Jeremiah 33:8,9.) This begets true tenderness of heart, true godly softness of spirit. This truly endears the affections to God; and in this true tenderness, softness, and endearedness of affection to God lies the very essence of this fear of the Lord, as is manifest by the fruit of this fear when we shall come to speak of it.

Seventh, this fear of God flows from a due consideration of the judgments of God that are to be executed in the world, yea, upon professors too: yea, further, God's people themselves, I mean as to themselves, have such a consideration of his judgments towards them, as to produce this godly fear. When God's judgments are in the earth, they effect the fear of his name in the hearts of his own people. "My flesh trembles for fear of you, and I am," said David, "afraid of your judgments." (Psalm 119:120.) When God smote Uzzah, David was afraid of God that day. (1 Chronicles 13:12.) Indeed, many regard not the works of the Lord, nor take notice of the operation of his hands, and such cannot fear the Lord; but others observe and regard, and wisely consider of his doings, and of the judgments that he executes, and that makes them fear the Lord. This God himself suggests as a means to make us fear him. Hence he commands the false prophet to be stoned, "that all Israel might hear and fear." Hence also he commanded that the rebellious son should be stoned, "that all Israel might hear and fear." False witness was also to have the same judgment of God executed upon him, "that all Israel might hear and fear." The man also that did aught presumptuously was to die, "that all Israel might hear and fear." (Deuteronomy 13:11; 21:21; 17:13; 19:20.) There is a natural tendency in judgments, as judgments, to beget a fear of God in the heart of man, as man; but when the observation of the judgments of God is made by him that has a principle of true grace in his soul, that observation being made, I say, by a gracious heart, produces a fear of God in the soul of its own nature, to wit, a gracious or godly fear of God.

Eighth, this godly fear also flows from a godly remembrance of our former distresses, when we were distressed with our first fears; for though our first fears were begotten in us by the Spirit's working as a spirit of bondage, and so are not always to be entertained as such, yet even that fear leaves in us, and upon our spirits, that sense and relish of our first awakenings and dread, as also occasions and produces this godly fear. "Take heed," says God, "and keep your soul diligently, lest you forget the things that your eyes have seen, and lest they depart from your heart all the days of your life, but teach them your sons, and your sons' sons." But what were the things that their eyes had seen that would so damn them, should they be forgotten? The answer is, "The things which they saw at Horeb; to wit, the fire, the smoke, the darkness, the earthquake, their first awakenings by the law, by which they were brought into a bondage fear; yea, they were to remember this especially. "Especially," says he, "the day that you stood before the Lord your God in Horeb, when the Lord your God said unto me, Gather me the people together, and I will make them hear my words, that they may learn to fear me all the days that they shall live upon the earth." (Deuteronomy 4:9-11.) The remembrance of what we saw, felt, feared, and trembled under the sense of, when our first fears were upon us, is that which will produce in our hearts this godly filial fear.

Ninth, this godly fear flows from our receiving of an answer of prayer, when we supplicated for mercy at the hand of God. See the proof for this. "If there be in the land famine, if there be pestilence, blasting, mildews, locust, or if there by caterpillars; if their enemies besiege them in the land of their cites, whatsoever plague, whatsoever sickness there be: whatever prayer and supplication be made by any man, or by all your people Israel, which shall know every man the plague of his own heart, and spread forth his hands towards this house: then hear you in heaven your dwelling-place, and forgive, and do, and give to every man according to his ways, whose heart you know, for you, even you only, know the hearts of all the children of men, that they may fear you all the days of their life, that they live in the land which you gave unto our fathers." (1 Kings 8:37-40.)

Tenth, this grace of fear also flows from a blessed conviction of the all-seeing eye of God; that is, from a belief that he certainly knows the heart, and sees every one of the turnings and returnings thereof; this is intimated in the text last mentioned. "Whose heart you know that they may fear you," to wit, so many of them as be, or shall be convinced of this. Indeed without this conviction this godly fear cannot be in us; the want of this conviction made the Pharisees such hypocrites. "You are they," said Christ, "that justify yourselves before men, but God knows your hearts." (Luke 16:15.) The Pharisees, I say, were not aware of this, therefore they so much preferred themselves before those that by far were better than themselves, and it is for want of this conviction that men go on in such secret sins as they do, so much without fear either of God or his judgments.

Eleventh, this grace of fear also flows from a sense of the impartial judgment of God upon men according to their works. This also is manifest from the text mentioned above. And give unto every man according to his works or ways, "that they may fear you," etc. This is also manifest by that of Peter (1 Peter 1:17): "And if you call upon the Father, who without respect of persons judges according to every man's work, pass the time of your sojourning here in fear." He that has godly conviction of this fear of God, will fear before him by which fear their hearts are posed, and works directed with trembling, according to the will of God.

Thus you see what a weighty and great grace this grace of the holy fear of God is, and how all the graces of the Holy Ghost yield mutually their help and strength to the nourishment and life of it; and also how it flows from them all, and has a dependence upon every one of them for its due working in the heart of him that has it. And thus much to show you from whence it flows. And now I shall come to the third thing, to wit, to show you what flows from this godly fear.

What flows from this godly Fear.

III. Having showed you what godly fear flows from, I come now, I say, to show you what proceeds or flows from this godly fear of God, where it is seated in the heart of man. And,

First, there flows from this godly fear a godly reverence of God. "He is great," said David, "and greatly to be feared in the assembly of his saints." God, as I have already showed you, is the proper object of godly fear, it is his person and majesty that this fear always causes the eye of the soul to be upon. "Behold," said David, "as the eyes of servants look unto the hand of their masters, and as the eyes of a maiden unto the land of her mistress: so our eyes wait upon the Lord our God, until he have mercy upon us." (Psalm 123:2.) Nothing awes the soul that fears God so much as does the glorious majesty of God.

1. His person is above all things feared by them. "I fear God," said Joseph. (Genesis 42:18.) That is, more than any other; I stand in awe of him, he is my dread, he is my fear; I do all my actions as in his presence, as in his sight; I reverence his holy and glorious majesty, doing all things as with fear and trembling before him.

2. This fear makes them have also a very great reverence of his word; for that also, I told you, was the rule of their

fear. "Princes," said David, "persecute me without a cause, but my heart stands in awe," in fear, "of your word." This grace of fear, therefore, from it flows reverence of the words of God; of all laws, "that man fears the word;" and no law that is not agreeing therewith. (Psalm 119:116.)

3. There flows from this godly fear, tenderness of God's glory. This fear, I say, will cause a man to afflict his soul, when he sees that by professors dishonor is brought to the name of God, and to his word. Who would not fear you, said Jeremiah, O king of nations, for to you does it appertain? He speaks it as being affected with that dishonor, that by the body of the Jews was continually brought to his name, his word, and ways; he also speaks it of a hearty wish that they once would be otherwise minded. The same saying in effect has also John in the Revelations, "Oh who would not fear the Lord," said he, "and glorify your name?" (Revelation 15:4) clearly concluding that godly fear produces a godly tenderness of God's glory in the world, for that appertains unto him; that is, it is due unto him, it is a debt which we owe unto him. "Give unto the Lord," said David, "the glory due unto his name." Now, if there be begotten in the heart of the godly, by his grace of far, a godly tenderness of the glory of God, then it follows of consequence, that where they that have this fear of God do see his glory diminished by the wickedness of the children of men, there they are grieved, and deeply distressed. "Rivers of waters," said David, "run down my eyes, because they keep not thy law." (Psalm 66:136.) Let me give you for this these following instances.

(1.) How was David provoked when Goliath defied the God of Israel! (1 Samuel 17:23-29, 45, 46.)

(2.) Also when others reproached God, he tells us that they reproach "was even as a sword in his bones." (Psalm 42:10.)

(3.)   How was Hezekiah afflicted when Rabshakeh railed upon his God! (Isaiah 37)

(4.)   David was, for the love that he had to the glory of God's word, ran the hazard and reproach of all the mighty people. (Psalm 119:151; 89:50.)

(5.)   How tender of the glory of God was Eli, Daniel, and the three children in their day! Eli died with trembling of heart when he heard that the ark of God was taken. (1 Samuel 4:14-18.) Daniel ran the danger of the lions' mouths, for the tender love that he had to the word and worship of God. (Daniel 6:10-16.) The three children ran the hazard of a burning fiery furnace, rather than they would dare to dishonor the way of their God. (Daniel 3:13, 16-20.)

This, therefore, is one of the fruits of this godly fear, to wit, a reverence of his name, and tenderness of his glory.

Second, there flows from this godly fear, watchfulness. As it is said of Solomon's servants, they "watched about his bed, because of fear in the night:" so it may be said of them that have this godly fear; it makes them a watchful people.

1. It makes them watch their hearts, and take heed to keep them with all diligence lest they should, by one or another of its flights, lead them to do that which in itself is wicked. (Proverbs 4:23. Hebrews 12:15.)

2. It makes them watch, lest some temptation from hell should enter into their heart to the destroying of them. (1 Peter 5:8.)

3. It makes them watch their mouths, and keep them also, at sometimes, as with a bit and bridle, that they offend not with their tongue, knowing that the tongue is apt, being an evil member, soon to catch the fire of hell, to the defiling of the whole body. (James 3:2-7.)

4. It makes them watch over their ways, look well to their goings, and to make straight steps for their feet. (Psalm 39:1. Hebrews 12:13.)

Thus this godly fear puts the soul upon its watch, lest from the heart within, or from the devil without, or from the world, or some other temptation, something should surprise and overtake the child of God to defile him or to cause him to defile the ways of God, and so offend the saints, open the mouths of men, and cause the enemy to speak reproachfully of religion.

Third, there flows from this fear, a holy provocation to a reverential converse with saints in their religious and godly assemblies, for their further progress in the faith and way of holiness. "Then they that feared the Lord spoke often one to another." Spoke, that is, of God, and his holy and glorious name, kingdom, and works, for their mutual edification; "a book of remembrance was written before him for them that feared the Lord, and that thought upon his name." (Malachi 3:16.) The fear of the Lord in the heart provokes to this in all its acts, not only of necessity, but of nature: it is the natural effect of this godly fear, to exercise the church in the contemplation of God, together and apart. Al fear, good and bad, has a natural propensity in it to incline the heart to contemplate upon the object of fear, and though a man should labor to take off his thoughts from the object of his fear, whether that object was men, hell, devils, etc., yet do what he could, the next time his fear had any act in it, it would return again to its object. And so it is with godly fear, that will make a man speak of, and think upon the name of God reverentially, (Psalm 89:7;) yea, and exercise himself in the holy thoughts of him in such sort that his soul shall be sanctified, and seasoned with such meditations. Indeed, holy thoughts of God, such as you see this fear does exercise the heart withal, prepare the heart to, and for God. This fear therefore it is that David prayed for, for the people, when he said, "Oh Lord God of Abraham, Isaac, and Israel, our fathers, keep this for ever in the imagination of the thoughts of the heart of your people, and prepare their heart unto you." (I Chronicles 29:18.)

Fourth, there flows from this fear of God, great reverence of his majesty, in and under the use and enjoyment of God's holy ordinances. His ordinances are his courts and palaces, his walks and places, where he gives his presence to those that wait upon him in them in the fear of his name. And this is the meaning of that of the Apostle: "Then had the churches rest throughout all Judea, and Galilee, and Samaria, and were edified; and, walking in the fear of the Lord, and in the comfort of the Holy Ghost, were multiplied." (Acts 9:31.) "And walking," that word intends their use of the ordinances of God. They walked in all the commandments and ordinances of the Lord blameless. This in Old Testament language is called, treading God's courts, and walking in his paths. This, says the text, they did here in the fear of God. That is in a great reverence of that God whose ordinances they were. "You shall keep my sabbaths, and reverence my sanctuary; I am the Lord." (Leviticus 19:30; 26:2.)

It is one thing to be conversant in God's ordinances, and another to be conversant in them with a due reverence of the majesty and name of that God whose ordinances they are; it is common for men to do the first, but none can do the last without this fear. "In your fear," said David, "will I worship." (Psalm 5:7.) It is this fear of God, therefore, from whence does flow that great reverence that his saints have in them, of his majesty, in and under the use and enjoyment of God's holy ordinances; and consequently, that makes our service in the performance of them acceptable to God through Christ. (Hebrews 12.) For God expects that we serve him with fear and trembling; and it is odious among men for a man in the presence, or about the service of his prince, to behave himself lightly, and without due reverence of that majesty, in whose presence and about whose business he is. And if so, how can their service to God have any thing like acceptation from the hand of God, that is done, not in, but without the fear of God? This service must needs be an abomination to him, and these servers must come off with rebuke.

Fifth, there flows from this godly fear of God, self-denial. That is, a holy abstaining from those things that are either unlawful or inexpedient; according to that of Nehemiah, "The former governors that had been before me were chargeable unto the people, and had taken of them bread and wine, besides forth shekels of silver, yea, even their servants bare rule over the people: but so did not I, because of the fear of God." (Nehemiah 5:15.) Here now was self-denial; he would not do as they did that went before him, neither himself, nor should his servants; but what was it that put him upon those acts of self-denial? The answer is, the fear of God: "but so did not I, because of the fear of God." Now whether by the fear of God in this place be meant his word, or the grace of fear in his heart, may perhaps be a scruple to some, but in my judgment the text must have respect to the latter, to wit, to the grace of fear, for without that be indeed in the heart, the word will not produce that good self-denial in us that here you find this good man to live in the daily exercise of. The fear of God, therefore, that was the cause of his self-denial, was this grace of fear in his heart. This made him to be, as was said before, tender of the honor of God, and of the salvation of his brother; yea, so tender, that rather than he would give an occasion to the weak to stumble or be offended, he would even deny himself of that which others never hesitated to do. Paul also, through the sanctifying operations of this fear of God in his heart, did deny himself even of lawful things for the profit and commodity of his brother. "I will not eat flesh while the world stands, lest I make my brother to offend." That is, if his eating of it would make his brother to offend. (1 Corinthians 8:13.) Men that have not this fear of God in them, will not, cannot deny themselves, (of love to God, and the good of the weak, who are subject to stumble at indifferent things,) but where this grace of fear is, there follows self-denial; there men are tender of offending; and count, that it far better becomes their profession to be of a self-denying, condescending conversation and temper, than to stand sturdily to their own liberty in things inexpedient, whoever is offended thereat. This grace of fear, therefore, is a very excellent thing, because it yields such excellent fruit as this. For this self-denial, of how little esteem may be with some, yet the want of it, if the words of Christ be true, as they are, takes quite away from even a professor the very name of a disciple. (Matthew 10:37, 38; Luke 14:26, 27, 33.) They, says Nehemiah, lorded it over the brethren, but so did not I. They took bread and wine, and forty shekels of silver of them, but so did not I; yea, even their servants bare rule over the people, "but so did not I, because of the fear of God."

Sixth, there flows from this godly fear of God, "singleness of heart." (Colossians 3:22.) Singleness of heart both to God and man; singleness of heart, that is it which in another place is called sincerity and godly simplicity; and it is this, when a man does a thing simply for the sake of him or of the law that commands it, without respect to this by-end, or that desire or praise or of vain-glory from others. I say, when our obedience to God is done by us simply, or alone for God's sake, for his word's sake, without any regard to this or that by-end or reserve, "not with eye-service, as men-pleasers, but with singleness of heart, fearing God." A man is more subject to nothing than to swerve from singleness of heart in his service to God, and obedience to his will. How does the Lord charge the children of Israel, and all their

205

obedience, and that for seventy years together, with the want of singleness of heart towards him! "When you fasted and mourned in the fifth and seventh month, even those seventy years, did you at all fast to me, even to me? And when you did eat, and when you did drink, did you not eat for yourselves, and drink for yourselves?" (Zechariah 7:5,6.) They wanted this singleness of heart in their fasting and in their eating, in their mourning and in their drinking; they had double hearts in what they did. They did not as the Apostle bids, "whether they eat or drink, or whatever they did, do all to the glory of God." And the reason of their want of this thing was, they wanted this fear of God; for that, as the Apostle here says, effects singleness of heart to God, and makes a man, as John said of Gaius, "do faithfully whatever he does." (3 John 5.) And the reason is, as has been already urged, for that grace of fear of God retains and keeps upon the heart, a reverent and awful sense of the dread majesty, and all-seeing eye of God, also a due consideration of the day of account before him; it likewise makes the soul against all discouragements; by this means, I say, the soul in its service to God or man is not so soon captivated as where there is not this fear, but through and by it its service is accepted, being single, sincere, simple, and faithful; when others, with what they do, are cast into hell for their hypocrisy, for they mix not what they do with godly fear. Singleness of heart in the service of God is of such absolute necessity, that without it, as I have hinted, nothing can be accepted, because where that is wanting, there wants love to God, and to that which is true holiness indeed. It was this singleness of heart that made Nathaniel so honorable in the eyes of Jesus Christ. "Behold," said he, "an Israelite indeed, in whom there is no guile." And it was the want of it that made him so much abhor the Pharisees. They wanted sincerity, simplicity, and godly sincerity in their souls, and so became an abhorrence in his esteem.

Now, I say, this golden grace, singleness of heart, it flows from this godly fear of God.

Seventh, there flows from this godly fear of God compassion and bowels to those of the saints that are in necessity and distress. This is manifest in good Obadiah; it is said of him, that "he took an hundred of the Lord's prophets and hid them by fifty in a save, and fed them with bread and water," in the days when Jezebel, that tyrant, sought their lives to destroy them. (1 Kings 18:3, 4.) But what was it that moved so upon his heart as to cause him to do this thing? Why, it was this blessed grace of the fear of God. "Now Obadiah," says the text, "feared the Lord greatly; for so it was, when Jezebel cut off the prophets of the Lord, that Obadiah took an hundred prophets and hid them by fifty in a cave, and fed them with bread and water." This was charity to the distressed, even to the distressed for the Lord's sake. Had no Obadiah served the Lord, yea, had he not greatly feared him, he would not have been able to do this thing, especially as the case then stood with him, and also with the church at that time; for then Jezebel sought to slay all that indeed feared the Lord; yea, and the persecution prevailed so much at that time, that even Elijah himself thought that she had killed all but him. But now, even now, the fear of God in this good man's heart put forth itself into acts of mercy, though attended with so imminent danger. See here, therefore, that the fear of God will put forth itself in the heart where God has put it, even to show kindness, and to have compassion upon the distressed servants of God, even under Jezebel's nose; for Obadiah dwelt in Ahab's house, and Jezebel was Ahab's wife, and a horrible persecutor, as was said before; yet Obadiah will show mercy to the poor, because he feared God; yea, he will venture her displeasure, his place, and neck and all, but he will be merciful to his brethren in distress. Cornelius also, being a man possessed with this fear of God, became a very free-hearted and open-handed man to the poor. "He feared God, and gave much alms to the people." Indeed, this fear, this godly fear of God, it is an universal grace; it will stir up the soul unto all good duties. It is a fruitful grace; from it, where it is, flows abundance of excellent virtues, nor without it can there be anything good, or done well, that is done. But,

Eighth, there flows from this fear of God, hearty, fervent, and constant prayer. This also is seen in Cornelius, that devout man. He feared God; and what then? Why, he gave much alms to the people, and prayed to God always. (Acts 10:1, 2.) Did I say that hearty, fervent, and constant prayer flowed from this fear of God? I will add, that if the whole duty, and the continuation of it, be not managed with this fear of God, it profits nothing at all. It is said of our Lord Jesus Christ himself, "He was heard in that he feared." He prayed, then, because he feared God, and therefore was his prayer accepted of him, even because he feared. "He was heard in that he feared." (Hebrews 5:7.) This godly fear is so essential to right prayer, and right prayer is such an inseparable effect and fruit of this fear, that you must have both or none; he that prays not fears not God, yea, he that prays not fervently and frequently fears him not; and so he that fears him not cannot pray; for if prayer be the effect of this fear of God, then without this fear, prayer, fervent prayer ceases. How can they pray or make conscience of the duty that fear not God? Oh prayerless man, you fear not God! You would not live so like a swine or a dog in the world as you do if you fear the Lord.

Ninth, there flows from this fear of God, a readiness, or willingness, at God's call, to give up our best enjoyments to his dispose. This is evident in Abraham, who at God's call, without delay, rose early in the morning to offer up his only and well-beloved Isaac a burnt-offering in the place where God shall appoint him. It was a rare thing that Abraham did, and had he not had this rare grace, this fear of God, he

208

would not, he could not have done to God's liking so wonderful a thing. It is true the Holy Ghost also makes this service of Abraham to be the fruit of his faith, "By faith Abraham offered up Isaac, and he that had the promises offered up his only son." (Hebrews 11; James 2.) Without doubt love unto God in Abraham was not wanting in this his service, nor was this grace of fear; nay, in the story where it is recorded, there it is chiefly accounted for the fruit of his godly fear, and that by an angel from heaven. "And the angel called out of heaven, and said, Abraham, Abraham. And he said, Here am I. And he said, Lay not your hand upon the lad, neither do you anything unto him, for now I know that you fear God, seeing you have not withheld your son, your only son from me." (Genesis 22:11, 12.) Now I know it; now, now you have offered up your only Isaac, your all, at the bidding of your God. Now I know it. The fear of God is not presently discerned in the heart and life of a man. Abraham had long before this done many a holy duty, and showed much willingness of heart to observe and do the will of God; yet you find not, as I remember, that he had this testimony from heaven that he feared God till now; but now he has it, now he has it from heaven. "Now I know that you fear God." Many duties may be done, though I do not say that Abraham did them, without the fear of God; but when a man shall not stick at, or withhold his darling from God, when called upon by God to offer it up unto him, that declares, yea, and gives conviction to angels, that now he fears God.

Tenth, there flows from this godly fear, humility. This is evident because when the Apostle cautions the Romans against the venom of spiritual pride, he directs them to the exercise of this blessed grace of fear as its antidote. "Be not high-minded," says he, "but fear." (Romans 11:20.) Pride, spiritual pride, which is here set forth by the word "high-minded," is a sin of a very high and damnable nature; it was the sin of the fallen angels, and is that which causes men to fall into the same condemnation: "Lest being puffed up with pride, he fall into the condemnation of the devil." Pride, I say, it damns a professor with the damnation of devils, with the damnation of hell, and therefore it is a deadly, deadly sin. Now against this deadly sin is set the grace of humility, that comely garment, for so the Apostle calls it, saying, "Be clothed with humility." But the question is now, how we should attain to, and live in the exercise of this blessed and comely grace? to which the Apostle answers, Fear be afraid with godly fear, and thence will flow humility. "Be not high-minded, but fear." That is, Fear, or be continually afraid and jealous of yourselves, and of your own naughty hearts, also fear lest at some time or other the devil, your adversary, should have advantage of you. Fear, lest by forgetting what you are by nature, you also forget the need that you have of continual pardon, support, and supplies from the Spirit of grace, and so grow proud of your own abilities, or of what you have received of God, and fall into the condemnation of the devil. Fear, and that will make you little in your own eyes, keep you humble, put you upon crying to God for protection, and upon lying at his foot for mercy; that will also make you have low thoughts of your own parts, your own doings, and cause you to prefer your brother before yourself, and so you will walk in humiliation, and be continually under the teachings of God, and under his conduct in your way. The humble God will teach; "the meek will he guide in judgment, the meek will he teach his way." From this grace of fear then flows this excellent and comely thing, humility; yea, it also is maintained by this fear. Fear takes off a man from trusting to himself, it puts a man upon trying of all things, it puts a man upon desiring counsel and help from heaven, it makes a man ready and willing to hear instruction, and makes a man walk lowly, softly, and so securely in the way.

Eleventh, there flows from this grace of fear, hope in the mercy of God. "The Lord takes pleasure in them that fear him, in them that hope in his mercy." (Psalm 147:11.) The latter part of the text is an explanation of the former: as if the Psalmist had said, They be the men that fear the Lord, even they that hope in his mercy; for true fear produces hope in God's mercy. And it is further manifest thus: Fear, true fear of God inclines the heart to a serious inquiry after that way of salvation which God himself has prescribed; now the way that God has appointed, by the which the sinner is to obtain the salvation of his soul, is his mercy as so and so set forth in the word; and godly fear has special regard to the word. To this way, therefore, the sinner with this godly fear submits his soul, rolls himself upon it, and so is delivered from that death into which others, for want of this fear of God, do headlong fall. It is, as I also hinted before, the nature of godly fear to be very much putting the soul upon the inquiry, which is, and which is not, the thing approved of God, and accordingly to embrace it, or shun it. Now I say, this fear having put the soul upon a strict and serious inquiry after the way of salvation, at last it finds it to be by the mercy of God in Christ; therefore this fear puts the soul upon hoping also in him for eternal life and blessedness; by which hope he does not only secure his soul; but becomes a portion of God's delight. "The Lord takes pleasure in them that fear him, in them that hope in his mercy." Besides, this godly fear carries in it self-evidence that the state of the sinner is happy, because possessed with this happy grace. Therefore, as John says, "We know we are passed from death to life, because we love the brethren." (1 John 3:14.) So here, "The Lord takes pleasure in them that fear him, in them that hope in his mercy." If I fear God, and if my fearing of him is a thing in which he takes such pleasure, then may I boldly venture to roll myself for eternal life into the bosom of his mercy, which is Christ. This fear also produces hope; if, therefore, poor sinner, you know yourself to be one that is possessed with this fear of God, suffer yourself to be persuaded therefore to hope in the mercy of God for salvation, for the Lord takes pleasure in you. And it delights him to see you hope in his mercy.

Twelfth, there flows from this godly fear of God, an honest and conscientious use of all those means which God has ordained that we should be conversant in for our attaining salvation. Faith and hope in God's mercy is that which secures our justification and hope, and as you have heard, they do flow from this fear. But now, besides faith and hope, there is a course of life in those things in which God has ordained us to have our conversation, without which there is no eternal life. "You have your fruit unto holiness, and the end everlasting life;" and again, "Without holiness no man shall see the Lord." Not that faith and hope are deficient, if they be right, but they are both of them counterfeit when not attended with a reverent use of all the means: upon the reverent use of which the soul is put by this grace of fear. "Wherefore, beloved," said Paul, " as you have always obeyed, not as in my presence only, but now much more in my absence, work out your own salvation with fear and trembling." (Romans 6:22; Hebrews 12:14; Philippians 2:12.) There is a faith and hope of mercy that may receive a man, though the faith of God's elect, and the hope that purifies the heart never will, because they are alone, and not attended with those companions that accompany salvation, (Hebrews 6:3-8); but now this godly fear carries in its bowels, not only a moving of the soul to faith and hope in God's mercy, but an earnest provocation to the holy and reverent use of all the means that God has ordained for a man to have his conversation in, in order to his eternal salvation. "Work our your salvation with fear." Not that work is meritorious, or such that can purchase eternal life, for eternal life is obtained by hope in God's mercy; but this hope, if it be right, is attended with this godly fear, which fear puts the soul upon a diligent use of all those means that may tend to the strengthening of hope, and so to the making of us holy in all manner of conversation, that we may be meet to be partakers of the inheritance of the saints in light. For hope purifies the heart, if fear of God shall be its companion, and so makes a man a vessel of mercy prepared unto glory. Paul bids Timothy to fly pride, covetousness, doting about questions, and the like, and to "follow after righteousness, godliness, faith, love, patience; to fight the good fight of faith, and to lay hold on eternal life." (1 Timothy 6.) So Peter bids that we "add to our faith virtue, and to virtue knowledge, and to knowledge temperance, and to temperance patience, to patience godliness, to godliness brotherly kindness, and to brotherly-kindness charity;" adding, "For if these things be in you and abound, they make you that you shall neither be barren nor unfruitful in the knowledge of our Lord Jesus Christ. Wherefore the rather, brethren, give diligence to make your calling and election sure; for if you do these things you shall never fall. For so an entrance shall be ministered unto you abundantly into the everlasting kingdom of our Lord and Savior Jesus Christ." (2 Peter 1:5-11.) The sum of all which is that which was mentioned before: to wit, "to work out our own salvation with fear and trembling." For none of these things can be conscientiously done, but by and with the help of this blessed grace of fear.

Thirteenth, there flowed from this fear, this godly fear, a great delight in the holy commands of God; that is, a delight in the holy commands of God; that is, a delight to be comfortable unto them. "Blessed is the man that fears the Lord, that greatly delights in his commandments." (Psalm 112:1.) This confirms that which was said before, to wit, that this fear provokes to a holy and reverent use of the means; for that cannot be, when there is not a holy, yea, a great delight

213

in the commandments. Wherefore this fear makes the sinner to abhor that which is sin, because that is contrary to the object of his delight. A man cannot delight himself at the same time in things directly opposite one to another, as sin and the holy commandment is; therefore Christ says of the servant, he cannot love God and mammon, "You cannot serve God and mammon." If he cleaves to the one, he must hate and despise the other; there cannot at the same time be service to both, because that themselves are at enmity one with the other. So is sin and the commandment. Therefore, if a man delights himself in the commandment, he hates that which is opposite, which is sin; how much more when he greatly delights in the commandment? Now, this holy fear of God, it takes the heart and affections from sin, and sets them upon the holy commandment. Therefore such a man is rightly esteemed blessed. For no profession makes an alienation of the heart from sin, nor does any thing do that, when this holy fear is wanting. It is from this fear, then, that love to, and delight in the holy commandment flows; and so by that the sinner is kept from those falls and dangers of miscarrying that other professors are so subject to: he greatly delights in the commandment.

Lastly, there flows from this fear of God, enlargement of heart. "Then you shall see, and flow together, and your heart shall fear, and be enlarged." (Isaiah 60:5.) "Thine heart shall fear, and be enlarged," enlarged to God-ward, enlarged to his ways, enlarged to his holy people, enlarged in love after the salvation of others. Indeed, when this far of God is wanting, though the profession be never so famous, the heart is shut up and straitened, and nothing is done in that princely free spirit which is called "th[RKHI]e spirit of the fear of the Lord," (Psalm 51:12; Isaiah 11:2) but with grudging, legally, or with desire of vain-glory; this enlargedness of heart is wanting, for that slows from this fear of the Lord.

Thus have I showed you both what this far of God is, what it flows from, and also what does flow from it. I come now to show you some of the privileges of them that thus do fear the Lord.

Of the Privileges of them that thus do fear the Lord.

Having thus briefly handled in particular thus far this fear of God, I shall now show you certain of the excellent privileges of them that fear the Lord; not that they are not privileges that have been already mentioned, for what greater privileges than to have this fear producing in the soul such excellent things, so necessary for us for good, both with reference to this world and that which is to come? but because those fourteen above-named do rather flow from this grace of fear where it is than from a promise to the person that has it; therefore, I have chosen rather to discourse of them as the fruits and effects of fear than otherwise. Now, besides all these, there is entailed by promise to the man that has this fear many other blessed privileges, the which I shall now in a brief way lay open unto you.

First, then, that man that fears the Lord has a grant and a license "to trust in the Lord;" with an affirmation that he is their help and their shield. "You that fear the Lord, trust in the Lord, he is their helper and shield." (Psalm 115:11.) Now what a privilege is this! An exhortation in general to sinners as sinners to trust in him, is a privilege great and glorious; but for a man to be singled out from his neighbors, for a man to be spoken to from heaven, as it were by name, and to be told that God has given him a license, a special and peculiar grant to trust in him, this is abundantly more; and yet this is the grant that God has given that man. He has, I say, a license to do it, a license indicted by the Holy Ghost, and left upon record for those to be born that shall fear the Lord, to trust in him; and not only so, but as the text affirms, "He is their help and their shield." Their help under all their weaknesses and infirmities, and a shield to defend

215

them against all the assaults of the devil and this world. So, then, the man that fears the Lord is licensed to make the Lord his stay and God of his salvation, the succor and deliverer of his soul. He will defend him because his fear is in his heart. O you servants of the Lord, you that fear him, live in the comfort of this; boldly make use of it when you area in straits, and put your trust under the shadow of his wings, for indeed he would have you do so, because you do fear the Lord.

Second, God has also proclaimed concerning the man that fears the Lord, that he will also be his teacher and guide in the way that he shall choose; and has moreover promised concerning such that their soul shall dwell at ease. "What man is he that fears the Lord?" says David, "him shall he teach in the way that he shall choose." (Psalm 25:12.) Now, to be taught of God, what like it? yea, what like to be taught in the way that you shall choose? You have chosen the way to life, God's way; but perhaps your ignorance about it is so great, and those that tempt you to turn aside so many and so subtle, that they seem to outwit you, and confound you with their guile. Well, but the Lord whom you fear will not leave you to your ignorance, nor yet to your enemies' power or subtlety, but will take it upon himself to be your teacher and your guide, and that in the way that you have chosen. Hear, then, and behold your privilege, O you that fear the Lord; and whoever wanders, turns aside, and swerves from the way of salvation, whoever is benighted, and lost in the midst of darkness, you shall find the way to the heaven and the glory that you have chosen.

Further, he does not only say that he will teach them the way (for that must of necessity be supplied), but he says also that he will teach such in it: "Him shall he teach in the way that he shall choose." This argues that, as you shall know, so the way shall be made, by the communion that you shall have with God therein, sweet and pleasant to you;

for this text promises unto the man that fears the Lord the presence, company, and discovery of the mind of God, while he is going in the way that he has chosen. It is said of the good scribe, that he is instructed unto, as well as into the way of the kingdom of God. Instructed unto, that is, he has the heart and mind of God still discovered to him in the way that he has chosen, even all the way from this world to that which is to come, even until he shall come to the very gate and door of heaven. (Matthew 13:52.) What the disciples said was the effect of the presence of Christ, to wit, "that their hearts did burn within them while he talked to them by the way," (Luke 24) shall be also fulfilled in you; he will meet with you in the way, talk with you in the way; he will teach you in the way that you shall choose.

Third, do you fear the Lord? he will open his secret unto you, even that which he has hid and keeps close from all the world, to wit, the secret of his covenant, and of your concern therein. "The secret of the Lord is with them that fear him, and he will show them his covenant." (Psalm 25:14.) This, then, further confirms what was said but just above; his secret shall be with them, and his covenant shall be showed unto them. His secret, to wit, that which has been kept hid from ages and generations, that which he manifests only to the saints, or holy ones; that is, his Christ, for he it is that is hid in God, "and that no man can know but he to whom the Father shall reveal him." (Matthew 11:27.) But, oh! what is there wrapped up in this Christ, this secret of God? Why, all treasures of life, of heaven and happiness. "In him are hid all the treasures of wisdom and knowledge;" and "in him dwells the fullness of the Godhead bodily." (Colossians 2.) This also is that hidden one that is so full of grace to save sinners, and so full of truth and faithfulness to keep promise and covenant with them, that their eyes must needs convey, even by every glance they make upon his person, offices, and relation, such affecting ravishments to the heart, that it would please them that see him, even to be killed with that sight. This secret of the Lord shall be, nay is, with them that far him, for he dwells in their heart by faith. "And he will show them his covenant;" that is, the covenant that is confirmed of God in Christ, that everlasting and eternal covenant; and show him too that he himself is wrapped up therein as in a bundle of life with the Lord his God. These are the thoughts, pur- poses, and promises of God to them that far him.

Fourth, do you fear the Lord? his eye is always over you for good, to keep you from all evil. "Behold the eye of the Lord is upon them that fear him, on them that hope in his mercy, to deliver their soul from death, and to keep them alive in famine." (Psalm 33:18, 19.) His eye is upon them, that is, to watch over them for good. He that keeps Israel neither slumbers nor sleeps. His eyes are upon them, and he will keep them as a shepherd does his sheep: that is, from those wolves that seek to devour them, and to swallow them up in death. His eyes are upon them, for they are the object of his delight, the rarities of the world, in whom, says he, is all my delight. His eye is upon them, as I said before, to teach and instruct them. "I will teach you and instruct you in the way that you shall go; I will guide you with my eye." (Psalm 32:8; 2 Chronicles 7:15, 16.) The eye of the Lord, therefore, is upon them, not to take advantage of them, to destroy them for their sins, but to guide, to help, and deliver them from death, from that death that would feed upon their souls, "To deliver their soul from death, and to keep them alive in famine." Take death here for death spiritual, and death eternal; and the famine here, not for that that is for want of bread and water, but for that which comes on many for want of the word of the Lord, (Revelation 20:14; Amos 8:12) and then the sense is this, the man that fears the Lord shall neither die spiritually nor eternally; for God will keep him with his eye from all those things that would in such a manner kill him. Again, should there be a famine of the word, should there want both the word and them that preach it in the place that you do dwell, yet bread shall be given you, and your water shall be sure; you shall not die of the famine, because you fear God. I say, that man shall not, behold he shall not, because he fears God, and this the next head does yet more fully manifest.

Fifth, do you fear God; fear him for this advantage more and more. "Oh fear the Lord, you his saints, for there is not want to them that fear him. The young lions do want and suffer hunger, but they that seek the Lord, that fear him, shall want no good thing." (Psalm 34:9, 10.) Not anything that God sees good for them, shall those men want that fear the Lord. If health will do them good, if sickness will do them good, if riches will do them good, if poverty will do them good, if life will do them good, if death will do them good, then they shall not want them, neither shall any of these come nigh them if they will not do them good. The lions, the wicked people of the world that far not God, are not made sharers in this great privilege; all things fall out to them contrary, because they fear not God. In the midst of their sufficiency they are in want of that good that God puts into the worst things that the man that fears God does meet with in the world.

Sixth, do you fear God? He has given charge to the armies of heaven to look after, take charge of, to camp about, and to deliver you. "The angel of the Lord encamps about them that fear him, and delivers them." (Psalm 34:7.) This also is a privilege entailed to them, that in all generations fear the Lord. The angels, the heavenly creatures, have it in commission to take the charge of them that fear the Lord; one of them is able to slay of men in one night 185,000. These are they that camped about Elisha like horses of fire, and chariots of fire, when the enemy came to destroy him. They also helped Hezekiah against the band of the enemy, because he feared God. (2 Kings 6:17. Isaiah 37:36. Jeremiah 26:19.) "The angel of the Lord encamps round about them," that is, lest the enemy should set upon them on any side; but let him come when he will, behind or before, on this side or that, the angel of the Lord is there to defend them. "The angel." It may be spoken in the singular number, perhaps, to show that every one that fears God has his angel to attend on him and serve him. When the church, in the Acts, was told that Peter stood at the door and knocked; at first they counted the messenger mad, but when she did constantly affirm it, they said, "It is his angel." (Acts 12:13-15.) So Christ says of the children that came unto him, "Their angels behold the face of my Father which is in heaven." Their angels; that is, those of them that feared God had each of them his angel, who had a charge from God to keep them in their way. We little think of this, yet this is the privilege of them that fear the Lord; yea, if need be, they shall all come down to help them, and to deliver them, rather than, contrary to the mind of their God, they should by any be abused. "Are they not all ministering spirits, sent forth to minister for them that shall be heirs of salvation?" (Hebrews 1.)

But how do they deliver them? for so says the text, "The angel of the Lord encamps about them that fear him, and delivers them." Answer: The way that they take to deliver them that fear the Lord, is sometimes by smiting of their enemies with blindness, that they may not find them; and so they served the enemies of Lot. (Genesis 19:10,11.) Sometimes by smiting of them with deadly fear; and so they served those that laid siege against Samaria. (2 Kings 7:6.) And sometimes by smiting of them even with death itself; and thus they served Herod, after he had attempted to kill the apostle James, and also sought to vex certain others of the church. (Acts xii.) These angels that are servants to them that fear the Lord, are them that will, if God does bid them, revenge the quarrel of his servants upon the stoutest monarch on earth. This therefore is a glorious privilege of the men that fear the Lord. Alas, they are some of them so mean, that they are counted not worth taking notice of by the high ones of the world, but their betters do respect them; the angels of God count not themselves too good to attend on them, and camp about them to deliver them. This then is the man that has his angel to wait upon him, even he that fears God.

Seventh. Do you fear the Lord? Salvation is nigh unto you. "Surely his salvation is nigh them that fear him, that glory may dwell in their land." (Psalm 85:9.) This is another privilege for them that fear the Lord. I told you before that the angel of the Lord did encamp about them, but now he says, "his salvation is also nigh them;' the which, although it does not altogether exclude the conduct of angels, but include them, yet it looks further. "Surely his salvation, his saving pardoning grace, is nigh them that fear him;" that is, to save them out of the hand of their spiritual enemies. The devil, and sin, and death, do always wait even to devour them that fear the Lord, but to deliver them from these his salvation does attend them. So then if Satan tempts, here is their salvation nigh; if sin, by breaking forth, beguiles them, here is God's salvation nigh them; yea, if death itself shall suddenly seize upon them, why here is their God's salvation nigh them.

I have seen that great men's little children must go no whither without their nurses be at hand. If they go abroad, their nurses must go with them' if they go to meals, their nurses must go with them; if they go to bed, their nurses must go with them; yea, and if they fall asleep, their nurses must stand by them. Oh, my brethren, those little ones that fear the Lord, they are the children of the Highest, therefore they shall not walk alone, be at their spiritual meats alone, go to their sick-beds, or to their graves alone; the salvation of their God is nigh them, to deliver them from the evil. This is then the glory that dwells in the land of them that fear the Lord.

Eighth. Do you fear the Lord/ hearken yet again. "The mercy of the Lord is from everlasting to everlasting on them that fear him, and his righteousness unto children's children." (Psalm 103:17.) This still confirms what was last asserted, that is, that his salvation is nigh unto them; his salvation, that is, pardoning mercy that is nigh them. But mind it, there he says, it is nigh them: but here it is upon them. His mercy is upon them, it covers them all over, it encompasses them about as with a shield. Therefore they are said in another place to be clothed with salvation, and covered with the robe of righteousness. The mercy of the Lord is upon them, that is, as I said, to shelter and defend them. The mercy, the pardoning preserving mercy, the mercy of the Lord is upon them, who is he then that can condemn them? (Romans viii.)

But there yet is more behind: "The mercy of the Lord is from everlasting to everlasting on them." It was designed for them before the world was, and shall be upon them when the world itself is ended; from everlasting to everlasting, it is on them that fear him. This from everlasting to everlasting is that by which, in another place, the eternity of God himself is declared. "From everlasting to everlasting you are God." (Psalm 15:3.) The meaning then may be this: that so long as God has his being, so long shall the man that fears him find mercy at his hand. According to that of Moses: "The eternal God is your refuge, and underneath are the everlasting arms; and he shall thrust out the enemy before you, and say, Destroy them." (Deuteronomy 33:27.)

Child of God, you that fear God, here is mercy nigh you, mercy enough, everlasting mercy upon you. This is long-lived mercy. It will live longer than your sin, it will live longer than temptation, it will live longer than your sorrows, it will live longer than your persecutors. It is mercy from everlasting to contrive your salvation, and mercy to everlasting to weather it out with all your adversaries. Now what can hell and death do to him that has this mercy of God upon him? And this has the man that fears the Lord. Take that other blessed word, and oh, you man that fear the Lord, hang it like a chain of gold about your neck: "As the heaven is high above the earth, so great is his mercy towards them that fear him." (Psalm 103:11.) If mercy as big, as high, and as good as heaven itself will be a privilege, the man that fears God shall have a privilege.

Ninth. Do you fear God? "Like as a father pities his children, so the Lord pities them that fear him." (Psalm 103:13.)

The Lord pities them that fear him; that is, condoles and is affected, feels, and sympathizes with them in all their afflictions. It is a great matter for a poor man to be in this manner in the affections of the great and might, but for a poor sinner to be thus in the heart and affections of God (and they that fear him are so), this is astonishing to consider. "In his love and in his pity he redeemed them." In his love and in his pity! "In all their afflictions he was afflicted, and the angel of his presence saved them; in his love and in his pity he redeemed them, and bare them, and carried them all the days of old." (Isaiah lxiii. 9.) I say, in that he is said to pity them, it is as much as to say, he condoles, feels, and sympathizes with them in all their afflictions and temptations. So that this is the happiness of him that fears God; he has a God to pity him, and to be touched with all his miseries. It is said in Judges, "His soul was grieved for the miseries of Israel," (Judges 10:16;) and in the Hebrews, "He is touched with the feeling of our infirmities, and can succor them that are tempted." (chapter 4:15; 2:17,\ 18.)

But further, let us take notice of the comparison. "As a father pities his children, so the Lord pities them that fear

him." Here is not only pity, but the pity of a relation, a father. It is said in another place, "Can a woman (a mother)
forget her sucking child, that she should not have compassion on the son of her womb? yea, she may, yet will not I
forget you." The pity of neighbors and acquaintances helps
in times of distress, but the pity of a father and a mother is
pity with an over and above. "The Lord," says James, "is
very pitiful and of tender mercy." Pharoah called Joseph his
tender father, because he provided for him against the
famine, but how tender a father is God! how full of bowels,
how full of pity! (Jas. 5:11; Genesis 41:32.) It is said that
when Ephraim was afflicted, God's bowels were troubled
for him, and turned within him towards him. Oh that the
man that fears the Lord did but believe the pity and bowels
that are in the heart of God and his Father towards him!
(Jeremiah 31:18-20.)

Tenth. Do you fear God? "He will fill the desire of them
that fear him, he will hear their cry, and will save them."
(Psalm 144:19.) Almost all those places that make mention of
the men that far God, do insinuate as if they still were under
affliction, or in danger by reason of an enemy. But, I say,
here is still their privilege, their God is their father, and pities them. "He will fulfill the desire of them that fear him."
Where now is the man that fears the lord? let him hearken
to this. What do you say, poor soul? will this content you,
the Lord will fulfill your desires? It is intimated of Adonijah,
that David his father did let him have his head and his will
in all things. "His father," says the text, "had not displeased
him at any time in (so much as) saying, Why have you done
so?" (I Kings i. 6.) But here is more; here is a promise to
grant you the whole desire of your heart, according to the
prayer of holy David, "The Lord grant you, according to
your own heart, and fulfill all your counsel." And again,
"The Lord fulfill all your petitions." (Psalm 20.)

Oh you that fear the Lord, what is your desire? "All your desire," says David, "is all my salvation," (2 Samuel 23: 5); so say you, "All my salvation is all my desire." Well, the desire of your soul is granted you, yea, God himself has engaged himself even to fulfill this your desire. "He will fulfill the desires of them that far him; he will hear their cry, and will save them." Oh this desire when it comes, "what a tree of life will it be to you!" You desire to be rid of your present trouble; the Lord shall rid you out of trouble. You desire to be delivered from temptation; the Lord shall deliver you out of temptation. You desire to be delivered from your body of death; and the Lord shall change this your vile body; that it may be like to his glorious body. You desire to be in the presence of God, and among the angels in heaven; this your desire also shall be fulfilled, and you shall be made and equal to the angels. (Exodus 6:6; 2 Peter 2:9; Philippians 3:20, 21. Luke 16:22; 20:35,36.) "Oh! but it is long first." Well, learn first to live upon your portion in the promise of it, and that will make your expectation of it sweet. God will fulfill your desires, God will do it, though it tarry long: wait for it, because it will surely come; it will not tarry.

Eleventh, do you fear God? "The Lord takes pleasure in them that fear him." (Psalm 147:11,12.) 1. They that fear God are among his chief delights. He delights in his Son, he delights in his works, and takes pleasure in them that fear him. As a man takes pleasure in his wife, in his children, in his gold, in his jewels; so the man that fears the Lord is the object of his delight. He takes pleasure in their prosperity (Psalm 35:27), and therefore sends them health from the sanctuary, and makes them drink of the river of his pleasures. "They shall be abundantly satisfied with the fatness of your house, and you shall make them drink of the river of your pleasures." (Psalm 36:8.)

2. That or those that we take pleasure in, that or those we love to beautify and adorn with many ornaments. We

count no cost too much to be bestowed on those in whom we place our delight, and whom we make the object of our pleasure: and even that it is with God; "For the Lord takes pleasure in his people;" and what follows? "he will beautify the meek with salvation." (Psalm 149:4.)

3. Those in whom we delight, we take pleasure in their actions; yea, we teach them and give them such rules and laws to walk by as may yet make them that we love more pleasurable in our eyes; therefore, they that fear God, since they are the object of his pleasure, are taught to know how to please him in everything. (1 Thessalonians 4:1.) And hence it is said that he is ravished with their looks; that he delights in their cry, and that he is pleased with their walking. (Song of Solomon 4:9, Proverbs 15:8; 11:20.)

4. Those in whom we delight and take pleasure, many things we will bear and put up that they do, though they be not according to our minds. A man will suffer that in, and put up that at, the hand of the child or wife of his pleasure, that he will not pass by nor put up in another. They are my jewels, says God, even them that fear me; and I will spare them, in all their comings short of my will, "even as a man spares his own son that serves him." (Malachi 3:16,17.) Oh, how happy is the man that fears God! His good thoughts, his good attempts to serve him, and his good life pleases him, because he fears God.

You know how pleasing in our eyes the actions of our children are, when we know that they do what they do even of a reverent fear and awe of us; yea, though that which they do amounts but to little, we take it well at their hands, and are pleased therewith. The woman that case in her two mites into the treasury, cast in not much, for they both did but make one farthing, (Mark. 12:40-43;) yet how does the Lord Jesus trumpet her up; he had pleasure in her, and in her action. This, therefore, that the Lord takes pleasure in them that fear him, is another of their great privileges.

Twelfth. Do you fear God? The least dram of that fear gives the privilege to be blessed with the biggest saint. "He will bless them that fear the Lord, small and great." (Psalm 115:13.) This word "small" may be taken three ways:—

1. For those that are small in esteem, for those that are but little accounted of. (Judges 6:15; 1 Samuel 18:23.) Are you small or little in this sense? yet if you fear God, you are sure to be blessed. "He shall bless them that fear him, small and great," be though never so small in the world's eyes, in your own eyes, in the saints' eyes (as sometimes one saint is little in another saint's eye); yet you, because you fear God, are put among the blessed.

2. By small, sometimes is meant those that are but small of stature or young in years; little children, that are easily passed by and looked over; as those that sang Hosanna in the temple were when the Pharisees deridingly said of them to Christ, "Do you hear what these say?" (Matthew 21:16.) Well, but Christ would not despise them, of them that feared God, but preferred them by the Scripture testimony far before those that did contemn them. Little children, however small, and although of never so small esteem with men, shall also, if they fear the Lord, be blessed with the greatest saints: "He shall bless them that fear him, small and great."

3. By "small" may sometimes be meant those that are small in grace or gifts; these are said to be the least in the church, that is, under this consideration, and so are by it least esteemed. Thus also is that of Christ to be understood, "Inasmuch as you did it not to one of the least of these, you did it not to me." (I Corinthians 6:4; Matthew 25:45.)

Are you in your own thoughts, or in the thoughts of others, of these last small ones, small in grace, small in gifts, small in esteem upon this account? yet if you fear God, if you fear God indeed, you are certainly blessed with the best of saints. The least star stands as fixed as the biggest of them all in heaven: "He shall bless them that fear him, small and great." He shall bless them, that is, with the same blessing of eternal life; for the different degrees of grace in saints does not make the blessing, as to its nature, differ: it is the same heaven, the same life, the same glory, and the same eternity of felicity that they are in the text promised to be blessed with. That is observable which I mentioned before, where Christ at the day of judgment particularly mentions and owns the least; "Inasmuch as yet did it not to one of the last." The least then was there, in his kingdom and in his glory, as well as the biggest of all: "He shall bless them that fear him, small and great." The small are named first in the text, and are so the first in rank; it may be to show, that though they may be slighted, and little set by in the world, yet they are much set by in the eyes of the Lord.

Are great saints only to have the kingdom, and the glory everlasting? Are great works only to be rewarded? works that are done by virtue of great grace, and the abundance of the gifts of the Holy Ghost? No: "Whosoever shall give to drink unto one of these little ones a cup of cold water only, in the some of a disciple, verily I say unto you, he shall in no wise lose a disciple's reward." Mark, here is but a little gift, a cup of cold water, and that given to a little saint: but both taken special notice of by our Lord Jesus Christ. (Matthew 10:42.) "He will give reward to his servants the prophets, and to his saints, and to them that fear his name, small and great." (Revelation 11:18.) The small, therefore, among them that fear God, are blessed with the great, as the great, with the same salvation, the same glory, and the same eternal life; and they shall have, even as the great ones also shall, as much as they can carry; as much as their hearts, souls, bodies, and capacities can hold.

Thirteenth. Do you fear God? Why, the Holy Ghost has on purpose indited for you a whole psalm to sing concerning yourself. So that you may even as you are in your calling, bed, journey, or whenever, sing out your own blessed and happy condition to your own blessed and happy condition to your own comfort and the comfort of your fellows. The psalm is called the 128th Psalm; I will set it before you, both as it is in the reading and in the singing psalms:

"Blessed is every one that fears the Lord; that walks in his ways. For you shall eat the labor of your hands; happy shalt you be, and it shall be well with you. Thy wife shall be as a fruitful vine by the sides of your house: your children like olive plants round about your table. Behold, that thus shall the man be blessed that fears the Lord. The Lord shall bless you out of Zion: and you shall see the good of Jerusalem, all the days of your life. Yea, you shall see your children's children, and peace upon Israel."

As it is sung:
"Blessed are you that fear God,
And walks in his way:
For of your labor you shall eat;
Happy are you, I say.
Like fruitful vines on your house side,
So does your wife spring out;
Thy children stand like olive plants,
Thy table round about.
"Thus are you blest that fears God,
And he shall let you see,
The promised Jerusalem,
And her felicity.
You shall your children's children see,
And likewise grace on Israel,
Prosperity and peace."

And now I have done with the privileges when I have removed one objection.

Objection: But the scripture says, "perfect love casts out fear," and therefore it seems that saints, after that a spirit of adoption is come, should not fear, but do their duty, as another scripture says, without it. (1 John 4:18; Luke 1:74, 75.)

Answer: Fear, as I have showed you, may be taken several ways. 1. It may be taken for the fear of devils. 2. It may be taken for the fear of reprobates. 3. It may be taken for the fear that is wrought in the godly by the Spirit as a spirit of bondage; or, 4. It may be taken for the fear that I have been now discoursing of.

Now the fear that perfect loves casts out cannot be that son-like gracious fear of God, that I have in this last place been treating of; because that fear that love casts out has torment, but so has not the son-like fear. Therefore, the fear that love casts out is either that fear that is like the fear of devils and reprobates, or that fear that is begot in the heart by the Spirit of God as a spirit of bondage, or both; for, indeed, all these kinds of fear have torment, and therefore may be cast out; and are so by the spirit of adoption, which is called the spirit of faith and love, when he comes with power into the soul; so that without this fear we should serve him. But to argue from these texts that we ought not to fear God, or to mix fear with the spirit of adoption we are made very rogues; for not to far God, is by the Scripture applied to such. (Luke 23:40.) But for what I have affirmed the Scripture does plentifully confirm, saying, "Happy is the man that fears always." And again, "It shall be well with them that far God, that fear before him." Fear, therefore, the spirit of the fear of the Lord is a grace that greatly beautifies a Christian, his words, and all his ways. "Wherefore now let the fear of the Lord be upon you; take heed, and do it, for there is no iniquity with the Lord our God, nor respect of persons, nor taking of gifts."

I come now to make some use and application of this
doctrine.

The Use of this Doctrine

Having proceeded thus far bout this doctrine of the fear
of God, I now come to make some use and application of
the whole; and my

First. Use shall be a Use of Examination—Is this fear of
God such an excellent thing? Is it attended with so many
blessed privileges? Then this should put us, every soul of us,
upon a diligent examination of ourselves, to wit, whether
this grace be in us or not; for if it be, then you are one of
these blessed ones to whom belong these glorious privileges, for you have an interest in ever of them; but if it shall
appear that this grace is not in you, then your state is fear-
fully miserable, as has partly been manifest already, and will
further be seen in what comes after.

Now, the better to help you to consider, and not to miss
in finding out what you are in your self-examination, I will
speak to this—First. In general. Second. In particular.

First. In general. No man brings this grace into the
world with him. Every one by nature is destitute of it, for
naturally none fear God; there is no fear of God, none of
this grace of fear before their eyes; they do not so much as
know what it is, for this fear flows, as was showed before,
from a new heart, faith, repentance, and the like; of which
new heart, faith and repentance, if you be void, you are also
void of this godly fear. Men must have a mighty change of
heart and life, or else they are strangers to this fear of God.
Alas! how ignorant are the most of this! yea, and some are
not afraid to say they are not changed, nor desire so to be.
Can these fear God? can these be possessed with this grace
of fear? No, "Because they have no changes, therefore they
fear not God." (Psalm 36:1; Romans 3:18; Psalm 55:19.)

Wherefore, sinner, consider, whoever you are, that are destitute of this fear of God, you are void of all other graces for this fear, as also I have showed, flows from the whole stock of grace where it is. There is not one of the graces of the Spirit, but this fear is in the bowels of it; yea, as I may say, this fear is the flower and beauty of every grace; neither is there anything, let it look as much like grace as it will, that will be counted so indeed, if the fruit thereof be not this fear of God, wherefore, I say again, consider well of this matter, for as you shall be found with reference to this grace, so shall your judgment be. I have but briefly treated of this grace, yet have endeavored with words as fit as I could, to display it in its colors before your face; first, by showing you what this fear of God is, then what it flows from, as also what does flow from it; to which, as was said before, I have added several privileges that are annexed to this fear, that by all, if it may be, you may see it, if you have it, and yourself without it, if you have it not. Wherefore I refer you thither again for information in this thing; or, if you are loath to give the book a second reading, but will go on to the end, now you are gotten hither; then

Second, and particularly, I conclude with these several propositions concerning those that gear not God.

1. "That man that is proud, and of a high and lofty mind, fears not God." This is plain from the exhortation: "Be not high-minded, but fear." (Romans 11:20.) Here you see that a high mind and the fear of God are set in direct opposition the one to the other; and there is in them, closely concluded by the Apostle, that where indeed the one is, there cannot be the other; where there is a high mind, there is not the fear of God; and where there is the fear of God, the mind is not high, but lowly. Can a man at the same time be a proud man and fear God, too? Why, then, is it said God beholds every one that is proud, and abases him? and again, He beholds the proud afar off? He, therefore, that is proud

of his person, of his riches, of his office, of his parts, and the like, fears not God. It is also manifest further, for God resists the proud, which he would not do if he feared him; but in that he sets him at such a distance from him, in that he testifies that he will abase him and resist him, it is evident that he is not the man that has this grace of fear; for that man, as I have showed you, is the man of God's delight, the object of his pleasure. (Psalm 138:6; James 4:6; 1 Peter 5:5; Malachi 4:1.)

2. The covetous man fears not God. This also is plain from the word, because it setteth covetousness and the fear of God in direct opposition. Men that fear God are said to hate covetousness. (Exodus 18:21.) Besides, the covetous man is called an idolater, and is said to have no part in the kingdom of Christ and of God. And again: "The wicked boasts himself of his heart's desire, and blesses the covetous, whom the Lord abhors." (Ezekiel 33:31; Ephesians 5:4,5. Psalm 10:3.) Hearken to this, you that hunt the world to take it; you that care not how you get, so you get the world. Also you that make even religion your stalking-horse to get the world, you fear not God. And what will you do whose hearts go after your covetousness? you who are led by covetousness up and down, as it were, by the nose; sometimes to swear, to lie, to cozen, and cheat and defraud, when you can get the advantage to do it. You are far, very far from the fear of God. "You adulterers and adulteresses"—for so the covetous are called—"know you not that the friendship of the world is enmity with God; whosoever, therefore, will be a friend of the world is the enemy of God." (James 4:4.)

3. The riotous eaters of flesh have not the fear of God: for this is done "without fear." (Jude 12.) Gluttony is a sin little taken notice of, and as little repented of by those that use it; but yet it is odious in the sight of God, and the practice of it a demonstration of the want of his fear in the heart; yea, so odious is it, that God forbids that his people should

so much as company with such: "Be not," says he, "among wine-bibbers, among rioters eaters of flesh." (Proverbs 23:20.) And he further tells us, that they that are such, are spots and blemishes to those that keep them company, for indeed they fear not God. (2 Peter 2:13; Romans 13:13; 1 Peter 4:4.) Alas! some men are as if they were for nothing else born but to eat and to drink, and pamper their carcasses with the dainties of this world, quite forgetting why God sent them hither; but such, as is said, fear not God, and so consequently are of the number of them upon whom the day of judgment will come at unawares. (Luke 21:34.)

4. The liar is one that fears to God. This also is evident from the plain text, "You have lied," says the Lord, "and have not remembered me, nor laid it to your heart; have not I held my peace even of old, says the Lord, and you fear me not?" (Isaiah 57:1) What lie this was is not material; it was a lie, or a course of lying that is here rebuked, and the person or persons in this practice, as is said, were such as feared not God; a course of lying and the fear of God cannot stand together. This sin of lying is a common sin, and it walks in the world in several guises. There is the profane scoffing liar; there is the cunning, artificial liar; there is the hypocritical religious liar, with liars of other ranks and degrees; but none of them all have the fear of God, nor shall any of them, they not repenting, escape the damnation of hell: "All liars shall have their part in the lake that burns with fire and brimstone." (Revelation 21:8.) Heaven and the New Jerusalem are not a place for such. "And there shall in no wise enter into it anything that defiles, neither whatsoever works abomination, or makes a lie" (verse 27.) Therefore another scripture says that all liars are without. "For without are dogs, and sorcerers, and whoremongers, and murderers, and idolaters, and whosoever loves and makes a lie." (Revelation 22:15.) But this should not be their sentence,

judgment, and condemnation, if they that are liars were such as had in them this blessed fear of God.

5. They fear not God who cry unto him for help in the time of their calamity, and when they are delivered, they return to their former rebellion. This Moses, in a spirit of prophecy, asserts at the time of the mighty judgment of the hail. Pharoah then desired him to pray to God that he would take away that judgment from him. Well, so I will," said Moses, "But as for you and your servants, I know that you will not yet fear the Lord God," (Exodus 9:30.) As who should say, I know that so soon as this judgment is removed, you will to your old rebellion again. And what greater demonstration can be given that such a man fears not God, than to cry to God to be delivered from affliction to prosperity, and to spend that prosperity in rebellion against him? This is crying for mercies that they may be spent, or that we may have something to spend upon our lusts, and in the service of Satan. (James 4:1-3.) Of these God complains the 16th of Ezekiel, and in the 2nd of Hosea: "You have," says God, "taken your fair jewels of my gold, and of my silver, which I had given you, and made to yourself images," etc. (Ezekiel 16:17.) This was for want of the fear of God. Many of this kind there be now in the world, both of men, and women, and children. Have you not read this book of this number? Have you not cried for health when sick, for wealth when poor, when lame for strength, when in prison for liberty, and then spent all that you got by your prayer in the service of Satan, and to gratify your lusts? Look to it, sinner; these things are signs that with your heart you fear not God.

6. They fear not God that waylay his people, and seek to overthrow them, or to turn them besides the right path, as they are journeying from hence to their eternal rest. This is evident from the plain text, "Remember," says God "what Amalek did unto you by the way when you were come

forth out of Egypt, how he met you by the way, and smote the hindmost of you, even all that were feeble behind you, when you were faint and weary, and he feared not God." (Deuteronomy 25:17,18.) Many such Amalekites there be now in the world, that have set themselves against the feeble of the flock, against the feeble of the flock especially, still smiting them, some by power, some with the tongue, some in their lives and estates, some in their names and reputations, by scandal, slanders, and reproach; but the reason of this their ungodly practice is this, they fear not God; for did they fear him, they would be afraid to so much as think, much more of attempting to afflict and destroy, and calumniate the children of God; but such there have been, such there are, and such there will be in the world, for all men fear not God.

7. They fear not God who see his hand upon backsliders for their sins, and yet themselves will be backsliders also. "I saw," says God, "when for all the causes whereby backsliding Israel committed adultery, I had put her away, and given her a bill of divorce; yet her treacherous sister Judah feared not, but went and played the harlot also." (Jeremiah 3:8; 2:19.) Judah saw that her sister was put away, and delivered by God into the hands of Shalmanezer, who carried her away beyond Babylon; and yet, though she saw it, she went and played the harlot also; a sign of great hardness of heart, and of the want of the fear of God indeed; for this fear, had it been in her heart, it would have taught her to have trembled at the judgment that was executed upon her sister, and not have gone and played the harlot also; and not to have done it while her sister's judgments as in the sight and memory. But what is it that a heart that is destitute of the fear of God will not do? No sin comes amiss to such; yea, they will sin; they will do that themselves, for the doing of which they believe some are in hell-fire, and all because they fear not God.

But, pray observe, if those that take not warning when they see the hand of God upon backsliders, are said to have none of the fear of God, have they it, think you, that lay stumbling-blocks in the way of God's people, and use devices to cause them to backslide, yea, rejoice when they can do this mischief to any? and yet many of this sort there are in the world, that even rejoice when they see a professor fall into sin, and go back from his profession, as if they had found some excellent thing.

8. They fear not God who can look upon a land as wallowing in sin, and yet are not humbled at the sight thereof. "Have you," said God by the prophet to the Jews, "forgotten the wickedness of your fathers, and the wickedness of the kings of Judah, and the wickedness of their wives, which they have committed in the land of Judah, and in the streets of Jerusalem? They are not humbled to this day, neither have they feared nor walked in my law." (Jeremiah 44:8-10.) Here is a land full of wickedness, and none to bewail it, for they wanted the fear of God, and love to walk in his law. But how say you, if they that are not humbled at their own and others' wickedness are said not to fear, or have the fear of God, what shall we think or say of such that receive, that nourish and rejoice in such wickedness? Do they fear God? Yea, what shall we say of such that are the inventors and promoters of wickedness, as of oaths, beastly talk, or the like? Do they, do you think, fear God? Once again, what shall we say of such that cannot be content to be wicked themselves, and to invent and rejoice in other men's wickedness, but must hate, reproach, vilify and abuse those that they cannot persuade to be wicked? Do they fear God?

9. They that take more heed to their own dreams than to the word of God, fear not God. This also is plain from the word: "For in the multitude of dreams there are also divers vanities, but fear you God," (Ecclesiastes 5:7; Isaiah 8:20) that is, take heed unto his word. Here the fearing of God is op-

posed to our overmuch heeding dreams; and there is implied that it is for want of the fear of God that men so much
heed those things. What will they say to this that give more
heed to a suggestion that arises from their foolish hearts, or
that is cast in thither by the devil, than they do to the holy
word of God? These are "filthy dreamers." Also, what shall
we say to those that are more confident of the mercy of God
to their soul, because he has blessed them with outward
things, than they are afraid of his wrath and condemnation,
though the whole of the word of God does fully verify the
same? These are "filthy dreamers" indeed.

A dream is either real, or so by way of semblance, and
so some men dream sleeping, and some waking. (Isaiah
29:7.) And as those that a man dreams sleeping are cause, either by God, Satan, business, flesh, or the like, so are they
that a man dreams waking, to pass by those that we have in
our sleep. Men, when bodily awake, may have drams, that
is, visions from heaven; such are all they that have a tendency to discover to the sinner his state, or the state of the
church, according to the word. But those that are from Satan, business, and the flesh, are such (especially the first and
last, to wit, from Satan and the flesh) as tend to embolden
men to hope for good in a way disagreeing with the word
of God. These Jude calls "filthy dreamers," such whose principles were their dreams, and they led them to defile the
flesh, that is, by fornication and uncleanness; to despise
dominion, that the reins might be laid upon the neck of
their lusts; "to speak evil of dignities;" of those that God had
set over them, for their governing in all the law and testament of Christ; these dreamt that to live like brutes, to be
greedy of gain, and to take away for it, as Cain and Balaam
did by their wiles, the lives of the owners thereof, would go
for good coin in the best of trials. These also Peter speaks of
in 2 Peter 2; and he makes their dreams that Jude calls so,
their principle and errors in life and doctrine. You may read

of them in that whole chapter, where they are called cursed children, and so by consequence such as fear not God.

10. They fear not God, who are sorcerers, adulterers, false swearers, and that oppress the hireling of his wages. It is a custom with some men to keep back by fraud from the hireling that which by covenant they agreed to pay for their labor; pinching, I say, and paring from them their due that of right belongs to them, to the making of them cry in the ears of the Lord of Sabaoth. (James 5:4.) These fear not God; they are reckoned among the worst of men, and in their day of account God himself will bear witness against them. "And I," says God, "will come near to you to judgment, and I will be a swift witness against false swearers, and against the adulterers, and against those that oppress the hireling in his wages, the widow and the fatherless, and that turn aside the stranger from his right, and fear not me, says the Lord."

11. They fear not God, who instead of pitying of, rail at God's people in their affliction, temptations, and persecutions, and rather rejoice and skip for joy, than sympathize with them in their sorrow. Thus did David's enemies, thus did Israel's enemies, and thus did the thief; he railed at Christ when he hanged upon the cross, and was for that, even by his fellow, accounted for one that feared not God. (Luke 23:40; Psalm 35:1,22-26. Read Obadiah 10-15; Jeremiah 48:2-7.) This is a common thing among the children of men, even to rejoice at the hurt of them that fear God, and it arises even of an inward hatred to godliness. "They hate you," says Christ, "because they hated me." Therefore Christ takes what is done to his, in this, as done unto himself, and so to holiness of life. But this falls hard upon such as despise at, and rejoice to see God's people in their griefs, and that take the advantage, as dogged Shimel did, to augment the griefs and afflictions of God's people. (2 Samuel 16:5-8.) There fear not God, they do this of enmity, and their sin is such as will hardly be blotted out. (1 Kings 2:8,9.)

12. They fear not God, who are strangers to the effects of fear. "If I be a master, where is my fear?" That is, show that I am so by your fear of me in the effects of your fear of me. "You offer polluted bread upon my altar." This is not a sign that you fear me, you offer the blind for sacrifices, where is my fear? you offer the lame and the sick, these are not the effects of the fear of God. (Malachi 1:6-8.) Sinner, it is one thing to say, I fear God, and another to fear him indeed. Therefore, as James says, "show me your faith by your works," so here God calls for a testimony of your fear by the effects of fear. I have already showed you several effects of fear; if you are a stranger to them, you are a stranger to this grace of fear. Therefore, to conclude this, it is not a feigned profession that will do; nothing is good here but what is salted with this fear of God, and they that fear him are men of truth, men of singleness of heart, perfect, upright, humble, holy men; wherefore, perfect, upright, humble, holy men; wherefore, reader, examine, and again, I say, examine, and lay the word and your heart together, before that you concludes that you fear God.

What! fear God, and in a state of nature? fear God, without a change of heart and life? What! fear God, and be proud and covetous, a wine-bibber, and a riotous eater of flesh! How! fear God and a liar, and one that cries for mercies to spend them upon your lusts; this would be strange. True, you may fear as devils do, but what will that profit? You may by your fear be driven away from God, from his worship, people, and ways, but what will that avail? It may be you may so fear at present, as to be a little stopped in your sinful course; perhaps you have got a knock from the word of God, and are at present a little dazzled and hindered from being in your former and full career after sin; but what of that? If by the fear that you have your heart is not united to God, and to the love of his Son, word, and people, your fear is nothing worth.

Supplement: *The Fear of God* by John Bunyan

Many men also are forced to fear God, as underlings are forced to fear those that are by force above them. If you only thus fears God, it is but a false fear; it flows not from love to God: this fear brings not willing subjection, which indeed brings the effect of right fear: but being over-mastered, like an hypocrite, you subjected yourself, (Proverbs 18:44) by feigned obedience, being forced, I say, by mere dread to do it. (Psalm 66:3.)

It is said of David, that "the fame of him went out into all lands, and the Lord brought the fear of him upon all nations." (1 Chronicles 14:17) But what, did they now love David? did they now choose him to be their king? No verily; they many of them rather hated him, and when they could, made resistance against him. They did even as you do, feared, but did not love; feared, but did not choose his government that ruled over them. It is also said of Jehoshaphat, when God had subdued before him Ammon, Moab, and Mount Seir, that "the fear of God was upon all the kingdoms of these countries, when they heard that the Lord fought against the enemies of Israel." (2 Chronicles 20:29.) But, I say, was this fear, that is called now the fear of God, anything else but a dread of the greatness and power of the king? No verily, nor did that dread bring them into a willing subjection to, and liking of his laws and government; it only made them, like slaves and underlings, stand in fear of his executing the vengeance of God upon them.

Therefore still, notwithstanding this fear, they were rebels to him in their hearts, and when occasion and advantage offered themselves, they showed it by rising in rebellion against Israel. This fear, therefore, provoked but feigned and forced obedience, a right emblem of the obedience of such, who being still enemies in their minds to God, are forced by virtue of present conviction to yield a little, even of fear, to God, to his word, and to his ordinances. Reader, whoever you are, think of this; it is your concern, therefore do it, and examine, and examine again, and look diligently to your heart in your examination, that it beguile you not about this your so great concern, as indeed the fear of God is.

One thing more, before I leave you, let me warn you of. Take heed of deferring to fear the Lord. Some men, when they have had conviction upon their heart that the fear of God is not in them, have, through the overpowering of their corruptions, yet deferred and put off the fear of God from them, as it is said of them in Jeremiah: "This people have a revolting and a rebellious heart, they are revolted and gone; neither said they in their heart, Let us now fear the Lord." (Jeremiah 5:22-24.) They saw that the judgments of God attended them because they did not yet fear God, but that conviction would not prevail with them to say, Let us now fear the Lord. They were for deferring to fear them still; they were for putting off his fear from them longer. sinner, have you deferred to fear the Lord? is your heart still so stubborn as not to say yet, Let us fear the Lord? Oh, the Lord has taken notice of this your rebellion, and is preparing some dreadful judgment for you. "Shall I not visit for these things?" says the Lord, "shall not my soul be avenged of such a nation as this?" (ver. 29.) Sinner, why should you pull vengeance down upon you? why should you pull vengeance down from heaven upon you? Look up, perhaps you have already been pulling this great while, to pull it down upon you. Oh, pull no longer why should you be your own executioner? Fall down upon your knees, man, and up with your heart and your hands to the God that dwells in the heavens; cry, yea cry aloud, Lord, unite my heart to fear your name, and do not harden my heart from your fear! Thus holy men have cried before you, and by crying have prevented judgment.

Before I leave this use, let me give you a few things that, if God will, may provoke you to fear the Lord.

1. The man that fears not God, carries it worse towards him than the beast, the brute beast, does carry it towards that man. "The fear of you, and the dread of you, shall be upon every beast of the earth, yea, and upon every fowl of the air, and upon all that moves upon the earth, and upon all the fishes in the sea." (Genesis 9:2.)

Mark, all my creatures shall fear you, and dread you, says God. None of them shall be so hardy as to cast off all reverence of you. But what a shame is this to man, that God should subject all his creatures to him, and he should refuse to stoop his heart to God! The beast, the bird, the fish, and all, have a fear and dread of man, yea, God has put it in their hearts to fear man, and yet man is void of ear and dread, I mean of godly far of him, that thus lovingly has put all things under him. Sinner, are you not ashamed, that a silly cow, a sheep, yea, a swine, should better observe the law of his creation, than you do the law of your God?

2. Consider, he that will not fear God, God will make him fear him whether he will or no. That is, he that does not, will not now so fear him, as willingly to bow before him, and put his neck into his yoke, God will make him fear him when he comes to take vengeance on him. Then he will surround him with terror and with fear on every side, fear within, and fear without; fear shall be in the way, even in the way that you go when you are going out of this world: and that will be a dreadful fear. (Ecclesiastes 12:5.) "I will bring their fears upon them, says the Lord." (Isaiah 66:4.)

3. He that fears not God now, the Lord shall laugh at his fears then. Sinner, God will be even with all them that choose not to have his fear in their hearts: for as he calls and they hear not now, so they shall cry, yea, howl then, and he will laugh at their fears. "I will laugh," says he, "as their destruction, I will mock when their fear comes, when your fear comes as desolation, and your destruction like a whirlwind, when distress and anguish comes upon you; then shall you

call upon me, but I will not answer; you shall seek me early, but you shall not find me, for that you hated knowledge, and did not choose the fear of the Lord." (Proverbs 1:26-29.)

Sinner! you think to escape the fear; but what will you do with the pit? You think to escape the pit; but what will you do with the snare. The snare, say you, what is that? I answer, it is even the work of your own hands. "The wicked is snared in the works of his own hands, he is snared by the words of his lips." (Psalm 9:16; Proverbs 12:13.)

Sinner! what will you do when you come into this snare; that is, into the guilt and terror that your sins will snaffle you with, when they, like a cord, are fastened about your soul? This snare will bring you back again to the pit, which is hell, and then how will you do to be rid of your fear? The fear, pit, and the snare shall come upon you, because you fear not God.

Sinner! are you one of them that have cast off fear? Poor man, what will you do when these three things beset you? whither will you fly for help? and where will you leave your glory? If you flee from the fear, there is the pit, if you flee from the pit, there is the snare.

The second Use is an Exhortation to fear God.

My next word shall be an Exhortation to fear God. I man, an exhortation to saints. "Oh fear the Lord, you his saints, for there is not want to them that fear him." Not but that every saint does fear God, but, as the Apostle says in another case, "I beseech you, do it more and more." The fear of the Lord, as I have showed you, is a grace of the new covenant, as other saving graces are, and so is capable of being stronger or weaker as other graces are. Wherefore, I beseech you, fear him more and more.

It is said of Obadiah, that he feared the Lord greatly: every saint fears the Lord, but every saint does not greatly fear him. Oh there are but few Obadiahs in the world! I mean, among the saints on earth. (See the whole relation of him, 1 Kings 18.) As Paul said of Timothy, I have none like-minded, so it may said of some concerning the fear of the Lord; they have scarce a fellow. So it was with Job: "There is none like him in all the earth, one that fears God," etc. (Job 1:8.) There was even none in Job's day that feared God like him, no, there was not one like him in all the earth, but doubtless there were more in the world that feared God; but this fearing of him greatly, that is the thing that saints should do, and that was the thing that Job did do, and in that he did outstrip his fellows. It is also said of Hananiah, that "he was a faithful man, and feared God above many." (Nehemiah 7:2.) He also had got, as to the exercise of, and growth in, this grace, the start of many of his brethren. "He feared God above many." Now then, seeing this grace admits of degrees, and is in some stronger, and in some weaker, let us be all awakened, as to other graces, so to this grace also. That like as you abound in everything, in faith, in utterance, in knowledge, and in all diligence, and in your love to us; see that you abound in this grace also. I will labor to enforce this exhortation upon you by several motives.

First, let God's distinguishing love to you be a motive to you to fear him greatly. He has put his fear in your heart, and has not given that blessing to your neighbor; perhaps not to your husband, your wife, your child, or your parent. Oh what an obligation should this consideration lay upon your heart, greatly to fear the Lord! Remember also, as I have showed in the first part of this book, that this fear of the Lord is his treasure, a choice jewel, given only to favorites, and to those that are greatly beloved. Great gifts naturally tend to oblige, and will do so, I trust, with you, when you shall ingeniously consider it. It is a sign of a very bad nature when the contrary shows itself; could God have done more for you than to have put his fear in your heart? This is better than to have given you a place, even in heaven, without it. Yea, had he given you all faith, all knowledge, and the tongue of men and angels, and a place in heaven to boot, they had all been short of this gift of the fear of God in your heart. Therefore love it, nourish it, exercise it, use all means to cause it to increase and grow in your heart, that it may appear it is set by, at your hand, poor sinner.

Second, another motive to stir you up to grow in this grace of the fear of God, may be the privileges that it lays you under. What, or where will you find in the Bible so many privileges so affectionately entailed to any grace, as to this of the fear of God? God speaks of this grace, and of the privileges that belong unto it, as if, to speak with reverence, he knew not how to have down blessing of the man that has it. It seems to me as if this grace of fear is the darling grace, the grace that God sets his heart upon at the highest rate. At it were, he embraces and hugs, and lays the man in his bosom, that has, and grows strong in this grace of the fear of God. See again the many privileges in which the man is interested that has this grace in his heart; and see also that there are but few of them, wherever mentioned, but have entailed to them the pronunciation of a blessing, or else that man is spoken of by way of admiration.

Third, another motive may be this. The man that grows in this grace of the fear of the Lord will escape those evils that others will fall into. Where this grace is, it keeps the soul from final apostasy: "I will put my fear in their hearts, and they shall not depart from me." (Jeremiah 32:40.) But yet, if there be not an increase in this grace, much evil may attend and be committed notwithstanding. There is a child that is healthy, and has its limbs, and can go, but it is careless. Now, the evil of carelessness does disadvantage it very much. Carelessness is the cause of stumblings, of falls, of knocks; and that it falls into the dirt, yea, that sometimes it is burned, or almost drowned. And thus it is even with God's people that fear him, because they add not to their fear a care of growing more in the fear of God; therefore they reap damage; whereas, were they more in his fear, it would keep them better, deliver them more, and preserve them from these snares of death.

Fourth, another motive may be this: To grow in this grace of the fear of God, is the way to be kept always in a conscientious performance of Christian duties. An increase in this grace, I say, keeps every grace in exercise; and the keeping of our graces in their due exercise produces a conscientious performance of duties. You have a watch, perhaps, in your pocket; but the hand will not as yet be kept in any good order, but does always give you the lie as to the hour of the day. Well, but what is the way to remedy this but to look well to the spring and the wheels within? for if they indeed go right, so will the hand do also. This is your case in spiritual things. You are a gracious man, and the fear of God is in you; but yet, for all that, one cannot well tell, by your life, what time a-day it is. You give no true and constant sign that you are indeed a Christian. Why, the reason is, you do not look well to this grace of the fear of God. You do not grow and increase in that, but suffers your heart to grow careless and hard, and so your life remiss and worldly. Job's growing great in the fear of God made him eschew evil. (Job 1:2.)

Fifth, another motive is: This is the way to be wise indeed. A wise man fears and departs from evil. It does not say, a wise man has the grace of fear, but a wise man fears, that is, puts this grace into exercise. There is no greater sign of wisdom that to grow in this blessed grace. Is it not a sign of wisdom to depart from sins, which are the snares of death and hell? Is it not a sign of wisdom for a man yet more and more to endeavor to interest himself in the love and protection of God? Is it not a high point of wisdom for a man to be always doing of that which lays him under the conduct of angels? Surely this is wisdom; and if it be a blessing to have this fear, is it not wisdom to increase in it? Doubtless it is the highest point of wisdom, as I have showed before; therefore grow therein.

Sixth, another motive may be this: It is seemly for saints to fear, and increase in this fear of God.

1. He is your Creator: is it not seemly for creatures to fear and reverence their Creator?
2. He is your King: is it not seemly for subjects to fear and reverence their King?
3. He is your Father: is it not seemly for children to reverence and fear their Father; yea, and to do it more and more?

Seventh, another motive may be: It is honorable to grow in this grace of fear. When Ephraim spoke trembling, he exalted himself in Israel. (Hosea 13:1.) Truly, to fear, and to abound in this fear, is a sign of a very princely spirit; and the reason is, when I greatly fear my God, I am above the fear of all others; nor can anything in this world, be it never so terrible and dreadful, move me at all to fear them; and hence it is that Christ counsels us to fear: "And I say unto you, my friends, says he, fear not them that kill the body, and after that have no more than they can do." (Ay, but this is a high pitch; how should we come by such princely spirits?) Well, I will forewarn you whom you shall fear, and by fearing of him arrive at this pitch: "Fear him who, after he has killed, has power to cast into hell; yea, I say unto you, fear him." (Luke 12:4, 5.) Indeed, this true fear of God sets a man above all the world; and therefore it says again, "Fear not their fear, but sanctify the Lord God in your heart, and let him be your fear, and let him be your dread." (Isaiah 8.)

Your great, ranting, swaggering roosters, that are ignorant of the nature of the fear of God, count it a poor, sneaking, pitiful, cowardly spirit in men to fear and tremble before the Lord, but who looks back to jails and gibbets, to the sword and burning stake, shall see that there, in them, has been the most mighty and invincible spirit that has been in the world.

Yea, see if God does not count that the growth of his people in this grace of fear is that which makes them honorable, when he positively excludes those from a dwelling-place in his house that do not honor them that fear him. (Psalm 15:4.) And he says, moreover, "A woman that fears the Lord, she shall be praised." If the world and godless men will not honor these, they shall be honored some way else. Such, says he, "that honor me I will honor," and they shall be honored in heaven, in the churches, and among the angels.

Eighth, another motive to grow in this fear of God may be, this fear, and the increase of it, qualifies a man to be put in trust with heavenly and spiritual things, yea, and with earthly things too.

1. For heavenly and spiritual things. "My covenant," says God, "was with Levi of life and peace, and I gave them to him, for the fear wherewith he feared me, and was afraid before my name." (Malachi 2:5.) Behold what a gift, what a mercy, what a blessing this Levi is entrusted with; to wit, with God's everlasting covenant, and with the life and peace that is wrapped up in this covenant. But why is it given to him? the answer is, "For the fear wherewith he feared me, and was afraid before my name." And the reason is good, for this fear of God teaches a man to put a due estimation upon every gift of God bestowed upon us; also it teaches us to make use of the same with reverence of his name, and respect to his glory in most godly wise, all which becomes him that is entrusted with any spiritual gift. The gift here was given to Levi to minister to his brethren doctrinally thereof, for he, says God, shall teach Jacob my statutes and Israel my law. See also Exodus 17:21 and Nehemiah 7:2, with many other places that might be named, and you will find that men fearing God and hating covetousness; that men that

fear God above others, are entrusted by God, yea, and by his church too, with the trust and ministration of spiritual things before any other in the world.

2. For earthly things. This fear of God qualifies a man to be put in trust with them rather than with another. Therefore God made Joseph lord of all Egypt; Obadiah, steward of Ahab's house; Daniel, Mordecai, and the three children were set over the province of Babylon; and this by the wonderful working hand of God, because he had to dispose of earthly things now, not only in a common way, but for the good of his people in special. True, when there is no special matter or thing to be done by God in a nation for his people, then who will, that is, whether they have grace or no, may have the dispose of those things; but if God has any thing in special to bestow upon his people of this world's goods, then he will entrust it in the hands of men fearing God. Joseph must now be made lord of Egypt, because Israel must be kept from starving. Obadiah must now be made steward of Ahab's house, because the Lord's prophets must be hid from, and fed in despite of, the rage and bloody mind of Jezebel. Denial, with his companions, and Mordecai also, they were all exalted to earthly and temporal dignity, that they might in that state, they being men that abounded in the fear of God, be serviceable to their brethren in their straits and difficulties. (Genesis 42:18; 41:39, 1 Kings 18:3; Esther, the two last chapters; Daniel 2:48; 3:30; 5:29; 6:1-3.)

Ninth, another motive to grow in this grace of fear is, Where the fear of God in the heart of any is not growing, there no grace thrives, nor duty done as it should.

1. There no grace thrives, neither faith, hope, love, nor any grace. This is evident from that general exhortation, "Perfect holiness is the fear of God." (2 Corinthians 7:1.) Perfect holiness, what is that? but, as James says of patience, let every grace have its perfect work, that you may be perfect and entire, lacking nothing. (James 1.) But this cannot be

done but in the fear of God, yea, in the exercise of that grace, and so consequently in the growth of it, for there is no grace but grows by being exercised. If, then, you would be perfect in holiness, if you would have ever grace that God has put into your souls grow and flourish into perfection, lay them, as I may say, a-soak in this grace of fear, and do all in the exercise of it; for a little done in the fear of the Lord is better than the revenues of the wicked. And again, the Lord will not suffer the soul of the righteous, the soul that lives in the fear of the Lord, to famish, but he casts away the abundance of the wicked. Bring abundance to God, and if it be not seasoned with godly fear, it shall not be acceptable to him, but loathsome and abominable in his sight; for it does not flow from the spirit of the fear of the Lord.

2. Therefore, where there is not a growth in this far, there is no duty done so acceptably. This flows from that which goes before, for if grace rather decays than grows, where this grace of fear is not in the growth and increase thereof, then duties in their glory and acceptableness decay likewise.

Tenth, another motive to stir you up to grow in the increase of this grace of fear is, It is a grace, do but abound therein, that will give you great boldness both with God and men. Job was a man, a none-such in his day, for one that feared God; and who so bold with God as Job? who so bold with God, and who so bold with men as he? How bold was he with God, when he wishes for nothing more than that he might come even to his seat, and concludes that if he could come at him, he would approach even as a prince unto him, and as such would order his cause before him. (Job 23:3-7; 31:35-37.) Also before his friends, how bold was he! For ever as they laid to his charge that he was an hypocrite, he repels them with the testimony of a good conscience, which good conscience he got, and kept, and maintained by increasing

251

in the fear of God; yea, his conscience was kept so good by this grace of fear, for it was by that that he eschewed evil, that it was common with him to appeal to God when accused, and also to put himself for his clearing under most bitter curses and imprecations. (Job 13:3-9; 18; 19:22,24; 31.)

This fear of God is it that keeps the conscience clean and tender, and so free from much of that defilement that even a good man may be afflicted with, for want of his growth in this fear of God. Yea, let me add, if a man can with a good conscience say that he desires to fear the name of God, it will add boldness to his soul in his approaches in to the presence of God. "O Lord," said Nehemiah, "I beseech you let your ear be attentive to the prayer of your servant, and servants, who desire to fear your name." (Nehemiah 1:11.) He pleaded his desire of fearing the name of God, as an argument with God to grant him his request; and the reason was, because God had promised before "to bless them that fear him, both small and great." (Psalm 115:13.)

Eleventh, another motive to stir you up to fear the Lord, and to grow in this fear, is, By it you may have your labors blessed to the saving of the souls of others. It is said of Levi, of whom mention was made before, that he feared God, and was afraid before his name, that he saved others from their sins: "The law of truth was in his lips, and he walked with me in peace and equity, and did turn away many from iniquity." (Malachi 2:6.) The fear of God that dwelt in his heart showed its growth in the sanctifying of the Lord by his life and words, and the Lord also blessed this his growth herein, by blessing his labors to the saving of his neighbors.

Would you save your husband, your wife, your children, etc? then be greatly in the fear of God. This Peter teaches: "Wives," says he, "be subject to your own husbands, that if any obey not the word, they may, without the word, be won by the conversation of the wives, while they behold your chaste conversation, coupled with fear." (1 Peter 3:1,2.) So, then if wives and children, yea, if husbands, wives, children, servants, etc., did but better observe this general rule of Peter, to wit, of letting their whole conversation be coupled with fear, they might be made instruments in God's hand of much more good than they are; but the misery is, the fear of God is wanting in actions, and that is the cause that so little good is done by those that profess. It is not a conversation that is coupled with a profession, for a great profession may be attended with a life that is not good, but scandalous; but it is a conversation coupled with fear of God, that is, with the impressions of the fear of God upon it; that is convicting, and that ministers the awakenings of God to the conscience, in order to saving the unbeliever. Oh, they are a sweet couple, to wit, a Christian conversation coupled with fear!

The want of this fear of God is that that has been a stumbling-block to the blind oftentimes. Alas! the world will not be convinced by your talk, by your notions, and by the great profession that you make, if they see not therewith mixed the lively impressions of the fear of God; but will, as I said, rather stumble and fall, even at your conversation and at your profession itself. Wherefore, to prevent this mischief, that is, of stumbling of souls, while you make your profession of God, by a conversation not becoming your profession, God bids you fear him; implying that a good conversation, coupled with fear, delivers the blind world from those falls that otherwise they cannot be delivered from: "You shall not curse the deaf, nor put a stumbling-block before the blind, but you shall fear your God; I am the Lord." (Leviticus 19:14.) But you shall fear your God; that is the remedy that will prevent their stumbling at you, at whatever they stumble. Wherefore Paul says to Timothy, "Take heed to yourself, and to your doctrine; continue in them for in so doing you shall both save yourself and them that hear you." (I Timothy 4:16.)

Twelfth, another motive to fear, and to grow in this fear of God is, This is the way to engage God to deliver you from many outward dangers, whoever falls therein. (Psalm 34:7.) This is proved from that of the story of the Hebrew mid-wives: "The midwives," said Moses, "feared God, and did not drown the men-children, as the king had commanded, but saved them alive." And what follows? "Therefore God dealt well with the midwives; and it came to pass that be-cause the midwives feared God, that he made them houses" (Exodus 1); that is, he sheltered them, and caused them to be hid from the rage and fury of the king, and that perhaps in some of the houses of the Egyptians themselves; for why might not the midwives be there hid as well as was Moses even in the King's court? And how many times are they that fear God said to be delivered both by God and holy angels? as also I have already showed.

Thirteenth, another motive to fear, and to grow in this fear of God is, This is the way to be delivered from errors and damnable opinions. There are some that perish in their righteousness; that is an error. There be some that perish in their wickedness; and that is an error also. Some, again, prolong their lives by their wickedness, and others are righteous over-much; and also some are over-wise; and all these are snares, and pits, and holes. But then, you say, how shall I escape? Indeed, that is the question; and the Holy Ghost resolves it thus: "He that fears God shall come out of them all." (Ecclesiastes 8:15-18.)

Fourteenth, another motive to fear, and to grow in this fear of God is, such have leave, be they never so dark in their souls, to come boldly to Jesus Christ, and to trust in him for life. I told you before that they that feared God have, in the general, a license to trust in him; but now I tell you, and that in particular, that they, and they especially, may do it, and that though in the dark. You that sit in dark-ness, and have no light, if this grace of fear be alive in your hearts, you have this boldness: "Who is among you that fears the Lord," (mark, that fears the Lord), "and obeys the voice of his servant, that walks in darkness, and has no light? Let him trust in the name of the Lord, and stay upon his God." (Isaiah 1:10.) It is no small advantage, you know, when men have to deal in difficult matters, to have a patent or license to deal; now to trust in the Lord is a difficult thing, yet the best and most gainful of all. But then, some will say, since it is so difficult, how may we do without danger? Why, the text gives a license, a patent to them to trust in his name, that have his fear in their hearts: "Let him trust in the name of the Lord, and stay upon his God."

Fifteenth, another motive to fear and grow in this grace of fear is, God will own and acknowledge such to be his, whoever he rejects; yea, he will distinguish and separate them from all others in the day of his terrible judgments. He will do with them as he did by those that sighed for the abominations that were done in the land (Ezekiel 9) command the man that had his inkhorn by his side, "to set a mark upon their foreheads," that they might not fall in that judgment with others. So in Malachi 3, God said plainly of them that feared the Lord, and that thought upon his name, that they should be writ in his book: "A book of remembrance was written before him for them that feared the Lord, and that thought upon his name; and they shall be my, says the Lord of hosts, in the day that I make up my jewels, and I will spare them as a man spares his own son that serves him." (Malachi 3:16, 17.) Mark; he both acknowledges them for his, and also promises to spare them, as a man would spare his own son; yea, and moreover will wrap them up as his chief jewels with himself in the bundle of life. Thus much for the motives.

How to grow in this Fear of God.

Having given you these motives to the duty of growing in this fear of God, before I leave this use I will, in few words, show you how you may grow in this fear of God.

First, then, if you would grow in this fear of God, learn aright to distinguish of fear in general. I mean, learn to distinguish between that fear that is godly and that which in itself is indeed ungodly fear of God; and know them well the one from the other, lest the one, the fear that in itself indeed is ungodly, get the place, even the upper hand of that which truly is godly fear. And remember, the ungodly fear of God is by God himself counted an enemy to him and hurtful to his people, and is therefore most plentifully forbidden in the word. (Genesis 1:15; 26:24; 46:3; Exodus 14:13; 20:20; Numbers 14:9; 21:34; Isaiah 41:10, 13, 14; 43:1; 44:2, 8; 54:4; Jeremiah 33:10; Daniel 10:12, 19; Joel 2:21; Haggai 2:4; Zechariah 8:13.)

Second, if you would grow in this godly fear, learn rightly to distinguish it from that fear in particular that is godly but for a time; even from that fear that is wrought by the spirit as a spirit of bondage. I say, learn to distinguish this from that, and also perfectly to know the bounds that God has set to that fear that is wrought by the spirit as a spirit of bondage; lest, instead of growing in the fear that is to abide with your soul for ever, you be overrun again with that first fear which is to abide with you but till the Spirit of adoption come. And that you may not only distinguish them one from the other, but also keep each in its due place and bounds, consider in general of what has already been said upon this head; and in particular, that the first fear is no more wrought by the Holy Spirit, but by the devil, to distress you, and make you to live, not like a son, but a slave. And for your better help in this matter, know that God himself has set bounds to this fear, and has concluded that after the Spirit of adoption is come, that other fear is wrought in your heart by him no more. (Romans 8:15; 2 Timothy 1:7.)

Again; before I leave this, let me tell you, that if you do not well bestir you in this matter, this bondage fear, to wit, that which is like it, though not wrought in you by the Holy Ghost, will, by the management and subtlety of the devil, the author of it, haunt, disturb, and make you live uncomfortably, and that while you are an heir of God and his kingdom. This is that fear that the Apostle speaks of, that makes men "all their lifetime subject to bondage." (Hebrews 2:14, 15.)

For though Christ will deliver you indeed at last, you having embraced him by faith, yet your life will be full of trouble; and death, though Jesus has abolished it, it will be always a living bugbear to you in all your ways and thoughts, to break your peace, and to make you to draw your loins heavily after him.

Third, would you grow in this godly fear? then as you should learn to distinguish of fears, so you should make conscience of which to entertain and cherish. If God would have his fear, and it is called his fear by way of eminency—"that this fear may be before you that you sin not," Exodus 20:20; Jeremiah 32:40—I say, if God would have this his fear be with you, then you should make conscience of this, and not so lightly give way to slavish fear, as is common for Christians to do.

There is utterly a fault among Christians about this thing; that is, they make not that conscience of resisting of slavish fear as they ought; they rather cherish and entertain it, and so weaken themselves and that fear that they ought to strengthen.

And this is the reason that we so often lie grabbling under the black and amazing thoughts that are engendered in our hearts by unbelief; for this fear nourishes unbelief: that is, now it does, to wit, if we give way to it after the Spirit of adoption is come, and readily closes with all the fiery darts of the wicked.

But Christians are ready to do with this fear as the horse does when the tines of the fork are set against his side, even lean to it until it enters into his belly. We lean naturally to this fear, I mean, after God has done good to our souls; it is hard striving against it, because it has even our sense and feeling of its side. But I say, if you would be a growing Christian, growing, I say, in the fear that is godly, in the fear that is always so; then make conscience of striving against the other, and against all these things that would bring you back to it. "Wherefore should I fear," said David, "In the days of evil, when the iniquities of my heels compasses me about?" (Psalm 99:5.)

What! not fear in the day of evil? What! not when the iniquity of your heels compasses you about? No, not then, says he; that is, not with that fear that would bring him again into bondage to the law, for he had received the Spirit of adoption before. Indeed, if ever a Christian has ground to give way to slavish fear it is at these two times, to wit, in the day of evil, and when the iniquity of his heels compasses him about. But you see, David would not then, no, not then give way thereto: nor did he see reason why he should. Wherefore should I, said he? Aye, wherefore indeed, since now you are become a son of God through Christ, and hat received the Spirit of his Son into your heart, crying, Father, Father.

Fourth, would you grow in this grace of godly fear? then grow in the knowledge of the new covenant, for that is indeed the girdle of our reins, and the strength of our souls. Hear what Zacharias says; "God," says he, "has raised up to us a horn of salvation in the house of his servant David, as he spoke by the mouth of all the holy prophets which have been since the world began." But what was it? what was it that he spoke? Why, "that he would grant us, that we, being delivered from the hand of our enemies, might serve him without fear," without this slavish bondage fear, "in holiness and righteousness before him all the days of our life." But upon what is this princely fearless service of God grounded? Why, "upon the holy covenant of God, upon the oath that he swore unto Abraham." (Luke 1:69-74.) Now, in this covenant is wrapped up all your salvation; in it is contained all your desire; and I am sure that then it contains the complete salvation of your soul: and I say, since this covenant is confirmed by promise, by oath, and by the blood of the Son of God, and that on purpose that you might serve your God without slavish fear, then the knowledge and faith of this covenant is of absolute necessity to bring us into this liberty, and out of our slavish terrors, and so, consequently, to cause us to grow in that son-like, godly fear, which became even the Son of God himself, and becomes all his disciplines to live in the growth and exercise of.

Fifth, would you grow in this godly fear? then labor even always to keep your evidences for heaven and of your salvation alive upon your heart; for he that loses his evidences for heaven will hardly keep slavish fear out of heart; but he that has the wisdom and grace to keep them alive and apparent to himself, he will grow in this godly fear. See how David words it; "From the ends of the earth," says he, "will I cry unto you, when my heart is overwhelmed; lead me to the rock that is higher than I. For you have been a shelter to me, and a strong tower from the enemy: I will abide in your tabernacle for ever. For you, God, have heard my prayer, you have given me the heritage of those that fear your name." (Psalm 61:5)

Mark a little; David does by these words in the first place suggest, that sometimes, to his thinking, he was as far off of his God as the ends of the earth are asunder, and that at such times he was subject to be overwhelmed, afraid. Secondly, the way that he took at such times to help himself was, 1. To cry to God to lead him again to Jesus Christ: "Lead me to the rock that is higher than I" for, indeed, without faith in him, and the renewing of that faith, there can be no evidence for heaven made to appear unto the soul. This, therefore, he prays for first. 2. Then he puts that faith into exercise, and that with respect to the time that was past, and also of the time that was to come. For the time past, says he, "You have been a shelter to me, and a strong tower from the enemy;" and for the time to come, he said, "I will abide in your tabernacle;" that is, in your Christ by faith, and in your way of worship by love, for ever. And observe it, he makes the believing remembrance of his first evidences for heaven the ground of this his cry and faith, "For you," says he, "Oh God, have given me the heritage of those that fear your name." You have made me meet to be a partaker of the mercy of your chosen, and have put me under the blessing of goodness wherewith you have blessed those that fear you.

Thus you see how David in his distresses musters up his prayers, faith, and evidences for eternal life, that he might deliver himself from being overwhelmed, that is, with slavish fear, and that he might also abound in that son-like fear of his fellow-brethren that is not only comely with respect to our profession, but profitable to our souls.

Sixth, would you grow in this fear of God? then set before your eyes the being and majesty of God; for that both begets, maintains, and increases this fear. And hence it is called the fear of God, that is, an holy and awful dread and reverence of his majesty. For the fear of God is to stand in awe of him; but how can that be done if we do not set him before us? And again, if we would fear him more, we must abide more in the sense and faith of his glorious majesty. Hence this fear and God's name is so often put together; as fear God, fear the Lord, fear your God, do this in the fear of the Lord, and you shall fear your God, I am the Lord. For these words, "I am the Lord your God," and the like, are on purpose put in, not only to show us whom we should fear, but also to beget, maintain, and increase in us that fear that is due from us to that glorious and fearful name, the Lord our God. (Deuteronomy 28:58.)

Seventh, would you grow in this grace of fear? then keep always close to your conscience the authority of the word; fear the commandment, as the commandment of a God both mighty and glorious, and as the commandment of a Father, both loving and pitiful. Let this commandment, I say, be always with your eye, with your ear, and with your heart; for then you will be taught, not only to fear, but to abound in the fear of the Lord. Every grace is nourished by the word, and without it there is no thrift in the soul. (Proverbs 13:13; 4:20-22; Deuteronomy 6:1,2.)

Eighth, would you grow in this grace of fear? then be much in the faith of the promise, of the promise that makes over to your soul an interest in God, by Christ, and of all good things. The promise naturally tends to increase in us the fear of the Lord, because this fear, it grows by goodness and mercy; they shall fear the Lord and his goodness. Now, this goodness and mercy of God it is wrapped up in, and made over to us by promise, for God gave it to Abraham by promise; therefore the faith and hope of the promise causes this fear to grow in the soul. "Having therefore these promises, dearly beloved, let us cleanse ourselves from all filthiness of flesh and spirit, perfecting holiness in the fear of God." (2 Corinthians 7:1) "Perfecting holiness in the fear of God;" therefore that fear by the promise must needs grow mighty, for by, with, and in it, you see holiness is perfected.

Ninth, would you grow in this grace of fear? Then remember the judgments of God that have or shall certainly overtake those professors that have either been downright hypocrites, or else unwatchful Christians. For both these sorts partake of the judgments of God; the one, to wit, the true Christian, for his unwatchfulness, for his correction; the other, to wit, the hypocrite, for his hypocrisy, to his destruction. This is a way to make you stand in awe, and to make you tremble, and grow in the grace of fear before your God. Judgments! You may say, what judgments?

Answer: Time will fail me here to tell you of the judgments that sometimes overtake God's people, and that always certainly overtake the hypocrite for his transgressions. For those that attend God's people, I would have you look back to the place in this book where they are particularly touched upon. And for those that attend the hypocrite, in general they are these: 1. Blindness of heart in this world. 2. The death of their hope at the day of their death. 3. And the damnation of their souls at the day of judgment. (Matthew 23:15-19; Job 8:13; 11:20; 18:14; 20:4-7; Matthew 23:33; 24:51; Luke 20:47.) The godly consideration of these things tends to make men grow in the fear of God.

Tenth, would you grow in this grace of fear? Then study the excellencies of the grace of fear, and what profit it yields to them that have it, and labor to get they heart into the love, both of the exercise of the grace itself, and also of the fruit it yields; for a man hardly grows in the increase of any grace, until his heart is united to it, and until it is made lovely in his eyes. Now the excellencies of this grace of fear have also been discoursed of in this book before, where by reading you shall find the fruit it bears, and the promises that are annexed to it, which, because they are many, I refer you also thither for your instruction.

Eleventh, would you grow in this grace of fear? Then remember what a world of privileges do belong to them that fear the Lord; as also I have hinted, namely, that such shall not be hurt, shall want no good thing, shall be guarded by angels, and have a special license, though in never so dreadful a plight, to trust in the name of the Lord, and stay upon their God.

Twelfth, would you grow in this grace of fear? Then be much prayer to God for abundance of the increase thereof.

To fear God, is that which is according to his will; and if we ask anything according to his will, he hears us. Pray, therefore, that God will unite your heart to fear his name; this is the way to grow in the grace of fear.

Lastly, would you grow in this grace of fear? Then devote yourself to it. (Psalm 119:38.) Devote myself to it, you will say, how is that? I answer, why give yourself to it, addict yourself to it. Solace yourself in the contemplation of God, and of a reverence of his name, and word, and worship. Then will you fear, and grow in this grace of fear.

What things they are that have a tendency in them to hinder the growth of the fear of God in our hearts.

And that I may yet be helpful to you, reader, I shall now give you caution of those things that will, if way be given to them, hinder your growth in this fear of God, the which, because they are very hurtful to the people of God, I would have you be warned by them. And they are these which follow:

First. If you would grow in this grace of fear, take heed of a hard heart, for that will hinder your growth in this grace. "Why have you hardened our hearts from your fear?" (Isaiah 58:17,) was a bitter complaint of the church heretofore; for it is not only the judgment that in itself is dreadful, and sore to God's people, but that which greatly hinders the growth of this grace in the soul. A hard heart is but barren ground for any grace to grow in, especially for the grace of fear; there is but little of this fear where the heart indeed is hard; neither will there ever be much therein.

Now if you would be kept from a hard heart, 1. Take heed of the beginnings of sin. Take heed, I say, of that, though it should be never so small; "A little leaven leavens the whole lump:" there is more in a little sin to harden, than in a great deal of grace to soften. David's look upon Bathsheba was, one would think, but a small matter: yet that beginning of sin contracted such hardness of heart in him, that it carried him almost beyond all fear of God. It did carry him to commit lewdness with her, murder upon the body of Uriah, and to abundance of wicked dissimulation; which are things, I say, that have direct tendency to quench and destroy all fear of God in the soul.

2. If you have sinned, lie not down without repentance; for the want of repentance, after one has sinned, makes the heart yet harder and harder. Indeed a hard heart is impenitent, and impenitence also makes the heart harder and harder. So that if impenitence be added to hardness of heart, or to the beginnings of sin which makes it so, it will quickly be with that soul, as is said of the house of Israel, it will have a whore's forehead, it will hardly be brought to shame. (Jeremiah 3:3.)

3. If you would be rid of a hard heart, that great enemy to the growth of the grace of fear, be much with Christ upon the cross in your meditations; for that is an excellent remedy against hardness of heart: a right sight of him, as he hanged there for your sins, will dissolve your heart into tears, and make it soft and tender. "They shall look upon me whom they have pierced, and mourn." (Zechariah 12:10, 11.) Now a soft, a tender, and broken heart, is a fit place for the grace of fear to thrive in. But,

Second, if you would have the grace of fear to grow in your soul, take heed also of a prayerless heart, for that is not a place for this grace of fear to grow in. Hence he that restrains prayer is said to cast off fear. "You cast off fear," said one of his friends to Job But how must he do that? why the next words show, "You restrain prayer before God." (Job 15:4.) Do you see a professor that prays not? that man thrusts the fear of God away from him. Do you see a man that prays but little? that man fears God but little; for it is the praying soul, the man that is might in praying, that has a heart for the fear of God to grow in. Take heed, therefore, of a prayerless heart, if you would grow in this grace of the fear of God. Prayer is as the pitcher that fetches water from the brook, therewith to water the herbs; break the pitcher, and it will fetch no water, and for want of water the garden withers.

Third, would you grow in this grace of fear? Then take heed of a light and wanton heart; for neither is such a heart good ground for the fear of God to grow in: wherefore it is said of Israel, 'She feared not, but went and played the harlot also." She was given to wantonness, and to be light and vain, and so her fear of God decayed. (Jeremiah 3:8.) Had Joseph been as wanton as his mistress, he had been as void of the fear of God as she: but he was of a sober, tender, godly, considerate spirit, therefore he grew in the fear of God.

Fourth, would you grow in this grace of fear? Then take heed of a covetous heart, for neither is that which is such an one good ground for this grace of fear to grow in. Therefore this covetousness, and the fear of God, are as enemies, set the one in opposition to the other: "one that fears God, and hates covetousness." (Exodus 18:21.) And the reason why covetousness is such an obstruction to the growth of this grace of fear, is because covetousness casts those things out of the heart which alone can nourish this fear. It casts out the word and love of God, without which no grace can grow in the soul, how then should the fear of God grow in a covetous heart? (Ezekiel 33:30-32; I John 2:15.)

Fifth, would you grow in this grace of fear? Then take heed of an unbelieving heart; for an unbelieving heart is not good ground for this grace of fear to grow in. An unbelieving heart is called "an evil heart" (Hebrews 3:12) because from it flows all the wickedness that is committed in the world. Now it is faith, or a believing heart, that nourishes this fear of God (Hebrews 11:7) and not the other: and the reason is that faith brings God, heaven, and hell, to the soul, and makes it duly consider of them all. This is, therefore, the

means of fear, and that which will make it grow in the soul:
but unbelief is a bane thereto.

Sixth, would you grow in this grace of fear? then take
heed of a forgetful heart. Such a heart is not a heart where
the grace of fear will flourish, "When I remember I am
afraid," etc. Therefore take heed of forgetfulness; do not
forget, but remember God, and his kindness, patience, and
mercy, to those that yet neither have grace nor special favor
from him; and that will beget and nourish his fear in your
heart; but forgetfulness of this or of any other of his judgments, is a great wound and weakening to this fear. (Job
21:6.) When a man well remembers that God's judgments
are so great a deep and mystery, as indeed they are, that
remembrance puts a man upon such considerations of God
and of his judgments as to make him fear. "Therefore," says
Job, "I am afraid of him." (See the place, Job 23:15.) "Therefore am I troubled at his presence; when I consider, I am
afraid of him;" when I remember and consider of the wonderful depths of his judgments toward man.

Seventh, would you grow in this grace of fear? then
take heed of a murmuring and repining heart, for that is not
a heart for this grace of fear to grow in. As, for instance,
when men murmur and repine at God's hand, at his dispensations, and at the judgments that overtake them, in
their persons, estates, families, or relations, that their murmuring tends to destroy fear; for a murmuring spirit is such
an one as seems to correct God, and to find fault with his
dispensations, and where there is that the heart is far from
fear. A murmuring spirit either comes from that wisdom
that pretends to understand that there is a failure in the nature and execution of things, or from an envy and spite at
the execution of them. Now if murmuring arises from this
pretended wisdom of the flesh, then instead of faring God,
his actions are judged to be either rigid or ridiculous, which
yet are done in judgment, truth, and righteousness. So that

a murmuring heart cannot be a good one for the fear of God to grow in. Alas! the heart where that grows must be a soft one, as you have it in Job 23:15, 16; and a heart that will stoop and be silent at the most abstruse of all his judgments. "I was silent, because you did it." The heart in which this fear of God does flourish is such, that it bows and is mute, if it can but espy the hand, wisdom, justice, or holiness of God in this or the other of his dispensations, and so stirs up the soul to fear before him. But if this murmuring arises from envy and spite, that looks so like to the spirit of the devil, that nothing need be said to give conviction of the horrible wickedness of it.

Eighth, would you grow in this grace of fear? then, take heed of a high and captious spirit, for that is not good ground for the fear of God to grow in. A meek and quiet spirit is the best, and there the fear of God will flourish most; therefore Peter puts meekness and fear together, as being most suited in their nature and natural tendency one to another. (I Peter 3:15.) Meekness of spirit is like that heart that has depth of earth in it, in which things may take root and grow; but a high and captious spirit is like to the stony ground, where there is not depth of earth, and consequently, where this grace of fear cannot grow; therefore, take heed of this kind of spirit, if you would that the fear of God should grow in your soul.

Ninth, would you grow in this grace of fear? then, take heed of an envious heart, for that is not a good heart for the fear of God to grow in. "Let not your heart envy sinners, but be you in the fear of the Lord all the day long." (Proverbs 23:17.) To envy any is a sign of a bad spirit, and that man takes upon him, as I have already hinted, to be a controller and a judge, yea, and a malicious executioner too, and that of that fury that arises from his own lusts and revengeful spirit, upon, perhaps, the man that is more righteous than himself. But suppose he is a sinner that is the object of your envy, why, the text sets that envy in direct opposition to the fear of God; "Envy not sinners, but be you in the fear of God." These two, therefore, to wit, envy to sinners and fearing of God, are opposites. You cannot fear God and envy sinners too. And the reason is, because he that envies a sinner has forgotten himself, that he is as bad, and how can he then fear God? He that envies sinners rejects his duty of blessing of them that curse, and praying for them that despitefully use us; and how can he that has rejected this fear God? He that envies sinners, therefore, cannot be of a good spirit, nor can the fear of God grow in his heart.

Lastly, would you grow in this grace of fear? then, take heed of hardening your heart at any time against convictions to particular duties, as to prayer, alms, self-denial, or the like. Take heed also of hardening your heart when you are under any judgment of God, as sickness, losses, crosses, or the like. I bid you before to beware of a hard heart, but now I bid you beware of hardening your soft ones. For to harden the heart is to make it worse than it is; harder, more desperate and bold against God, than at the present it is. Now, I say, if you would grow in this grace of fear, take heed of hardening your heart, and especially of hardening of it against convictions to good; for those convictions are sent of God, like seasonable showers of rain, to keep the tillage of your heart in good order, that the grace of fear may grow therein; but this stifling of convictions makes the heart as hard as a piece of the nether millstone. Therefore happy is he that receives conviction, for so he does keep in the fear of God, and that fear thereby nourished in his soul; but cursed is that that does otherwise. "Happy is the man that fears always, but he that hardens his heart shall fall into mischief." (Proverbs 28:14.)

A Use of Encouragement.

I come now to a use of encouragement to those that are blessed with this grace of fear. The last text that was mentioned says, "Happy is the man that fears always," and so does many more. Happy already, because blessed with his grace, and happy for time to come, because this grace shall abide, and continue till the soul that has it is brought unto the mansion-house of glory. "I will put my fear in their heart, and they shall not depart from me." Therefore, as here it says, Happy is he, so it says also, It shall go well with him, that is, in time to come. "It shall go well with them that fear the Lord." (Ecclesiastes 8:12.)

Had God given you all the world, yet cursed had you been if he had not given you the fear of the Lord; for the fashion of this world is a fading thing, but he that fears the Lord shall abide for ever and ever. This, therefore, is the first thing that I would propound for your encouragement, you man that fears the Lord. This grace will dwell in your heart, for it is a new covenant grace, and will abide with you for ever. It is sent to you from God, not only to join your heart unto him, but to keep you from final apostasy. "I will put my fear in their heart, and they shall not depart from me." (Jeremiah 32.) That you may never forsake God is his design and therefore to keep you from that wicked thing, he has put his fear in your heart. Many are the temptations, difficulties, snares, traps, trials, and troubles that the people of God pass through in the world, but how shall they be kept, how shall they be delivered, and escape? Why, the answer is, the fear of God will keep them. "He that fears God shall come out of them all."

Is it not, therefore, a wonderful mercy to be blessed with this grace of fear, that you by it may be kept from final, which is damnable apostasy? Bless God, therefore you blessed man, that have this grace of fear in your soul. There are five things in this grace of fear that have a direct tendency in them to keep you from final apostasy.

1. It is seated in the heart, and the heart is, as I may call it, the main fort in the mystical world, man. It is not placed

in the head, as knowledge is; nor in the mouth, as utterance is; but in the heart, the seat of all. "I will put my fear in their heart." If a king will keep a town secure to himself, let him be sure to man sufficiently the main fort thereof. If he have twenty thousand men well armed, yet if they lie scattered here and there, the town may be taken for all that; but if the main fort be well manned, then the town is more secure. What if a man had all the parts, yea, all the arts of men and angels? that will not keep the heart to God. But when the heart, this principal fort, is possessed with the fear of God, then he is safe, but not else.

2. As the heart in general, so the will in special. That chief and great faculty of the soul, is the principle that is acted by this fear. The will, which way that goes, all goes; if it be to heaven or hell. Now the will, I say, is the main faculty that is governed by this fear that does possess the soul, therefore all is like to go well with it. This Samuel insinuates where he says "If you will fear the Lord." Fearing of God is a voluntary act of the will, and that being so, the soul is kept from rebellion against the commandment, because by the will, where this fear of God is placed, and which it governs, is led all the rest of the powers of the soul. (1 Samuel 12:14.) In this will, then, is this fear of God placed, that this grace may the better be able to govern the soul, and so by consequence the whole man; for as I said before, look what way the will goes, look what the will does, thither goes, and that does the whole man. (See Psalm 110:3.) Man, when his will is alienate from God, is reckoned rebellious throughout, (John 5:40) and that not without ground, for the will is the principal faculty of the soul as to obedience, and therefore things done without the will are as if they were not done at all. The spirit is willing; if you be willing; "she has done what she could," and the like; by these and such like sayings the goodness of the heart and action is judged, as to the subjective part thereof. Now this fear that we have been

speaking of is placed in the soul, and so consequently in the will, that the man may thereby the better be kept from final and damnable apostasy.

3. This fear, as I may say, even above every other grace, is God's well-wisher; and hence it is called, as I also have showed you, his fear. As he also says in the text mentioned above, "I will put my fear in their heart." These words, his and my, they are intimate and familiar expressions, bespeaking not only great favor to man, but a very great trust put in him; as who should say, this fear is my special friend, it will subject and bow the soul and the several faculties thereof to my pleasure; it is my great favorite, and subdues sinners to my pleasure. You shall rarely find faith or repentance, or parts, go under such familiar characters as this blessed fear of the Lord does. Of all the counselors and mighty men that David had, Hushai only was called the king's friend, (2 Samuel 15:37; 16:16.) So of all the graces of the Spirit, this of the fear of God goes mostly, if not always, by the title of My fear, God's far, His fear, etc. I told you before, if the king will keep a town, the main fort therein must be sufficiently manned: and now I will add, that if he have not to govern those men some trusty and special friends, such as Hushai was David, he may find it lost when it should stand him in greatest stead. If a soul should be possessed with all things possible, yet if this fear of God be wanting, all other things will give place in time or rebellion, and the soul shall be found in and under the conduct of hell, when it should stand up for God and his truth in the world. This fear of God, it is God's special friend, and therefore it has given unto it the chief seat of the heart, the will, that the whole man may now be, and also be kept hereafter, in the subjection and obedience of the gospel. For,

4. This grace of fear is the softest and most tender of God's honor of any other grace. It is that tender, sensible, and trembling grace that keeps the soul upon its continual

watch. To keep a good watch is, you know, a wonderful safety to a place that is in continual danger because of the enemy. Why this is the grace that setteth the watch, and that keeps the watchman awake. (Song of Solomon 3:7,8.) A man cannot watch as he should if he be destitute of fear: let him be confident, and he sleeps; he unadvisedly lets into the garrison those that should not come there. Israel's fault when they came to Canaan was, that they made a covenant with the inhabitants of the land (to wit, the Gibeonites) without asking counsel of God. But would they have done so, think you, if at the same time the fear of God had had its fully play in the soul, in the army? no, they at that time forgot to fear. The grace of fear had not at that time its full stroke and sway among them.

5. This grace of fear is that which, as I may so say, first affects the hearts of saints with judgments, after we have sinned, and so is as a beginning grace to bring again that to rights that by sin is put out of frame. Oh, it is a precious grace of God! I know what I say in this matter, and also where I had been long ago, through the power of my lusts, and the wiles of the devil, had it not been for the fear of God.

But, secondly, another encouragement for those that are blessed with this blessed grace of fear is this: this fear fails not to do this work for the soul, if there in truth, be it never so small in measure. A little of this leaven "leavens the whole lump." True, a little will not do, or help the soul to do, those worthy exploits in the heart or life as well, as a bigger measure thereof; nor indeed can a little of any grace do that which a bigger measure will: but a little will preserve the soul from final apostasy, and deliver it into the arms of the Son of God at the final judgment. Wherefore, when he says, "I will put my fear in their heart," he says not, I will put so much of it there, such a quantity, or such a degree; but, "I will put my fear there." I speak not this in the least to tempt the godly man to be content with the least degree of the fear of God in his heart. True, men should be glad that God has put even the least degree of this grace into their souls, but they should not be content therewith; they should earnestly covet more, pray for more, and use all lawful, that is, all the means of God's appointing, that they may get more.

There are, as I have said already, several degrees of this grace of fear, and our wisdom is to grow in it, as in all the other graces of the Spirit. The reasons why, I have showed you, and also the way to grow therein; but the least measure thereof will do as I said, that is, keep the soul from final apostasy. There are, as I have showed you, those that greatly fear the Lord, that fear exceedingly, and that fear him above many of their brethren; but the small in this grace are saved as well as those that are great therein: "He will save them that fear him, both small and great." This fear of the Lord is the pulse of the soul; and as some pulses beat stronger, some weaker, so is this grace of fear in the soul. They that beat best are a sign of best life, but they that beat worst show that life is present. As long as the pulse beats, we count not that the man is dead, though weak; and this fear, where it is, preserves to everlasting life. Pulses there are also that are intermitting; to wit, such as have their times for a little; a little time to stop, and beat again; true, these are dangerous pulses, but yet, too, a sign of life. This fear of God also is sometimes like this intermitting pulse; there are times when it forbears to work, and then it works again. David had an intermitting pulse, Peter had an intermitting pulse, as also many other of the saints of God. I call that an intermitting pulse, with reference to the fear we speak of, when there is some obstruction by the workings of corruptions in the soul; I say, some obstruction from, and hindrance of the continual motion of this fear of God; yet none of these, though they are various, and some of them signs of weakness, are signs of death, but life. "I will put my fear in their heart, and they shall not depart from me."

But you may say, How shall I know that I fear God?

Answer: If I should say that desires, true sincere desires to fear him, is fear itself, I should not say amiss. (Nehemiah 1:11.) For, although a desire to be or do so and so, makes not a man to be in temporal or natural things what he desires to be—for a sick, or poor, or imprisoned man may desire to be well, to be rich, or to be at liberty, and yet be as they are, sick, poor, or in prison; yet in spirituals, a man's desire to be good, to believe, to love, to hope, and fear God, does flow from the nature of grace itself.

I said before, that in temporals a man could not properly be said to be what he was not; yet a man, even in naturals or temporals, shows his love to that thing that he desires, whether it be health, riches, or liberty; and in spirituals, desires of, from love to this or that grace of God, sincere desires of it flow from the roof of the grace itself. "Thy servants that desire to fear your name." Nehemiah bore himself before God upon this, "that he desired to fear his name." And hence again it is said concerning desires, true desires, "The desires of a man is his kindness. (Proverbs 19:22.) For a man shows his heart, his love, his affections, and his delights, in his desires; and since the grace of fear of God is a grace so pleasant in the sight of God, and of so sanctifying a nature in the soul where it is, a true sincere desire to be blessed with that grace must needs flow from some being of this grace in the soul already.

True, desires are lower than higher acts of grace, but God will not look over desires. "But now they desire a better country, that is, an heavenly; wherefore God is not ashamed to be called their God, for he has prepared for them a city." Mark, they desire a country, and they shall have a city. At this low place, to wit, sincere desires, God will meet the soul, and will tell him that he has accepted of his desires, that his desires are his kindness, and flow from grace itself. "He will fulfill the desires of them that fear him." Therefore, desires are not rejected of God; but they would, if they did not flow from a principle of grace already in the soul. Therefore, since you fear God, and it is evident by your desires that you do so do, you are happy now in this your fear, and shalt be happy for ever hereafter in the enjoyment of that which God in another world has laid up for them that fear him.

Thirdly. Another encouragement for those that have this grace of fear is this; this grace can make that man, that in many other things is not capable of serving of God, serve him better than those that have all, without it. Poor Christian man, you have scarce been able to do any thing for God all your days, but only to fear the Lord. You are no preacher, and so cannot do him service that way; you are no rich man, and so cannot do him service with outward substance; you are no wise man, and so cannot do any thing that way: but here is your mercy, you fear God. Though you cannot preach, you fear God. Though you cannot preach, you can fear God. Though you have no bread to feed the belly, nor fleece to clothe the back of the poor, you can fear God. Oh, how "blessed is the man that fears the Lord," because this duty of fearing of God is an act of the mind, and may be done by the man that is destitute of all things but that holy and blessed mind. Blessed, therefore, is that man, for God has not laid the comfort of his people in the doing of external duties, nor the salvation of their souls, but in believing, loving, and fearing God. Neither has he laid these things in actions done in their health, nor in the due management of their most excellent parts, but in the receiving of Christ, and fear of God. The which, good Christian, you may do, and do acceptably, even though you should lie bedrid all your days; you may also be sick, and believe; be sick and love; be sick and fear God, and so be a blessed man.

And here the poor Christian has something to answer them that reproach him for his ignoble pedigree, and shortness of the glory of the wisdom of the world. True, may that man say, I was taken out of the dunghill, I was born in a base and low estate, but I fear God. I have no worldly greatness, nor excellency of natural parts, but I fear God.

When Obadiah met with Elijah, he gave him no worldly and fantastical compliment, nor did he glory in his promotion by Ahab, the king of Israel, but gravely and after a gracious manner said, "I your servant fear the Lord from my youth." Also, when the mariners inquired of Jonah, saying, "What is your occupation, and whence do you come? What is your country, and of what people are you?" This was the answer he gave them, "I am a Hebrew, and I fear the Lord, the God of heaven, which has made the sea and the dry land." Indeed, this answer is the highest and most noble in the world, nor are there any, save a few, that in truth can thus express themselves, though other answers they have enough. Most can say, I have wisdom, or might, or riches, or friends, or health, or the like; these are common, and are greatly boasted in by the most; but he is the man that fears God, and he that can say, when they say to him, What are you? "I your servant do fear the Lord;" he is the man of many, he is to be honored of men: though this, to wit, that he fears the Lord, is all that he has in the world. He has the thing, the honor, the life, and glory, that is lasting; his blessedness will abide when all men's but his is buried in the dust, in shame and contempt.

A Word to Hypocrites.

Hypocrites, my last word is to you. The hypocrite is one that would appear to be that in men's eyes, that he is nothing of in God's. You hypocrite, that would be esteemed to be one that loves and that fears God, but does not; I have this to say to you; your condition is damnable, because you are a hypocrite, and seek to deceive both God and man with guises, vizards, masks, shows, pretenses, and your formal, carnal, feigned subjection to the outside of statutes, laws, and commandments; but within you are full of rottenness and all excess.

Hypocrite, you may by your cunning shifts be veiled and hid from men; but you are naked before the eyes of God, and he knows that his fear is not in your heart. (Luke 16:15.)

Hypocrite, be admonished that there is not obedience accepted of God, where the heart is destitute of this grace of fear. Keeping of the commandments is but one part of the duty of man; and Paul did that, even while he was a hypocrite. (Philippians 3.) To "fear God and keep his commandments, that is the whole duty of man." (Ecclesiastes 12:13.) This (fear God) the hypocrite cannot as a hypocrite do; and therefore as such cannot escape the damnation of hell.

Hypocrite, you must fear God first, even before you do offer to meddle with the commandments, that is, as to the keeping of them; indeed, you should read therein, that you may learn to fear the Lord; but yet fear God goes before the command to keep his commandments; and if you do not fear God first, you transgress instead of keeping of the commandments.

Hypocrite, this word "fear God" is that which the hypocrite quite forgets, although it is that which sanctifies the whole duty of man; for this is that, and nothing without it, that can make a man sincere in his obedience. The hypocrite looks for applause abroad, and forgets that he is condemned at home; and both these he does because he lacks the fear of God.

Hypocrite, be admonished that none of the privileges that are spoken of in the former part of the book belongs to you, because you are a hypocrite; and if you hope, your hope shall be cut off; and if you lean upon your house, both you and it shall fall into hell-fire. Triumph, then; your triumph is but for a while. Joy, then; but the joy of the hypocrite is but for a moment. (Job 8:13, 15; 20:4-6.)

Perhaps you will not let go now what, as a hypocrite, you have got: "But what is the hope of the hypocrite, when God shall take away his soul?" (Job 27:8.)

Hypocrite, you should have chosen the fear of God, as you have chosen a profession without it; but you have cast off fear, because you are a hypocrite; and because you are such, you shall have the same measure that you meet; God will cast you off because you are a hypocrite. God has prepared a fear for you, because you did not choose the fear of God; and that fear shall come upon you like desolation, and like an armed man, and shall swallow you up, you and all that you are. (Proverbs 1:27.)

Hypocrite, read this text and tremble: "The sinners in Zion are afraid, fearfulness has surprised the hypocrite. Who among us shall dwell with devouring fire? who among us shall dwell with everlasting burnings?" (Isaiah 33:13,14.)

Hypocrite, you are not under the fatherly protection of God, because you are a hypocrite, and lack his fear in your heart. The eyes of the Lord are upon them that fear him, to deliver them; but the fearless man, or hypocrite, is left to the snares, and wiles of the devil, to be caught therein and overcome, because he is destitute of the fear of God.

Hypocrite, you are like to have no other reward of God for your labor than that which the goats shall have. The hypocrite, because he is a hypocrite, shall not stand in God's sight. The gain of your religion you spend as you get it; you will not have one farthing over at death and judgment.

Hypocrite, God has not entrusted you with the least dram of his saving grace, nor will he because you are a hypocrite; and as far what you have, you have stolen it, even every man of you, from his neighbor; still pilfering out of their profession, even as Judas did out of the bag. You come like a thief into your profession, and like a thief you shall go out of the same. Jesus Christ has not counted you faithful to commit to you any of his jewels to keep, because you fear him not: he has given his "banner to them that fear him, that it may be displayed because of the truth." (Psalm 60:4.)

Hypocrite, you are not true to God nor man, nor your own soul, because you are a hypocrite. How should the Lord put any trust in you? Why should the saints look for any good from you? Should God give you his word, you will sell it; should men commit their souls to you, you will destroy them, by making merchandise of them for your own hypocritical designs. Yea, if the sun waxes hot, you will throw all away, and not endure the heat, because you are a hypocrite.

THE FEAR OF GOD
BY JOHN GILL

The fear of God has so great a concern in divine worship, that it is sometimes put for the whole of it; and a worshipper of God is frequently described in scripture by one that fears him; and particularly internal worship, or experimental religion, as distinguished from an external observance of the divine commands, is expressed by it; for, according to the wise man, the whole of religion, experimental and practical religion, lies in these two things, to *fear God and keep his commandments*, Ecclesiastes 20:13, and to worship itself is expressed by the fear of God, so the manner in which it is to be performed is directed to be in it and with it, for God is to be served *with reverence and godly fear*; see Psalm 2:11 and 5:7 and 89:7; Hebrews 12:28, concerning which may be observed,

I. The object of fear, not the creature, but God the Creator. There is a fear due to men, *fear to whom fear*; that is, it should be rendered to whom it is due, Romans 13:7, there is a fear and reverence due to parents from their children, Leviticus 19:3; Hebrews 12:9, which is shown by the honor and respect paid unto them, and the obedience yielded them, Ephesians 6:1,2. and the argument from hence is strong to the fear and reverence of God the Father of spirits, Hebrews 12:9; 1 Peter 1:14,17. There is a fear and reverence in the conjugal state, due from wives to their husbands, Ephesians 5:33; 1 Peter 3:5,6, and this relation affords a reason and argument why the church should fear and serve the Lord her God, because he is her husband, Psalm 14:11. There is a fear and reverence which servants should show to their masters, Ephesians 6:5, and if such masters are to be obeyed with fear, much more our Master which is in heaven; and this is the argument the Lord himself uses, *If I be a Master, where is my fear?* Malachi 1:6. there is a fear and reverence which ministers of the word should be had in, by those to whom they minister, 1 Samuel 12: 18. This is one part of that double honor they are worthy of, to be esteemed very highly for their work sake. Herod, though a wicked man, *feared John,* that is, not dreaded him, but respected him, for *he heard him gladly,* Mark 6:20. There is a fear and reverence to be rendered to magistrates, Romans 13:7, and especially to the king, the chief magistrate, Proverbs 24:21, and if an earthly king is to be feared and reverenced, much more the King of kings and Lord of lords, *Who would not fear you, O king of nations?* Jeremiah 10:7.

But then men are not so to be feared by the people of God, let them be in whatsoever character, relation, and station as to be deterred by them from the service of God; *the fear of man* too often *brings a snare* in this respect. God is to be hearkened to, served and obeyed, rather than men in the highest class and rank; they are not to be afraid of losing their favor and esteem, and of gaining their ill will thereby, as the Pharisees, who, though convinced that Jesus was the Christ, confessed him not, lest they should be put out of the synagogue, loving the praise of men more than the praise of God; nor should they be afraid of the revilings and reproaches of men, and be intimidated by them from serving the Lord their God, but with Moses should esteem reproach for the Lord's sake greater riches than the treasures of Egypt; nor should they be frightened from a profession of religion, and from an attention to it, by the threats and menaces of men, and by all the persecutions they may endure from them. They are not to be feared who can kill the body, but God is to be feared who can destroy both body and soul in hell; and such who fear men, so as to neglect the worship of God, are the *fearful* ones, who shall have their part in the lake of fire and brimstone, Matthew 10:28; Revelation 21:8. If God is on the side of his people, as he most certainly is, they have no reason to fear what man can do unto them.

God only is the object of fear, *You shall fear the Lord they God, and serve him*; that is, him only, Deuteronomy 6:13 and 10:20. That is the principal thing God requires of his people, and they are bound in duty to render to him; *Now, O Israel, what does the Lord your God require of you, but to fear the Lord your God?* this is the first thing, others follow, Deuteronomy 10:12. Hence because he is so much the object of the fear of good men, he is called *fear* itself; so the *fear of Isaac* is used for the God of Isaac, Genesis 31:42, and by whom Jacob swore, ver. 53. who could be no other than the God of his father Isaac. In the Chaldee paraphrase the word *fear*, is sometimes put for the true God, as well as used of idols; and with some, the Greek word for God, is by them derived from *fear* and by the Lacedemonians fear was worshipped as a deity, and had a temple for it; as Pavor and Pallor, fearfulness and paleness, were by Tullus Hostilius among the Romans; but none but the true God is the object of fear. And,

First, he is to be feared because of his name and nature; *Holy and reverend is his name*, particularly his name Jehovah, expressive of his essence and nature; *that you may fear this fearful and glorious name, The Lord your God*, Deuteronomy 28:58, a name peculiar to him; there is no name of God but is to be revered; and that by which he is commonly spoken of ought always to be used in a reverend manner, and not upon slight and trivial occasions, and with great irreverence, as it too often is, and when at every turn, men are apt to say, O Lord! O God! good God! etc. especially men profession the fear of God, should be careful of such language, for it is no other than taking the name of God in vain.

Secondly, God not only essentially but personally considered is to be feared, God, Father, Son, and Spirit; it is said of the Jews in the latter day, that they shall *seek the Lord their God, and David their king, and shall fear the Lord and his goodness in the latter days,* Hosea 3:5, where the Lord, who and his goodness will be feared by them, is Jehovah the Father, as distinguished from the Messiah the Son of God, and David their king, who will be sought for by them. So in Malachi 4:2. *Unto you that fear my name,* whose name is Jehovah, the Lord of hosts, *shall the Sun of righteousness arise with healing in his wings*; even the Son of God, who is the brightness of his Father's glory, and the express image of his person, and so is distinguished from him whose name is feared. Jehovah the Son is also the object of divine fear and reverence, *Let him be your fear, and let him be your dread*; that is, the object of your fear and reverence; and what follows shows which of the divine Persons is meant; and *he shall be for a sanctuary* to worship in, and a place of refuge for his people in times of distress; *but for a stone of stumbling, and for a rock of offense,* Isaiah 8:13,14, which phrases are applied to Christ, and can only be said of him, Romans 9:32, 33; 1 Peter 2:7,8. Jehovah the Father, the lord of the vineyard, after sending many of his servants who had been ill used, says, *I will send my beloved Son,* meaning Christ, the only begotten Son of the Father, it *may be, they will reverence him when they see him,* Luke 20:13. They ought to have done it; reverence should be given to him, the heir of the vineyard, his church, the son in his own house, whose house believers are, and therefore should reverence him. Jehovah the Spirit also is and should be the object of fear; the Israelites in the wilderness rebelled against him, and vexed him, and they smarted for it, for *he turned to be their enemy, and fought against them,* Isaiah 63:10. Lying to the Holy Ghost, which was a most irreverent treatment of him, was punished with death in Ananias and Sapphira; and saints should be careful that they *grieve* not the holy Spirit by their unbecoming carriage to him, from whom they receive many blessings and favors.

Thirdly, God, in his perfections and because of them, is the object of fear; as his majesty and greatness in general; God is clothed with majesty, and majesty and honor are before him, and *with him is terrible majesty*, such as is sufficient to command an awe of him; particularly his omnipotence, for *he is excellent in power*, Job 37:22,23. As also his omniscience, for nothing can be hid from his sight; the most enormous actions committed in the dark are seen by him, with whom the darkness and the light are alike; and his omnipresence, from whence there is no fleeing, for he fills heaven and earth with it; to which may be added, the justice and holiness of God, which make his majesty the more terrible and to be revered, since he is not only excellent in power, but also *in judgment, and in plenty of justice*, Job 37:23. (See 2 Chronicles 19:7.) And a fearful thing it is to fall into the hands of a just and sin-avenging God, the living God, the everlasting King, at whose wrath the nations tremble, and are not able to bear his indignation, Jeremiah 10:10.

Fourthly, the works of God make him appear to be a proper object of fear and reverence; his works of creation, the Psalmist on mention of them says, Psalm 33:5-8. *Let all the earth fear the Lord, let all the inhabitants of the world stand in awe of him*; who has made such a display of his greatness and goodness in them, as show him worthy of fear and reverence. The prophet instances in what may seem small, yet a most wonderful thing, and enough of itself to command an awe of the divine Being; *Fear you not me, says the Lord? will you not tremble at my presence? which has placed the sand for the bound of the sea, by a perpetual decree that it cannot pass it*; and at the same time the stupidity of the people is observed, how, notwithstanding the goodness of God in his works of providence towards them, yet were wanting in their fear and reverence of him: *Neither say they in their hearts, Let us now fear the Lord our God that gives rain, the former and latter rain in its season; he reserves unto us the appointed weeks of the harvest,* Jeremiah 5:22,24, which, though common providential blessings, yet are what should engage men to fear the Lord and his goodness; and especially God's works of grace should have such an effect upon the hearts of his people, as they have when they come with a divine power; particularly the pardoning grace and mercy of God; *There is forgiveness with you that you may be feared,* Psalm 130:4. See Hosea 3:5.

Fifthly, the judgments of God, which he threatens, and sometimes inflicts, and the promises of grace he makes and always fulfils, render him an object of fear and reverence. The judgments of God on sinners, are awful to the saints themselves, and strike their minds with fear of God; says David, *My flesh trembles for fear of you, and I am afraid of your judgments,* Psalm 119:120, not as coming upon himself, but as terrible to behold on others; and these are dreadful and formidable to sinners, when they see them near approaching, who go into the holes and clefts of rocks, and into the caves *for fear of the Lord, and the glory of his majesty, when he arises to shake terribly the earth* (Isaiah 2:19,21), and nothing has a greater influence on a filial and godly fear in the saints, and to stir them up to the exercise of it, than the free, absolute, and unconditional promise of grace in the covenant; thus after the apostle had observed such promises, strongly urges to *perfecting holiness in the fear of God,* 2 Corinthians 6:16, 18, and 7:1.

II. The nature and kind of fear. There is a fear which is not good nor commendable, and it is of different sorts; there is an idolatrous and superstitious fear, a fear of demons, which the city of Athens was greatly addicted to, observed to them by the apostle when there, to their disgrace; *I perceive that in all things you are too superstitious,* or given to the fear and worship; of false deities; such is all will worship, worship not founded in the word of God, which brings on a spirit of bondage unto fear; and all such false and vain imaginations which inject dread and terrors into the minds of men, and cause them to *fear where no fear is,* or where there is no reason for it; such as the pains of purgatory after death, invented by the Papists to extort money from men; and the beating of the body in the grave, a figment of the Jews.

There is an external fear of God, an outward show and profession of it, which is taught by the precept of men, as in the men of Samaria, who pretended to fear the Lord, as the priest instructed them, and yet served their own gods; and such an external fear of the true God, Job's friends supposed was all that he had, and that even he had cast off that, Job 15:4.

There is an hypocritical fear, when men draw nigh to God with their mouths and honor him with their lips, and their hearts are removed far from him; and when they fear and serve him for same sinister end and selfish view, which Satan insinuated was Job's case, *Does Job fear God for nothing?* and perhaps the same is suggested by Eliphaz, *Is not this your fear?* Job 1:9. and 4:6.

And there is a servile fear, such as that of some servants, who serve their masters, not from love but from fear of punishment; and such a *spirit of bondage to fear* the Jews were much subject to, under the legal dispensation; but now saints being *delivered out of the hands* of sin, Satan, and the law, they *serve* the Lord *without fear,* without slavish fear and with a filial one, Romans 8:15. Luke 1:74, 75.

And this sort of fear arises:

1. From a sense of sin, and the guilt of it on the conscience, without a view of pardon; thus no sooner were Adam and Even sensible of their sin and their nakedness by it, but they fled through fear from the presence of God, and hid themselves among the trees of the garden, as yet having no discovery of pardoning grace made to them; for said

Adam to God, calling for him, *I heard your voice in the garden, and I was afraid; because I was naked, and I hid myself*, Genesis 3:10. Thus a wicked man, conscious of his guilt, flees when no man pursues, and is like Pashur, a Magor-missabib, fear round about, a terror to himself and others.

2. From the law entering the conscience of a sinner, having broken it and working wrath in it; for the law, when it comes with powerful convictions of sin, and with menaces of punishment for it, *it works* present *wrath*, or a sense of it in the conscience, and leaves a *fearful looking for of judgment* to come, and of *fiery indignation* which shall consume *the adversaries* of God; when persons in such condition and circumstances would be glad of rocks and mountains to fall on them and hide them from the wrath of God, which appears to them intolerable.

3. From the curse of the law, and the weight of it on the conscience. The voice of the law is terrible, it is a voice of words which they that heard intreated they might hear no more. It accuses of sin, pronounces guilty for it, is a ministration of condemnation and a killing letter; its language is, *Cursed is every one that continues not in all things which are written in the book of the law to do them*, Galatians 3:10, which to hear is dreadful, when the conscience of a sinner is awakened; but how much more terrible is it, when a sinner fells as it were in his own apprehension all the curses of the law upon him, as he does when *the anger of the Lord, and his jealously smoke against* him, *and all the curses written* in the law *lie upon him*, Deuteronomy 29:20, with what slavish fear must he be then filled?

4. From a view of death as the demerit of sin; *The ages of sin is death*, the just desert of it; sin is the sting of death, gives it its venom and fatal influence, and makes it that terrible thing it is; and some *through fear of death* are *all their lifetime subject to bondage*, and are under a continual servile fear of it.

5. From a dread of hell and everlasting damnation. This fear is of the same kind with that of devils, who believe there is one God and tremble; tremble at present wrath and future torment. So wicked men, who have a fearful apprehension of everlasting punishment, it appears to them greater than they can bear, as it did to Cain.

But there is a fear of God different from this and opposite to it, and may be called a filial fear, such as that of a son to a father; the scriptures call it , and which is rendered *godly fear*, Hebrews 12:28, and the same word is used of the fear and reverence of Christ to his divine Father, who was *heard in that he feared,* or *because of fear*, Hebrews 5:7, his filial fear of his Father which lay in honoring him, in obedience to him, and in submission to his will, even when with supplications he deprecated death; and now a fear like this in the saints arises:

1. From the spirit of adoption, who delivers the people of God from a servile fear, and gives them a filial one, by witnessing their sonship to them; *You have not received*, says the apostle, *the spirit of bondage again to fear, but you have received the spirit of adoption, whereby we cry, Abba, Father*, and so are freed from a spirit of bondage which induces a servile fear, Romans 8:17. They that fear the Lord are in the relation of children to him; wherefore their fear of him, which he takes notice of and regards, must be a child-like one, arising from their being put among the children, and their sense of it; and which seems to be implied in Psalm 103:13. *Like as a father pities his children, so the Lord pities them that fear him,* where they that fear the Lord, in the latter clause, answer to children in the former.

2. From the love of God shed abroad in the heart by the Spirit, which produces love to God again; *there is no fear,* no slavish fear, *in love, but perfect love*, a sense of the perfect, everlasting, and unchangeable love of God *casts out* such kind of fear; for the true fear of God is no other than a reverential

affection for God flowing from a sense of his love; such do not dread his wrath, but desire his presence and communion with him, and say, *Whom have I in heaven but you? and there is none on earth that I desire besides you*, Psalms 73:25.

3. This filial fear is attended with faith and trust in God; it is a fiducial fear; hence they that fear the Lord and who trust in him, are characters put together, and which describe the same persons; and they that fear the Lord are exhorted and encouraged to trust in him, Psalm 31:19. and 115:11. Job was a man that feared God, and yet such was his faith and confidence in him, that he could say, *Though he slay me, yet will I trust in him*; and what a strong expression of his faith in Christ as his living Redeemer have we in chap. 19:25. (See Job 1:1 and 13:15.

4. It is a fear that is consistent with great joy in the Lord, *Serve the Lord with fear, and rejoice with trembling*, Psalm 2:11. and with the utmost courage and magnanimity of mind; it is a fearless fear; a man that fears the Lord has no reason to fear anything, or what any man or devil can do unto him; he may say as David did, *The Lord is my light and my salvation, whom shall I fear*, etc. Psalm 27:1, 3.

5. Such a fear is opposed to pride and self-confidence; it is an humble fear, a diffidence of a man's self, placing his trust and hope alone in God; *Be not high-minded, but fear*, Romans 11:20, that is that *fear* and *trembling*, or that modesty and humility, with which the saints are exhorted to *work* about or employ themselves in things that accompany *salvation*; as knowing that *both to will and to do*, the disposition and ability to perform any duty aright, are owing to the efficacious operation of the Spirit of God, and that it is by the grace of God they are what they are, and do what they do; they that fear the Lord are such who *rejoice in Christ Jesus, and have no confidence in the flesh*, declaring that when they have done all they can, they are but unprofitable servants, Philippians 2:12, 13 and 2:3.

III. Wherein the fear of God appears, and by what it is manifest.

1. In an hatred of sin. *The fear of the Lord is to hate evil*, Proverbs 8:13. as nothing is more opposite to good than evil, nothing is more to be abhorred; it is to be hated with a Stygian hatred, as hell itself, *abhor that which is evil*, Romans 12:9, and a man that fears God, who has a reverential affection for him, will hate it as being contrary to him, *You that love the Lord, hate evil*, Psalm 97:10, every thing that is evil is hated by such a man; as evil thoughts, which are only evil and that continually; the heart is full of evil thoughts, and out of it they daily proceed, and these are the object of a good man's hatred, *I hate vain thoughts*, says David, Psalm 119:113, and now as no one but a man himself is conscious of them and privy to them, to hate them shows that the fear of God is in his heart. Evil words are also hated by him; not only cursing, swearing, blasphemy, and all obscene and filthy language, but every vain and idle word, foolish and frothy expression, which comes out of his mouth when not on his guard, gives him uneasiness, as being displeasing to God, grieving to his Spirit, and what must be accounted for in the day of judgment; as *in many words* there are *divers vanities*, the wise man opposes the *fear of* God unto them, Ecclesiastes 5:7. And if evil thoughts and evil words are hated by such, then most certainly evil actions; and not only those of others, as the deeds of the Nicolaitans, the garment, the outward conversation-garment spotted with the flesh, the filthy conversation of the wicked, but his own actions springing from corrupt nature, done by him contrary to the law of his mind; *What I would, that do I not, but what I hate, that I do*, Romans 7:15. Evil men and their company are abhorrent to those that fear the Lord, and are shunned and avoided by them; they choose not to have any fellowship with the unfruitful works of darkness, and the workers of them; society with them is a grief and burden to them, as it

was to Lot, David, Isaiah, Jeremiah, and others, nay hateful to them: *Do I not hate them that hate you? I hate them with perfect hatred*, Psalm 139:21, 22, see Proverbs 4:14, 15. All evil and false ways, not only of immorality, but of superstition and will worship, are rejected with abhorrence by men that fear the Lord, and make his word the rule of their faith and practice. Wisdom herself, or Christ, has set an example, proving the truth of the assertion in Proverbs 8:13. *Pride and arrogance, and the evil way, and the froward mouth, do I hate*; and wisdom is justified of her children; says David, who was one of them, *I hate every false way*, Psalm 119:128. Yea, all evil doctrines which reflect on the divine persons in the godhead, on the free grace of God in man's salvation, on the person and offices of Christ, and the operations of the Spirit, are the object of the hatred and aversion of one that fears God; he cannot bear them that are evil, neither receive them into his house, nor wish them God speed. In short, every thing that is evil in its nature, as sin is in every shape exceeding sinful, a breach of the law of God, contrary to his nature, that abominable thing his righteous soul hates, is also hateful to a good man, to a man that fears the Lord, and hereby the fear of the Lord is manifested by him.

2. It shows itself by departing from evil; *By the fear of the Lord men depart from evil*, Proverbs 16:6. See chap. 3:7. Not only from open and public sins, but from private and secret ones; Job was a man that feared God and eschewed evil, avoided and departed from it, as every wise man does; yea to depart from evil is understanding, this shows a man both to be a wise man and one that fears the Lord, Job 1:1 and 28:28; Proverbs 14:16, yea such an one will abstain from all appearance of evil, from every thing that looks like it or leads unto it; will shun every avenue, every by-path, that has a tendency to ensnare into it, taking the wise man's advice. *Enter not into the path of the wicked, etc.* Proverbs 4:14, 15.

3. The fear of God appears in men in not allowing themselves to do what others do, and what they themselves formerly did; so Nehemiah, speaking of some ill things done by former governors, says, *So did not I, because of the fear of God*, Nehemiah 5:15. Not that such who fear God are without sin; Job feared God, but was not free from sin; he was sensible of it, acknowledged it, and implored the pardon of it; but they cannot give themselves that liberty to sin that others do, and walk as other Gentiles walk, in the vanity of their minds, and in a sinful course of life; they have not so learned Christ, and the grace of God teaches them other things.

4. The fear of God manifests itself by a carefulness not to offend God nor man; such study to exercise a conscience void of offense to both, and would willingly give no offense to Jew nor Gentile, nor to the church of God; and next to God they are careful that they offend not against the generation of his children, either by word or deed, and even to put no stumbling block before any, but fear the Lord their God, for to do otherwise would be contrary to it, Leviticus 19:14. Nay, such are not only on their guard to avoid sin and give no offense by it, but they are in an opposition to it; the spiritual part in them lusts against the carnal part; there are as it were a company of two armies in them fighting one against another; they strive against sin, acting the part of an antagonist to it, take to themselves the whole armor of God, and make use of it against it.

5. The fear of God in men is seen by a constant attendance on the worship of God, and by a strict regard to his will and the observation of it; the fear of God has so great a share and concern in divine worship, as has been observed, that it is sometimes put for the whole of it, both internal and external; such who fear the Lord cannot be easy in the neglect of the worship of God, but as they desire to be filled with the knowledge of his will, so to be found in the prac-

tice of it; and, like Zacharias and Elizabeth, to walk in all the ordinances and commands of the Lord blameless; and to fear God, and keep his commandments, is the whole required of man; and such who make a custom of it to forsake the assembling of themselves together to worship God, do interpretatively cast off the fear of God.

6. The fear of God is seen and known in men by their withholding nothing from God, though ever so dear unto them, whenever he requires it of them; so Abraham, when he so readily offered up his son at the command of God, received this testimony from him, *Now I know*, says the Lord, *that you fear God*, Genesis 22:12; on the contrary, when men keep back a part from God of what he expects from them, as in the case of Ananias and Sapphira, it is a proof that the fear of God is not before their eyes and in their hearts.

IV. The springs and causes of the fear of God, or from whence it flows.

1. It is not from nature, nor is it in natural men; the want of it is a part of the description of corrupt nature, and of men in a nature state; *There is no fear of God before their eyes*, Romans 3:18, it may be said of the heart of every natural man, what Abraham said of Gerar, *Surely the fear of God is not in this place*, Genesis 20:11, and which may be concluded from the wickedness that is in it, and that by what comes out of it; *The transgression of the wicked,* discovered by his words and works, his life and actions, *says within my heart,* suggests this to my mind, speaks as plainly as well can be, it is an observation of David, *that there is no fear of God before his eyes,* Psalm 36:1.

2. It arises from the grace of God, it is a gift and grant of grace; *O that there were such an heart in them that they would fear me*, or *who will give such an heart?* Deuteronomy 5:29, none but God can give it, and he has promised it in convent; it is a blessing of his grace, which he has provided in it; *I will give them one heart and one way, that they may fear me*

for ever. I will put my fear in their hearts, that they shall not depart from me, Jeremiah 32:39, 40. In consequence of which promise and covenant:

3. It is implanted in the heart in regeneration; it is planted in the heart in regeneration; it is put there by the Spirit of God, where it was not before, and where it never could have been, had he not put it there, and it appears as soon in a regenerate man as any grace whatever; upon first conversion there is quickly found a tenderness of conscience with respect to sin, and a carefulness not to offend God; and indeed *the fear of the Lord is the beginning of wisdom*, Psalm 111:10, Proverbs 9:10. No man is truly wise until he fears God, and as soon as he fears the Lord he begins to be wise, and not before; yea the fear of the Lord is wisdom itself it is that wisdom and truth which God desires and puts into the inward and hidden part of the heart, Job 28:28. Psalm 51:6.

4. The word and prayer are the means of attaining it; the fear of the Lord, as it is a duty, and expressive of worship, is to be learned; *Come you children, hearken unto me*, says David, *I will teach you the fear of the Lord*, Psalm 19:7,8, but as a grace, it is diligently sought after and earnestly importuned of God; the heart must not only be instructed but united to fear the Lord, and which is to be prayed for, Psalm 86:11; Proverbs 2:3-5.

5. It is encouraged, promoted, and increased by fresh discoveries of the grace and goodness of God, *They shall fear the Lord and his goodness*; the goodness of God made know, bestowed, and applied, greatly influences the fear of him, Hosea 3:5, especially an application of his pardoning grace and mercy, *There is forgiveness with you that you may be feared*, Psalm 130:4.

V. The happiness of those that fear the Lord. There is scarce any one character by which the people of God are described, under which more promises of good things are made unto them, than this.

First, with respect to things temporal, Godliness in general, and this part of it, the fear of the Lord, in particular, has the promise of this life, as well as of that which is to come.

1. It is promised they shall have no want, not of temporal good things, *O fear the Lord, you his saints, for there is no want to them that fear him*, Psalm 34:9, 10, not of any good thing; that is, which is suitable and convenient for them, and God in his wisdom sees fit and proper for them; and rather than they shall want, he will do wonders for them, and open sources of relief they never thought of, Isaiah 41:17, 18. and 43:19, 20.

2. Though they may have but little of the good things of this world, yet *better is little with the fear of the Lord, than great treasures and troubles therewith,* Proverbs 15:16, this with the fear of God and with righteousness, is better than great revenues without right, and better than the riches of many wicked, Proverbs 16:8. Psalm 37:16.

3. Yea wealth and riches are promised to be in the house of that man that fears the Lord, and that by humility and the fear of the Lord are riches, and honor, and life, Psalm 107:1,3; Proverbs 22:4, which can only be understood of some, not of all that fear the Lord; unless spiritual wealth, riches, honor, and life, are intended, since the fear of the Lord itself is the good man's treasure, Isaiah 33:6, it is a treasure of itself.

4. It is said that the man that fears the Lord shall eat of the labor of his hands, and he shall not only be happy, and it shall be well with him in his person, but in his family; his wife shall be as a fruitful vine by the sides of his house, and his children shall be as olive plants round about his table.

5. They that fear the Lord are in the utmost safety; in his fear is strong confidence, and they have no reason to be afraid of any thing; they shall not be visited with evil, yea the angle of the Lord encamps round about them and pro-

tects, defends, and delivers them from all dangers and from all enemies, Proverbs 14:26, and 19:23; Psalm 34:7.

6. The fear of the Lord prolongs days, or adds unto them, Proverbs 10:27, which was always reckoned a great temporal blessing; the wise man says of a sinner, *though his days be prolonged*, as they may be, and he not happy, *yet surely*, says he, *I know that it shall be well with them that fear God, which fear before him*, Ecclesiastes 8:12, be their days more or fewer.

Secondly, with respect to things spiritual, much is promised to them that fear the Lord, and they are spoken of as most happy persons.

1. The Lord is said to take pleasure in them that fear him, so having the utmost complacency and delight in them, being his special and peculiar people, his Hephzibah in whom he delights, his Beulah to whom he is married, Psalm 142:11.

2. They are accepted of him, and are acceptable to him; *Of a truth* says Peter, *I perceive that God is no respecter of persons, but in every nation he that fears him and works righteousness, is accepted with him,* Acts 10:34, 35. his person is accepted with him in Christ, the beloved, and his sacrifices of prayer and praise are acceptable to him through Jesus Christ.

3. The heart of God is towards them; he has a sympathy and fellow-feeling with them in all their distresses, trials, and exercises; in all their afflictions he is afflicted, and he comforts and supports them; *like as a father pities his children, so the Lord pities them that fear him*, Psalm 103:13.

4. The eye of the Lord is upon them for good; *the eye of the Lord is upon them that fear him*, Psalm 33:18, not only his eye of providence, which runs to and fro throughout the earth to show himself strong on their behalf, to protect and defend them, and to avenge himself on their enemies; but his eye of special love, grace, and mercy, is upon them, and

is never withdrawn from them, but is ever delighting in them and caring for them, Psalm 103:11,17; Luke 1:50.

5. His hand is open and ready to communicate to them; he *gives meat to them that fear him,* spiritual food, the blessings of his covenant, of which he is ever mindful; the comforts of his Spirit in which they walk, who walk in the fear of the Lord; he gives them grace, fresh and rich supplies of it, and at last gives them glory; and in the meanwhile withholds no good thing from them, to support their faith, encourage their hope, and engage their trust in him and dependence on him.

6. *The secret of the Lord is with them that fear him;* the secrets of his heart's love to them, and of his gracious designs towards them, are disclosed unto them, but which he uses them as his most intimate and bosom friends; and *he will show them his covenant,* the blessings and promises of it, and their interest in them, Psalm 35:14, what is said of Christ the head of the covenant, is true of all the covenant ones in their measure, Malachi 2:5, to which may be added, that the Lord grants the requests and fulfills the desires of them that fear him, hears the cries and saves them, Psalm 145:19.

7. They are remembered by him with the favor he bears to his own people, with his tender mercies and loving kindness, which have been ever of old; he remembers them when in a low estate, and brings them out of it; he remembers his promises to them, and fulfills them; *a book of remembrance* is said to be *written before him for them that feared the Lord,* Malachi 3:16.

8. It is promised to them *that fear the name* of the Lord, that *unto* them *the Sun of righteousness shall arise with healing in his wings,* Malachi 4:2, Christ the Savior shall come and show himself with a discovery and application of pardoning grace and mercy; nay, one that *fears the Lord,* though he *walks in darkness and has no light;* yet he is encouraged to *trust in the name of the Lord, and stay upon his God,* Isaiah 1:10.

9. Salvation, a fresh view of interest in it, a renewed application of it, as well as the full enjoyment of it, *is night unto them that fear* the Lord, Psalm 85:9, for that is nearer to them than when they first believed, and had the fear of God first implanted in them, and were set a seeking after it, and had first hope of interest in it.

10. Great and good things are laid up for such persons in the heart of God, in the covenant of grace, and in the hands of Christ, and in heaven; even a blessed hope, a crown of righteousness, and things which eye has not seen, nor ear heard of, nor has it entered into the heart of man to conceive of; *O how great is they goodness, which you have laid up for them that fear you!* Psalm 31:19.

SINNERS IN THE HANDS OF AN ANGRY GOD
BY JONATHAN EDWARDS

Their foot shall slide in due time. —*Deuteronomy 32: 35*

In this verse is threatened the vengeance of God on the wicked unbelieving Israelites, who were God's visible people, and who lived under the means of grace; but who, notwithstanding all God's wonderful works towards them, remained (as verse 28) void of counsel, having no understanding in them. Under all the cultivations of heaven, they brought forth bitter and poisonous fruit; as in the two verses next preceding the text. The expression I have chosen for my text, Their foot shall slide in due time, seems to imply the following doings, relating to the punishment and destruction to which these wicked Israelites were exposed.

That they were always exposed to *destruction;* as one that stands or walks in slippery places is always exposed to fall. This is implied in the manner of their destruction coming upon them, being represented by their foot sliding. The same is expressed, Psalm 73:18—"Surely you set them in slippery places; you cast them down into destruction."

2. It implies, that they were always exposed to sudden unexpected destruction. As he that walks in slippery places is every moment liable to fall, he cannot foresee one moment whether he shall stand or fall the next; and when he does fall, he falls at once without warning: Which is also expressed in Psalm 73: 18, 19—" Surely you set them in

299

slippery places; you cast them down into destruction. How are they brought into desolation as in a moment!"

3. Another thing implied is, that they are liable to fall *of themselves*, without being thrown down by the hand of another; as he that stands or walks on slippery ground needs nothing but his own weight to throw him down.

4. That the reason why they are not fallen already, and do not fall now, is only that God's appointed time is not come. For it is said, that when that due time, or appointed time comes, *their foot shall slide*. Then they shall be left to fall, as they are inclined by their own weight. God will not hold them up in these slippery places any longer, but will let them go; and then at that very instant, they shall fall into destruction; as he that stands on such slippery declining ground, on the edge of a pit, he cannot stand alone, when he is let go he immediately falls and is lost.

The observation from the words that I would now insist upon is this: There is nothing that keeps wicked men at any one moment out of hell, but the mere pleasure of God. By "the mere pleasure of God," I mean his sovereign pleasure, his arbitrary will, restrained by no obligation, hindered by no manner of difficulty, any more than if nothing else but God's mere will had in the least degree, or in any respect whatsoever, any hand in the preservation of wicked men one moment.

The truth of this observation may appear by the following considerations. 1. 1. There is no want of *power* in God to cast wicked men into hell at any moment. Men's hands cannot be strong when God rises up. The strongest have no power to resist him, nor can any deliver out of his hands. He is not only able to cast wicked men into hell, but he can most easily do it. Sometimes an earthly prince meets with a great deal of difficulty to subdue a rebel, who has found means to fortify himself, and has made himself strong by the numbers of his followers. But it is not so with God. There is no fortress that is any defense from the power of God. Though hand join in hand, and vast multitudes of God's enemies combine and associate themselves, they are easily broken in pieces. They are as great heaps of light chaff before the whirlwind; or large quantities of dry stubble before devouring flames. We find it easy to tread on and crush a worm that we see crawling on the earth; so it is easy for us to cut or singe a slender thread that any thing hangs by: thus easy is it for God, when he pleases, to cast his enemies down to hell. What are we, that we should think to stand before him, at whose rebuke the earth trembles, and before whom the rocks are thrown down?

2. They deserve to be cast into hell; so that divine justice never stands in the way, it makes no objection against God's using his power at any moment to destroy them. Yea, on the contrary, justice calls aloud for an infinite punishment of their sins. Divine justice says of the tree that brings forth such grapes of Sodom, "Cut it down, why cumbereth it the ground?" Luke 13:7 The sword of divine justice is every moment brandished over their heads, and it is nothing but the hand of arbitrary mercy, and God's mere will, that holds it back.

3. They are already under a sentence of condemnation to hell. They do not only justly deserve to be cast down thither, but the sentence of the law of God, that eternal and immutable rule of righteousness that God has fixed between him and mankind, is gone out against them, and stands against them; so that they are bound over already to hell.

John 3:18—"He that believeth not is condemned already."
So that every unconverted man properly belongs to hell;
that is his place; from thence he is, John 8:23—"You are
from beneath." And thither be is bound; it is the place that
justice, and God's word, and the sentence of his unchangeable law assign to him.

4. They are now the objects of that very same anger and
wrath of God, that is expressed in the torments of hell. And
the reason why they do not go down to hell at each moment, is not because God, in whose power they are, is not
then very angry with them; as he is with many miserable
creatures now tormented in hell, who there feel and bear
the fierceness of his wrath. Yea, God is a great deal more
angry with great numbers that are now on earth: yea,
doubtless, with many that are now in this congregation,
who it may be are at ease, than he is with many of those
who are now in the flames of hell.

So that it is not because God is unmindful of their wickedness, and does not resent it, that he does not let loose his
hand and cut them off. God is not altogether such an one as
themselves, though they may imagine him to be so. The
wrath of God burns against them, their damnation does not
slumber; the pit is prepared, the fire is made ready, the furnace is now hot, ready to receive them; the flames do now
rage and glow. The glittering sword is whet, and held over
them, and the pit has opened its mouth under them.

5. The devil stands ready to fall upon them, and seize
them as his own, at what moment God shall permit him.
They belong to him; he has their souls in his possession, and
under his dominion. The scripture represents them as his
goods (Luke 11:12). The devils watch them; they are ever by
them at their right hand; they stand waiting for them, like

greedy hungry lions that see their prey, and expect to have it, but are for the present kept back. If God should withdraw his hand, by which they are restrained, they would in one moment fly upon their poor souls. The old serpent is gaping for them; hell opens its mouth wide to receive them; and if God should permit it, they would be hastily swallowed up and lost.

6. There are in the souls of wicked men those hellish principles reigning, that would presently kindle and flame out into hell fire, if it were not for God's restraints. There is laid in the very nature of carnal men, a foundation for the torments of hell. There are those corrupt principles, in reigning power in them, and in full possession of them, that are seeds of hell fire. These principles are active and powerful, exceeding violent in their nature, and if it were not for the restraining hand of God upon them, they would soon break out, they would flame out after the same manner as the same corruptions, the same enmity does in the hearts of damned souls, and would beget the same torments as they do in them. The souls of the wicked are in scripture compared to the troubled sea (Isaiah 52:20). For the present, God restrains their wickedness by his mighty power, as he does the raging waves of the troubled sea, saying, "Up to here shall you come, but no further;" but if God should withdraw that restraining power, it would soon carry all before it. Sin is the ruin and misery of the soul; it is destructive in its nature; and if God should leave it without restraint, there would need nothing else to make the soul perfectly miserable. The corruption of the heart of man is immoderate and boundless in its fury; and while wicked men live here, it is like fire pent up by God's restraints, whereas if it were let loose, it would set on fire the course of nature; and as the heart is now a sink of sin, so if sin was not restrained, it

would immediately turn the soul into a fiery oven, or a furnace of fire and brimstone.

7. It is no security to wicked men for one moment, that there are no visible means of death at hand. It is no security to a natural man, that he is now in health, and that he does not see which way he should now immediately go out of the world by any accident, and that there is no visible danger in any respect in his circumstances. The manifold and continual experience of the world in all ages, shows this is no evidence, that a man is not on the very brink of eternity, and that the next step will not be into another world. The unseen, unthought of ways and means of persons going suddenly out of the world are innumerable and inconceivable. Unconverted men walk over the pit of hell on a rotten covering, and there are innumerable places in this covering so weak that they will not bear their weight, and these places are not seen. The arrows of death fly unseen at noonday; the sharpest sight cannot discern them. God has so many different unsearchable ways of taking wicked men out of the world and sending them to hell, that there is nothing to make it appear, that God had need to be at the expense of a miracle, or go out of the ordinary course of his providence, to destroy any wicked man, at any moment. All the means that there are of sinners going out of the world, are so in God's hands, and so universally and absolutely subject to his power and determination, that it does not depend at all the less on the mere will of God, whether sinners shall at any moment go to hell, than if means were never made use of, or at all concerned in the case.

8. Natural men's prudence and care to preserve their own lives, or the care of others to preserve them, do not secure them a moment. To this, divine providence and universal experience do also bear testimony. There is this

clear evidence that men's own wisdom is no security to
them from death; that if it were otherwise we should see
some difference between the wise and politic men of the
world, and others, with regard to their liability to early and
unexpected death: but how is it in fact? Ecclesiastes 2:16—
"How does the wise man die? Even as the fool."

9. All wicked men's pains and contrivance which they
use to escape hell, while they continue to reject Christ, and
so remain wicked men, do not secure them from hell one
moment. Almost every natural man that hears of hell, flatters himself that he shall escape it; he depends upon himself
for his own security; he flatters himself in what he has done,
in what he is now doing, or what he intends to do. Every
one lays out matters in his own mind how he shall avoid
damnation, and flatters himself that he contrives well for
himself, and that his schemes will not fail. They hear indeed
that there are but few saved, and that the greater part of
men that have died heretofore are gone to hell; but each one
imagines that he lays out matters better for his own escape
than others have done. He does not intend to come to that
place of torment; he says within himself, that he intends to
take effectual care, and to order matters so for himself as not
to fail.

But the foolish children of men miserably delude themselves in their own schemes, and in confidence in their own
strength and wisdom; they trust to nothing but a shadow.
The greater part of those who heretofore have lived under
the same means of grace, and are now dead, are undoubtedly gone to hell; and it was not because they were not as
wise as those who are now alive: it was not because they
did not lay out matters as well for themselves to secure their
own escape. If we could speak with them, and inquire of

them, one by one, whether they expected, when alive, and when they used to hear about hell ever to be the subjects of that misery: we doubtless, should hear one and another reply, "No, I never intended to come here: I had laid out matters otherwise in my mind; I thought I should contrive well for myself: I thought my scheme good. I intended to take effectual care; but it came upon me unexpected; I did not look for it at that time, and in that manner; it came as a thief: Death outwitted me: God's wrath was too quick for me. Oh, my cursed foolishness! I was flattering myself, and pleasing myself with vain dreams of what I would do hereafter; and when I was saying, Peace and safety, then suddenly destruction came upon me."

10. God has laid himself under no obligation, by any promise to keep any natural man out of hell one moment. God certainly has made no promises either of eternal life, or of any deliverance or preservation from eternal death, but what are contained in the covenant of grace, the promises that are given in Christ, in whom all the promises are yea and amen. But surely they have no interest in the promises of the covenant of grace who are not the children of the covenant, who do not believe in any of the promises, and have no interest in the Mediator of the covenant.

So that, whatever some have imagined and pretended about promises made to natural men's earnest seeking and knocking, it is plain and manifest, that whatever pains a natural man takes in religion, whatever prayers he makes, till he believes in Christ, God is under no manner of obligation to keep him a moment from eternal destruction.

So that, thus it is that natural men are held in the hand of God, over the pit of hell; they have deserved the fiery pit, and are already sentenced to it; and God is dreadfully pro-

voked, his anger is as great towards them as to those that
are actually suffering the executions of the fierceness of his
wrath in hell, and they have done nothing in the least to
appease or abate that anger, neither is God in the least
bound by any promise to hold them up one moment; the
devil is waiting for them, hell is gaping for them, the flames
gather and flash about them, and would almost lay hold on
them, and swallow them up; the fire pent up in their own
hearts is struggling to break out: and they have no interest
in any Mediator, there are no means within reach that can
be any security to them. In short, they have no refuge,
nothing to take hold of, all that preserves them every moment is the mere arbitrary will, and uncovenanted,
unobliged forbearance of an incensed God.

APPLICATION

The use of this awful subject may be for awakening unconverted persons in this congregation. This that you have
heard is the case of every one of you that are out of Christ.-
That world of misery, that lake of burning brimstone, is ex-
tended abroad under you. There is the dreadful pit of the
glowing flames of the wrath of God; there is hell's wide
gaping mouth open; and you have nothing to stand upon,
nor any thing to take hold of, there is nothing between you
and hell but the air; it is only the power and mere pleasure
of God that holds you up.

You probably are not sensible of this; you find you are
kept out of hell, but do not see the hand of God in it; but
look at other things, as the good state of your bodily constitution, your care of your own life, and the means you use
for your own preservation. But indeed these things are
nothing; if God should withdraw his band, they would avail

307

no more to keep you from falling, than the thin air to hold up a person that is suspended in it.

Your wickedness makes you as it were heavy as lead, and to tend downwards with great weight and pressure towards hell; and if God should let you go, you would immediately sink and swiftly descend and plunge into the bottomless gulf, and your healthy constitution, and your own care and prudence, and best contrivance, and all your righteousness, would have no more influence to uphold you and keep you out of hell, than a spider's web would have to stop a falling rock. Were it not for the sovereign pleasure of God, the earth would not bear you one moment; for you are a burden to it; the creation groans with you; the creature is made subject to the bondage of your corruption, not willingly; the sun does not willingly shine upon you to give you light to serve sin and Satan; the earth does not willingly yield her increase to satisfy your lusts; nor is it willingly a stage for your wickedness to be acted upon; the air does not willingly serve you for breath to maintain the flame of life in your vitals, while you spend your life in the service of God's enemies. God's creatures are good, and were made for men to serve God with, and do not willingly subserve to any other purpose, and groan when they are abused to purposes so directly contrary to their nature and end. And the world would spew you out, were it not for the sovereign hand of him who has subjected it in hope. There are black clouds of God's wrath now hanging directly over your heads, full of the dreadful storm, and big with thunder; and were it not for the restraining hand of God, it would immediately burst forth upon you. The sovereign pleasure of God, for the present, stays his rough wind; otherwise it would come with fury, and your destruction would come like a whirlwind, and you would be like the chaff of the summer threshing floor.

Supplement: *Sinners in the Hands of an Angry God* by
Jonathan Edwards

The wrath of God is like great waters that are dammed for the present; they increase more and more, and rise higher and higher, till an outlet is given; and the longer the stream is stopped, the more rapid and mighty is its course, when once it is let loose. It is true, that judgment against your evil works has not been executed hitherto; the floods of God's vengeance have been withheld; but your guilt in the mean time is constantly increasing, and you are every day treasuring up more wrath; the waters are constantly rising, and waxing more and more mighty; and there is nothing but the mere pleasure of God, that holds the waters back, that are unwilling to be stopped, and press hard to go forward. If God should only withdraw his hand from the flood-gate, it would immediately fly open, and the fiery floods of the fierceness and wrath of God, would rush forth with inconceivable fury, and would come upon you with omnipotent power; and if your strength were ten thousand times greater than it is, yea, ten thousand times greater than the strength of the stoutest, sturdiest devil in hell, it would be nothing to withstand or endure it.

The bow of God's wrath is bent, and the arrow made ready on the string, and justice bends the arrow at your heart, and strains the bow, and it is nothing but the mere pleasure of God, and that of an angry God, without any promise or obligation at all, that keeps the arrow one moment from being made drunk with your blood. Thus all you that never passed under a great change of heart, by the mighty power of the Spirit of God upon your souls; all you that were never born again, and made new creatures, and raised from being dead in sin, to a state of new, and before altogether unexperienced light and life, are in the hands of an angry God. However you may have reformed your life in many things, and may have had religious affections, and may keep up a form of religion in your families and closets, and in the house of God, it is nothing but his mere pleasure that keeps you from being this moment swallowed up in everlasting destruction. However unconvinced you may now be of the truth of what you hear, by and by you will be fully convinced of it. Those that are gone from being in the like circumstances with you, see that it was so with them; for destruction came suddenly upon most of them; when they expected nothing of it, and while they were saying, Peace and safety: now they see, that those things on which they depended for peace and safety, were nothing but thin air and empty shadows.

The God that holds you over the pit of hell, much as one holds a spider, or some loathsome insect over the fire, abhors you, and is dreadfully provoked: his wrath towards you burns like fire; he looks upon you as worthy of nothing else, but to be cast into the fire; he is of purer eyes than to bear to have you in his sight; you are ten thousand times more abominable in his eyes, than the most hateful venomous serpent is in ours. You have offended him infinitely more than ever a stubborn rebel did his prince; and yet it is nothing but his hand that holds you from falling into the fire every moment. It is to be ascribed to nothing else, that you did not go to hell the last night; that you was suffered to awake again in this world, after you closed your eyes to sleep. And there is no other reason to be given, why you have not dropped into hell since you arose in the morning, but that God's hand has held you up. There is no other reason to be given why you have not gone to hell, since you have sat here in the house of God, provoking his pure eyes by your sinful wicked manner of attending his solemn worship. Yea, there is nothing else that is to be given as a reason why you do not this very moment drop down into hell.

Supplement: *Sinners in the Hands of an Angry God* by
Jonathan Edwards

O sinner, consider the fearful danger you are in! It is a great furnace of wrath, a wide and bottomless pit, full of the fire of wrath, that you are held over in the hand of that God, whose wrath is provoked and incensed as much against you, as against many of the damned in hell. You hang by a slender thread, with the flames of divine wrath flashing about it, and ready every moment to singe it, and burn it asunder; and you have no interest in any Mediator, and nothing to lay hold of to save yourself, nothing to keep off the flames of wrath, nothing of your own, nothing that you ever have done, nothing that you can do, to induce God to spare you one moment. And consider here more particularly:

1. Whose wrath it is: it is the wrath of the infinite God. If it were only the wrath of man, though it were of the most potent prince, it would be comparatively little to be regarded. The wrath of kings is very much dreaded, especially of absolute monarchs, who have the possessions and lives of their subjects wholly in their power, to be disposed of at their mere will. Proverbs 20:2—"The fear of a king is as the roaring of a lion: Whoso provoketh him to anger, sinneth against his own soul." The subject that very much enrages an arbitrary prince, is liable to suffer the most extreme torments that human art can invent, or human power can inflict. But the greatest earthly potentates in their greatest majesty and strength, and when clothed in their greatest terrors, are but feeble, despicable worms of the dust, in comparison of the great and almighty Creator and King of heaven and earth. It is but little that they can do, when most enraged, and when they have exerted the utmost of their fury. All the kings of the earth, before God, are as grasshoppers; they are nothing, and less than nothing: both their love and their hatred is to be despised. The wrath of the

311

great King of kings, is as much more terrible than theirs, as his majesty is greater. Luke 12:4, 5—"And I say unto you, my friends, Be not afraid of them that kill the body, and after that, have no more that they can do. But I will forewarn you whom you shall fear: fear him, which after he has killed, has power to cast into hell. I say unto you, Fear him."

2. It is the fierceness of his wrath that you are exposed to. We often read of the fury of God, as in Isaiah 59:18—"According to their deeds, accordingly he will repay fury to his adversaries." Also in Isaiah 66:15—"For behold, the Lord will come with fire, and with his chariots like a whirlwind, to render his anger with fury, and his rebuke with flames of fire." And in many other places. So, Revelation 19:15, we read of "the wine press of the fierceness and wrath of Almighty God." The words are exceeding terrible. If it had only been said, "the wrath of God," the words would have implied that which is infinitely dreadful: but it is "the fierceness and wrath of God." The fury of God! the fierceness of Jehovah! Oh, how dreadful must that be! Who can utter or conceive what such expressions carry in them! But it is also "the fierceness and wrath of Almighty God." As though there would be a very great manifestation of his almighty power in what the fierceness of his wrath should inflict, as though omnipotence should be as it were enraged, and exerted, as men are wont to exert their strength in the fierceness of their wrath. Oh! then, what will be the consequence! What will become of the poor worms that shall suffer it! Whose hands can be strong? And whose heart can endure? To what a dreadful, inexpressible, inconceivable depth of misery must the poor creature be sunk who shall be the subject of this!

Consider this, you that are here present, that yet remain in an unregenerate state. That God will execute the fierce-

ness of his anger, implies, that he will inflict wrath without
any pity. When God beholds the ineffable extremity of your
case, and sees your torment to be so vastly disproportioned
to your strength, and sees how your poor soul is crushed,
and sinks down, as it were, into an infinite gloom; he will
have no compassion upon you, he will not forbear the executions of his wrath, or in the least lighten his hand; there
shall be no moderation or mercy, nor will God then at all
stay his rough wind; he will have no regard to your welfare,
nor be at all careful lest you should suffer too much in any
other sense, than only that you shall not suffer beyond what
strict justice requires. Nothing shall be withheld, because it
is so hard for you to bear. Ezekiel 8:18—"Therefore will I
also deal in fury: mine eye shall not spare, neither will I
have pity; and though they cry in mine ears with a loud
voice, yet I will not hear them." Now God stands ready to
pity you; this is a day of mercy; you may cry now with
some encouragement of obtaining mercy. But when once
the day of mercy is past, your most lamentable and dolorous
cries and shrieks will be in vain; you will be wholly lost and
thrown away of God, as to any regard to your welfare. God
will have no other use to put you to, but to suffer misery;
you shall be continued in being to no other end; for you will
be a vessel of wrath fitted to destruction; and there will be
no other use of this vessel, but to be filled full of wrath. God
will be so far from pitying you when you cry to him, that it
is said he will only "laugh and mock" (Proverbs 1:25, 26,
etc.).

How awful are those words, Isa. 63:3, which are the
words of the great God. "I will tread them in mine anger,
and will trample them in my fury, and their blood shall be
sprinkled upon my garments, and I will stain all my raiment." It is perhaps impossible to conceive of words that

carry in them greater manifestations of these three things, vis. contempt, and hatred, and fierceness of indignation. If you cry to God to pity you, he will be so far from pitying you in your doleful case, or showing you the least regard or favor, that instead of that, he will only tread you under foot. And though he will know that you cannot bear the weight of omnipotence treading upon you, yet he will not regard that, but he will crush you under his feet without mercy; he will crush out your blood, and make it fly, and it shall be sprinkled on his garments, so as to stain all his raiment. He will not only hate you, but he will have you, in the utmost contempt: no place shall be thought fit for you, but under his feet to be trodden down as the mire of the streets.

The misery you are exposed to is that which God will inflict to that end, that he might show what that wrath of Jehovah is. God has had it on his heart to show to angels and men, both how excellent his love is, and also how terrible his wrath is. Sometimes earthly kings have a mind to show how terrible their wrath is, by the extreme punishments they would execute on those that would provoke them. Nebuchadnezzar, that mighty and haughty monarch of the Chaldean empire, was willing to show his wrath when enraged with Shadrach, Meshech, and Abednego; and accordingly gave orders that the burning fiery furnace should be heated seven times hotter than it was before; doubtless, it was raised to the utmost degree of fierceness that human art could raise it. But the great God is also willing to show his wrath, and magnify his awful majesty and mighty power in the extreme sufferings of his enemies. Romans 9:22—"What if God, willing to show his wrath, and to make his power known, endure with much long-suffering the vessels of wrath fitted to destruction?" And seeing this is his design, and what he has determined, even to show how terrible the unrestrained wrath, the fury and fierceness of

Jehovah is, he will do it to effect. There will be something accomplished and brought to pass that will be dreadful with a witness. When the great and angry God has risen up and executed his awful vengeance on the poor sinner, and the wretch is actually suffering the infinite weight and power of his indignation, then will God call upon the whole universe to behold that awful majesty and mighty power that is to be seen in it. Isaiah 33:12-14—"And the people shall be as the burnings of lime, as thorns cut up shall they be burnt in the fire. Hear, you that are far off, what I have done; and you that are near, acknowledge my might. The sinners in Zion are afraid; fearfulness has surprised the hypocrites," etc.

Thus it will be with you that are in an unconverted state, if you continue in it; the infinite might, and majesty, and terribleness of the omnipotent God shall be magnified upon you, in the ineffable strength of your torments. You shall be tormented in the presence of the holy angels, and in the presence of the Lamb; and when you shall be in this state of suffering, the glorious inhabitants of heaven shall go forth and look on the awful spectacle, that they may see what the wrath and fierceness of the Almighty is; and when they have seen it, they will fall down and adore that great power and majesty. Isaiah 66:23, 24—"And it shall come to pass, that from one new moon to another, and from one sabbath to another, shall all flesh come to worship before me, says the Lord. And they shall go forth and look upon the carcasses of the men that have transgressed against me; for their worm shall not die, neither shall their fire be quenched, and they shall be an abhorring unto all flesh."

4. It is everlasting wrath. It would be dreadful to suffer this fierceness and wrath of Almighty God one moment; but you must suffer it to all eternity. There will be no end to this

exquisite horrible misery. When you look forward, you shall see a long for ever, a boundless duration before you, which will swallow up your thoughts, and amaze your soul; and you will absolutely despair of ever having any deliverance, any end, any mitigation, any rest at all. You will know certainly that you must wear out long ages, millions of millions of ages, in wrestling and conflicting with this almighty merciless vengeance; and then when you have so done, when so many ages have actually been spent by you in this manner, you will know that all is but a point to what remains. So that your punishment will indeed be infinite. Oh, who can express what the state of a soul in such circumstances is! All that we can possibly say about it, gives but a very feeble, faint representation of it; it is inexpressible and inconceivable: For "who knows the power of God's anger?"

How dreadful is the state of those that are daily and hourly in the danger of this great wrath and infinite misery! But this is the dismal case of every soul in this congregation that has not been born again, however moral and strict, sober and religious, they may otherwise be. Oh that you would consider it, whether you be young or old! There is reason to think, that there are many in this congregation now hearing this discourse, that will actually be the subjects of this very misery to all eternity. We know not who they are, or in what seats they sit, or what thoughts they now have. It may be they are now at ease, and hear all these things without much disturbance, and are now flattering themselves that they are not the persons, promising themselves that they shall escape. If we knew that there was one person, and but one, in the whole congregation, that was to be the subject of this misery, what an awful thing would it be to think of! If we knew who it was, what an awful sight would it be to see such a person! How might all the rest of the congregation lift up a lamentable and bitter cry over

him! But, alas! instead of one, how many is it likely will remember this discourse in hell? And it would be a wonder, if
some that are now present should not be in hell in a very
short time, even before this year is out. And it would be no
wonder if some persons, that now sit here, in some seats of
this meeting-house, in health, quiet and secure, should be
there before to-morrow morning. Those of you that finally
continue in a natural condition, that shall keep out of hell
longest will be there in a little time! your damnation does
not slumber; it will come swiftly, and, in all probability, very
suddenly upon many of you. You have reason to wonder
that you are not already in hell. It is doubtless the case of
some whom you have seen and known, that never deserved
hell more than you, and that heretofore appeared as likely
to have been now alive as you. Their case is past all hope;
they are crying in extreme misery and perfect despair; but
here you are in the land of the living and in the house of
God, and have an opportunity to obtain salvation. What
would not those poor damned hopeless souls give for one
day's opportunity such as you now enjoy!

And now you have an extraordinary opportunity, a day
wherein Christ has thrown the door of mercy wide open,
and stands in calling and crying with a loud voice to poor
sinners; a day wherein many are flocking to him, and
pressing into the kingdom of God. Many are daily coming
from the east, west, north and south; many that were very
lately in the same miserable condition that you are in, are
now in a happy state, with their hearts filled with love to
him who has loved them, and washed them from their sins
in his own blood, and rejoicing in hope of the glory of God.
How awful is it to be left behind at such a day! To see so
many others feasting, while you are pining and perishing!
To see so many rejoicing and singing for joy of heart, while

317

you have cause to mourn for sorrow of heart, and howl for vexation of spirit! How can you rest one moment in such a condition? Are not your souls as precious as the souls of the people at Suffield,1 where they are flocking from day to day to Christ?

Are there not many here who have lived long in the world, and are not to this day born again? and so are aliens from the commonwealth of Israel, and have done nothing ever since they have lived, but treasure up wrath against the day of wrath? Oh, sirs, your case, in an especial manner, is extremely dangerous. Your guilt and hardness of heart is extremely great. Do you not see how generally persons of your years are passed over and left, in the present remarkable and wonderful dispensation of God's mercy? You had need to consider yourselves, and awake thoroughly out of sleep. You cannot bear the fierceness and wrath of the infinite God.-And you, young men, and young women, will you neglect this precious season which you now enjoy, when so many others of your age are renouncing all youthful vanities, and flocking to Christ? You especially have now an extraordinary opportunity; but if you neglect it, it will soon be with you as with those persons who spent all the precious days of youth in sin, and are now come to such a dreadful pass in blindness and hardness. And you, children, who are unconverted, do not you know that you are going down to hell, to bear the dreadful wrath of that God, who is now angry with you every day and every night? Will you be content to be the children of the devil, when so many other children in the land are converted, and are become the holy and happy children of the King of kings?

---

1 A town in the neighborhood.

Supplement: *Sinners in the Hands of an Angry God* by
Jonathan Edwards

And let every one that is yet out of Christ, and hanging over the pit of hell, whether they be old men and women, or middle aged, or young people, or little children, now harken to the loud calls of God's word and providence. This acceptable year of the Lord, a day of such great favors to some, will doubtless be a day of as remarkable vengeance to others. Men's hearts harden, and their guilt increases apace at such a day as this, if they neglect their souls; and never was there so great danger of such persons being given up to hardness of heart and blindness of mind. God seems now to be hastily gathering in his elect in all parts of the land; and probably the greater part of adult persons that ever shall be saved, will be brought in now in a little time, and that it will be as it was on the great out-pouring of the Spirit upon the Jews in the apostles' days; the election will obtain, and the rest will be blinded. If this should be the case with you, you will eternally curse this day, and will curse the day that ever you was born, to see such a season of the pouring out of God's Spirit, and will wish that you had died and gone to hell before you had seen it. Now undoubtedly it is, as it was in the days of John the Baptist, the axe is in an extraordinary manner laid at the root of the trees, that every tree which brings not forth good fruit, may be hewn down and cast into the fire. Therefore, let every one that is out of Christ, now awake and fly from the wrath to come. The wrath of Almighty God is now undoubtedly hanging over a great part of this congregation: Let every one fly out of Sodom: "Haste and escape for your lives, look not behind you, escape to the mountain, lest you be consumed."

ABOUT THE AUTHOR

Robert A. Morey is the Executive Director of the California Institute of Apologetics and the author of over forty books, some of which have been translated into French, German, Italian, Polish, Finish, Dutch, Spanish, Norwegian, Swedish, Farsi, and Chinese. He is a internationally recognized scholar in the fields of philosophy, theology, comparative religion, the cults and the occult. He has also written:

The Trinity: Evidences and Issues
Satan's Devices
The Islamic Invasion
The Truth About Masons
Death and The Afterlife
Studies In The Atonement
Battle of The Gods
How to Keep Your Faith While in College
The New Atheism and the Erosion of Freedom
An Introduction to Defending the Faith
An Analysis of the Hadith
When Is It Right to Fight?
How to Answer a Jehovah's Witness
How to Answer A Mormon
Reincarnation and Christianity
Horoscopes and the Christian

Worship Is All of Life
How to Keep Your Kids Drug-Free
An Examination of Exclusive Psalmody
Is Allah Just Another Name for God?
Here Is Your God
The Reformation View of Roman Catholicism
Is Sunday the Christian Sabbath?
The Dooyeweerdian Concept of The Word of God
The New Life Notebook vol. I
The New Life Notebook vol. II
The Doctrine of Jihad According to the Qur'an and the Hadith
Will Islam Cause World War Three?

For more information on Dr. Morey's books, audio tapes, and video tapes, write to: The California Institute of Apologetics, Post Office Box 7447, Orange, CA 92863 or dial 1-800-41-TRUTH.

ABOUT THE CD-ROM

This book includes a CD-ROM containing a Microsoft PowerPoint™ slide presentation based on the text of *Fearing God*. The presentation is divided into eleven chapters for instruction over eleven weeks as an adult Sunday School course or as a course for week-night Bible studies. Permission to reproduce the speaker's notes included in the presentation is granted to the purchaser of this book. The purchaser is also granted a license by the publisher to reproduce and distribute the presentation handouts provided that the handouts are distributed at no charge to attendees of any study based on *Fearing God*. If a charge is made for attendance at a study based on *Fearing God*, the charge may not exceed the list price of the book.

The disk also contains software with dozens of study aids, including the entire text of the International Standard Version® New Testament. The ISV® has been called the most readable and accurate English translation of the Bible ever produced. The disk is designed to run under the Windows 95™ or Windows 98™ operating system only. Technical support for the software is provided by the software publisher. *Please note that Davidson Press does not provide any technical support for the software; please do not contact Davidson Press with questions about installing or using the software.*

And be sure to visit the Davidson Press StudyCenter™ at http://davidsonpress.com, where you can access the complete text of all of the Davidson Press family of books on line, including *Fearing God* and the ISV Bible.

INDEX

Psalm 99:9 79
Psalm 102:15 82
Psalm 103:11 40
Psalm 103:17 40
Psalm 104:24 83
Psalm 111:10 ....37, 46
Psalm 111:5 39
Psalm 111:9 82
Psalm 112 97
Psalm 112:1 ....35, 58
Psalm 112:2-4 36
Psalm 114:7 53
Psalm 116:1 32
Psalm 119:120 57
Psalm 119:161 82
Psalm 119:42 32
Psalm 119:63 58
Psalm 119:97 32
Psalm 128 97
Psalm 128:1-3 37
Psalm 130:3-4 37
Psalm 130:4 84
Psalm 145:17 83
Proverbs 1:7................................ 1, 97
Proverbs 3:5-6............................... 32
Proverbs 4:7.................................. 48
Proverbs 9:10...........................46, 48
Proverbs 14:27............................... 40
Proverbs 19:23............................... 41
Ecclesiastes 3:14 58
Isaiah 8:13.................................... 54
Isaiah 9:6..................................... 11
Isaiah 26:17................................... 52
Isaiah 29:23................................... 54
Isaiah 33:6.................................... 41
Isaiah 59:2.................................... 89
Isaiah 66:2.................................... 82
Isaiah 66:5.................................... 82
Jeremiah 5:22................................. 53
Jeremiah 5:22-24............................. 83
Jeremiah 31:31-33............................ 43
Jeremiah 32:38-40......................43, 74
Jeremiah 32:40............................... 69
Ezekiel 20:40 47
Ezekiel 48:14 48
Daniel 5:19 56
Daniel 6:26 ....56, 81
Hosea 1:2..................................... 48
Habakkuk 3:2................................. 57

Jonah 3:5-10 71
Malachi 1:14.................................. 82
Matthew 3:7................................... 70
Matthew 10:28............................. 1, 84
Matthew 10:28-29............................ 62
Matthew 16:18................................ 25
Matthew 22:37................................ 32
Matthew 25:31-34............................ 91
Matthew 25:41................................ 91
Matthew 25:46................................ 91
Luke 12:4-5................................... 61
Luke 12:5..................................... 70
John 14:1-2................................... 36
John 14:23.................................... 12
John 3:16...................................... 5
John 3:20..................................... 86
John 3:36...................................... 5
John 6:67-68.................................. 69
Acts 2:42-43.................................. 71
Acts 2:43..................................... 98
Acts 2:47..................................... 98
Acts 5:5...................................... 71
Acts 5:11.................................71, 98
Acts 9:31......................2, 44, 62, 71
Acts 13:26.................................... 67
Acts 19:17.................................... 71
Acts 20:27.................................... 25
Romans 1:12-23............................... 65
Romans 1:18 70
Romans 3:4 23
Romans 3:18 ....19, 44
Romans 12:1-2................................ 21
1 Corinthians 10:31.......................... 71
2 Corinthians 3:1-11 36
2 Corinthians 5:10........................... 70
2 Corinthians 5:11........................... 60
2 Corinthians 7:1..........................2, 62
Ephesians 1:11 83
Colossians 3:1-2............................. 36
Colossians 3:22.............................. 100
1 Thessalonians 1:10........................ 70
2 Timothy 4:2................................. 23
Titus 3:15.................................... 12
Hebrews 4:1 60
Hebrews 4:13 86
Hebrews 7:18-8:13............................ 42
Hebrews 8:8-13............................... 43
Hebrews 9:27................................. 88
Hebrews 10:11-18............................ 43

OTHER DAVIDSON PRESS PUBLICATIONS

Davidson Press publishes an ever-growing family of fine works by some of America's finest Christian scholars and writers. In a day when many publishers are refusing to publish works of substance and depth, Davidson Press is pleased to offer conservative works on topics of vital interest which will stimulate you to further growth in your spiritual life. Here are some examples:

The Myth of Adolescence: Raising Responsible Children in an Irresponsible Society **by Dr. David Alan Black**

Dr. David Alan Black looks at the social theory of adolescence and finds it seriously flawed. This fascinating study looks at the origins of the theory of adolescence and thoroughly refutes it. The biblical pattern is for young people to take their responsibilities as adults in their twelfth or thirteenth year. Dr. Black serves as Professor of New Testament and Greek at Southeastern Baptist Theological Seminary in Wake Forest, North Carolina.

Worldviews at War: The Biblical Worldview and Its Place in Society **by Dr. N. Allan Moseley.**

Dr. N. Allan Moseley looks at the Biblical worldview and how it fits in with all aspects of our life and culture. Some of his topics include Christians, God and Government; Homosexuality and the Christian Worldview; When Jesus Is Not Politically Correct; the Myth of Disposable People; and many others. Dr. Moseley serves as Dean of Students at

Southeastern Baptist Theological Seminary in Wake Forest, North Carolina.

Christ and the Qur'an: A Guide to Muslim Outreach
by Dr. Gleason L. Archer and Dr. Robert A. Morey

Dr. Archer and Dr. Morey have assembled this compact volume which provides Christians with a tool to present Christ to Muslims. *Christ and the Qur'an* first examines the portrait of Christ from the Qur'an and from other Islamic literature. Dr. Archer and Dr. Morey then correct that portrait by presenting the Christ of the Bible. This fine reference work includes complete citations from the Qur'an in English and in Arabic. Dr. Archer served as Professor of Old Testament at Trinity Evangelical Divinity School in Deerfield, Illinois.

The Divorce Decision: What It Will Do to Your Family, Your Friends, Your Finances and Your Future
by Gary Richmond

So, you think a divorce is the answer to your marital problems? Think again. Gary Richmond, long-time Single Parents Pastor at the Evangelical Free Church of Fullerton, California, outlines the devastating effects which the divorce decision has on your children, your finances, your emotions, your relationships, and your future. Based on literally thousands of hours of divorce counseling, *The Divorce Decision* will open your eyes to the life-long costs of going though that divorce. His conclusion: work out your problems; the divorce decision is usually the wrong decision.

Other Davidson Press Publications

The Answer Book: A Devotional Guide from the International Standard Version New Testament

Looking for answers to problems in your life? Look no further. The publisher of the ISV New Testament has assembled the answers to your life questions through clear and concise quotations from the Bible. You will love this book, and it makes a perfect gift!

ORDER FORM

You can order these fine works from Davidson Press by visiting our website on the Internet at http://davidsonpress.com or by calling the toll-free Davidson Press order line at 1-877-478-WORD (1-877-478-9673). You can also make a copy of **both sides** of the form below, fill it out, and send it in with your payment to the address indicated. Credit card orders can be faxed to 714-692-8874. Shipping, handling, and local taxes where applicable have been included with the price of each work.

Return this form with payment to:
Davidson Press, Inc.
23621 La Palma Avenue, #H460
Yorba Linda, CA 92887-5536

Qty	Item #	Description	$	Price
	1891833111	*International Standard Version New Testament with CD-ROM*	35.00	
	1891833510	*The Myth of Adolescence: Raising Responsible Children in an Irresponsible Society* by Dr. David Alan Black	23.00	
	1891833510T	*The Myth of Adolescence* teacher's package (6 copies)	100.00	
	1891833529	*Fearing God: The Key to the Treasure House of God* by Dr. Robert Morey	25.00	
	1891833529T	Fearing God teacher's package (6 copies)	110.00	
	1891833537	*Worldviews at War: The Christian World View and Its Place in Society* by Dr. N. Allan Moseley	25.00	
	1891833537T	*Worldviews at War* teacher's package (includes 6 copies)	110.00	
	1891833545	*Christ and the Qur'an* Dr. Gleason Archer, Dr. Robert Morey, et. al.	25.00	
	1891833545T	*Christ and the Qur'an* teacher's package (includes 6 copies)	110.00	

Qty	Item #	Description	Price	Total
		Subtotal from other side:		
	1891833561	*The Divorce Decision* by Gary Richmond	25.00	
	1891833561T	*The Divorce Decision* by Gary Richmond teacher's package (includes 6 copies)	110.00	
	1891833316	*The Answer Book: A Devotional Guide from the ISV New Testament*	5.00	
			Subtotal:	
1	1891833316	*The Answer Book* (1 copy is free with orders over $30.00)	0.00	0.00
			Total:	

Payment Type

❑ Check Enclosed ❑ Visa ❑ MC ❑ Discover ❑ American Express

Card Number (if applicable)	Expires

Name on Card	Ship to Address No PO Boxes

Ship to City	ST	ZIP

Cardholder signature required for credit card sales.	Date
X	